The Gospel According to St Matthew

Alexander Jones

The
Gospel
According to
St Matthew

A Text and Commentary for Students

GEOFFREY CHAPMAN
LONDON—DUBLIN 1966

By the same author

GOD'S LIVING WORD
THE GOSPEL ACCORDING TO ST MARK
UNLESS SOME MAN SHOW ME

First Published 1965
© 1965, Alexander Jones
Reprinted 1966

NIHIL OBSTAT: R. D. PETRUS GRIFFIN B.A., S.T.L., L.S.S., CENSOR DEPUTATUS
IMPRIMATUR H. GIBNEY, VICARIUS GENERALIS.
DATUM SOUTHWARCI, DIE 2A NOVEMBRIS, 1964

The Nihil obstat and Imprimatur are a declaration that a book or pamphlet is considered to be free from doctrinal or moral error; and it is in no way implied that those who have granted the Nihil obstat and the Imprimatur agree with the style or the contents nor with the opinions or statements expressed.

Made and printed in Great Britain by Fletcher & Son Ltd.
Norwich for the publisher, Geoffrey Chapman Ltd.
18, High Street, Wimbledon, London S.W.19

Note

With the kind permission of the publishers, we have adopted for this edition the text of the Revised Standard Version, copyrighted 1946 and 1962, by the Division of Christian Education, National Council of Churches, U.S.A.

The text of the Commentary in this book is adapted and revised from the Commentary which first appeared in *A Catholic Commentary on Holy Scripture*, Thomas Nelson and Sons Ltd., 1953.

CONTENTS

7

The Nucleus of the Kingdom: The Twelve
13:53—18:35

The Approaching Advent of the Kingdom
19:1—25:46

Passion and Resurrection 26:1—28:20

Foreword

"The evangelists wrote the music, the saints sing it". And indeed, the purpose of the Gospels was practical: the acceptance and imitation of Christ. St Mark thought it enough to present this Model in action: it is true that he emphasized the *fact* that Jesus taught (he uses the verb "to teach" and the noun "teaching" twenty times of Jesus) but he recorded relatively little of what our Lord had to say. St Matthew had other ideas. Doubtless he felt that his readers would be grateful for more articulate instruction. The Greeks collected the dicta of the philosophers, the Jews the sayings of the Rabbis, Matthew—the scribe instructed in the kingdom of the heavens—collected and ordered the words of the Son of God. His is the Gospel of discourses.

Now since discourses are commonly more obscure than narrative, the reader will find this Gospel more difficult than Mark's and will need to consult notes. This is unfortunate but inevitable. Why not let Jesus speak for himself? After all, he knew how to talk to simple people like ourselves. Simple, yes; but not like ourselves. They had a background that we lack: the notes are meant to supply this want. Furthermore, there is a second person to interpret—the inspired author who has so powerfully imposed his own synthesis on the various sayings of Jesus. Let this be sufficient apology. It is willingly admitted that notes to such a text are always an impertinence. With this in mind, we have kept these servants of the text to the servants' quarters so that their master may speak consecutively and not in staccato jerks on successive pages.

Alexander Jones

St Vincent's Lodge, Liverpool, 1964.

15

Introduction

Introduction

It is worth reminding ourselves of the frequently forgotten commonplace that there is only one Gospel, one "Good News": the good news of Jesus Christ: news of a climactic intervention of God in the history of fallen man. Now, although what Jesus *was* and what he *did* is effectively brought out in the 657 verses of Mark, (and only one-twentieth of this is absent from Matthew and Luke) what he *said* is treated much more briefly—Mark omits the Sermon on the Mount for instance. The Gospel in its Matthean form has 1068 verses (Luke: 1149), and this extra material (with the exception of 48 verses of Infancy narrative, absent from Mark) is devoted to Christ's discourses. It will be seen from a reference to our circular presentation (facing p. 32) how systematically these discourses are arranged. There is no doubt that the inspired author of our present Matthew had a power of synthesis which he did not hesitate to use in the interests of the early Christian community. One might almost sense the mentality of a civil servant behind it, and its form may be more attributable to Matthew the tax-collector than many are prepared to admit. In any case, it is a "scribe trained for the kingdom of heaven" (Mt 13:52) who is writing.

Each evangelist has his own gift, and in Matthew we may miss the freshness of Mark (though not always, e.g. the absence of Mt 15:23 from Mark), but we gain much from an orderly presentation which has made this Gospel the favourite for liturgical use and the most familiar to the Christian ear. From this emerges a practical advantage for the student of Matthew: any passage or section which is common to Matthew, Mark, and Luke (called the "Synoptic" Gospels) will most easily be located in Matthew. But it also follows, since a logical arrangement is often bound to conflict with a chronological one, that the time element will take second place. Hence, if we wish to date some saying of Christ's—a matter of secondary importance anyway—we should do better to consult Luke. For example, Matthew puts the Lord's Prayer in the Sermon on the Mount, the inaugural discourse, Luke places it at the end of the Public Ministry (Mt 6:9-15; Lk 11:2-4). Remembering Matthew's love of logical arrangement and synthesis, one might well prefer Luke's chronology here. So also with many sayings grouped together in this same Sermon but scattered in various places in Luke. Nor does this sacrifice of chronology apply only to discourses: compare, for example the order of Mt 8:1—9:34 with Mark's ordering of the same events.

2. THE STRUCTURE OF THE GOSPEL

Prescinding from the prologue (the Infancy narrative of ch. 1-2) and from the epilogue (the Passion and Resurrection account of ch. 26-28) the Gospel appears to fall naturally into five great parts. The evangelist marks these divisions with the repetition of a stereotyped formula (or its near equivalent) used nowhere else in the Gospel: "And it came to pass when Jesus had ended these words . . .", 7:28; 11:1; 13:53; 19:1; 26:1. Each part has its predominantly narrative section followed by a long discourse for which the narrative forms an apt preparation thus:

1. I. Narrative ch. 3-4   (The indispensable preliminary *mise en scène*).

  II. Discourse ch. 5-7   (Inaugural discourse: the "Sermon").

2. I. Narrative ch. 8-9   (Opening of our Lord's ministry; miracles).

  II. Discourse ch. 10   (Instruction for apostles' ministry).

3. I. Narrative ch. 11-12   (Opposition to the "kingdom").

  II. Discourse ch. 13   (Kingdom's mysterious nature explains opposition).

4. I. Narrative ch. 14-17   (Formation of disciples and of Peter).

  II. Discourse ch. 18   (Duties of the disciples).

5. I. Narrative ch. 19-23   (Mounting opposition of Judaism).

  II. Discourse ch. 24-25   (Messianic judgment on Judaism, etc.).

3. THE CHARACTERISTIC THEME

One might hesitate between two possible titles for our Gospel: the "Gospel of fulfilment" or the "Gospel of the kingdom" but, in effect, these are but two aspects of the one theme. The coming of the kingdom is a fulfilment of the old promises and the kingdom itself is not entirely a new thing, but a perfecting of the old. There is a true continuity here, as Mt insists in one sentence which he alone quotes: "The kingdom of God will be taken from you, and be given to a nation producing the fruits of it", 21:43.

The Gospel of Fulfilment.
Mt sees both kingdom and king not as unforeseen and un-

prepared phenomena, but as the supernatural climax of a divine plan announced and developing in the history of Israel. On twelve occasions the evangelist formally asserts that the old Scriptures were "fulfilled" in Jesus and his work (1:22, 2:23; 4:14; 8:17; 12:17; 13:35; 21:4; 26:54; 27:9 cf 3:15 note). From the first verses of the Gospel this is evident. The descent of Jesus from Abraham, not traced back to Adam as in Lk, implicitly links Jesus with the promise of Genesis (Gen 13:15; 17:8; cf Gal 3:16) and the Infancy narrative is punctuated with O.T. references eagerly sought out to reduce the surprise of the early opposition to the Messiah, 2:15, 17, 23. Alone among the evangelists Mt, 4:15, sees the opening of our Lord's public preaching as the shining of the great Messianic light already spoken of by Isaiah (9:1), and the first works of healing as the prophesied function of the Isaian "Servant of God", Mt 8:16-17. This second passage with its hint of suffering prepares the reader for the remaining O.T. citations chosen for circumstances more sombre: our Lord's withdrawal from the opposition of his people's leaders, the blindness of the people themselves, the flight of his own disciples, the moral treachery of one of them—even these are not the frustration of the divine plan but its fulfilment, 12:17; 13:35; 26:54, 56; 27:9.

As for the new order itself, it too is a fulfilment of the old and not its destruction, 5:17; ritual laws may pass, but the ancient moral code is protected, 15:3-6, and reinforced with a strong inner spirit, 5:20-48; though the new era is on a higher plane the old had looked towards it, 11:11-13. The message of the new kingdom is addressed first to the subjects of the old, 10:5f.; if it passes from Israel it is through Israel's fault, 21:28-44, and even Christ's farewell words to his people hold a hint of hope for the nation elect of old (23:39 note). The very refusal of its Messiah by Israel is no break with the past, but rather the climax of its melancholy history: Israel's response to God's invitations was never generous,

23:35, and Matthew's readers, largely converts from Judaism, need not be surprised nor scandalized that their own nation as a body has rejected the new offer, 23:34.

The Gospel of the kingdom

Fifty-one times (as against 14 in Mk, 39 in Lk) Mt speaks of "the kingdom", but whereas Mk and Lk consistently use the expression "kingdom of God", Mt uses it, at most, 5 times only and prefers (32 or 33 times) "kingdom of the heavens". This last is almost certainly the formula used by our Lord himself, the plural form of "heavens" reproducing Aramaic (and Hebrew) usage and the term itself being the contemporary respectful equivalent for "God", 1 Mac 3:60; 4:24. Since the two expressions are in practice synonymous it follows that the phrase "kingdom of the heavens" does not necessarily imply a kingdom in another world than this. Nevertheless the expression lends itself of its very nature to a certain ambiguity and the context will have to decide the exact formality of its use in any given passage. Sometimes it is the messianic kingdom of God on earth, sometimes the apotheosis of that kingdom in heaven, sometimes the recognition of God's royal rights by the individual soul. The perspectives will often merge since the kingdom on earth is designed as the antechamber to the kingdom in heaven, e.g. 8:11-12. In some cases the distinction will be clear, as when the kingdom of the Son (the kingdom on earth) is distinguished from the kingdom of the Father which is in heaven (cf 1 Cor 15:28); this is most deliberately done in Mt 13:41-43. Thus to the kingdom of the Son refer 13:41; 16:28; 20:21; and cf 19:28; to the kingdom of the Father: 13:43; 25:34; 26:29. On occasions the characteristics of the kingdom are such as to exclude a formal reference to heaven; thus, in the case of the parables of ch 13, the coexistence in the kingdom of good and bad, the hidden nature of the kingdom, its slow and secret growth. Similarly the disciples' ambition in 18:1-4 clearly has an earthly kingdom for its object; the same may be said of the request of the sons of Zebedee, 20:21. Likewise when the kingdom is said to have come, 12:28, or when it is given a human authority, 16:17-19, the aspect of a kingdom on earth is foremost. It is upon this aspect that Mt's emphasis lies because, for him, the kingdom is successor to God's ancient kingdom which was Israel, a kingdom of God upon this earth. The kingdom is on the threshold when the Baptist speaks, 3:2, and his words are echoed by Jesus, 4:17, with whose ministry the day of Sion's kingdom had dawned (11:5; cf Is 35:5; 61:1). It has manifestly come with the great work of exorcism, 12:28, and is a matter of present experience, 13:16-19. But its "coming", though hidden and constant like the great works of nature, may break through into observable history in spectacular fashion from time to time; in this sense it may have many "comings". Such a thrust is said to be near at hand, 16:28, 24:34; when the old temple falls the new kingdom will be known for its excelling successor (ch. 24 notes). Matthew's Gospel is therefore in some sort a theology of history, a sustained reflection upon the origin and nature and fortune and final destiny of the permanent and permeating force which God, through Christ, has infused into the affairs of the world. The Epistle to the Romans sees this revolutionary thing as the saving justice of God manifested in his Son, the Gospel sees it as God's kingdom established by the Son; its theology is less elaborate than St Paul's, but it is no less profound and its arrangement is admirable. The skilful synthesis and distribution of our Lord's discourses provides the reader with a growing understanding of the kingdom which is Mt's central theme. His first discourse describes the true subjects of the kingdom and their spirit; his second instructs its missionaries; the third illustrates its hidden but irresistible power; the fourth the mutual obligations of its citizens; the fifth its establishment in power on the ruins of Judaism—nor

does this last discourse end until the king ushers his faithful
subjects into the lasting kingdom of his Father. It is small
wonder that the marked preference for the Gospel of
Matthew in the early Church has remained to this day,
because it is the Gospel of God's kingdom on earth, the
"ecclesiastical Gospel", the Gospel of "the Church".

4. THE FIRST READERS OF THE GOSPEL

It seems clear that the Gospel was written for those Jews
who did not see in Jesus an ambitious heretic but a fulfilment
of the ancient promise and the hope of Judaism for the
future. Historical tradition asserts this and the evidence of
the Gospel text confirms it. We have already seen (in para-
graph 3) how the pervading theme or themes imply a Jewish
audience, and this is supported by closer examination. The
reader is expected to recognize words and phrases like "the
holy city" (4:5; "Jerusalem" in the parallel Lk 4:9), "an
adulterous generation" (in the O.T. sense of "faithless";
12:39, cp. Lk 11:29 which omits "adulterous"), "bind and
loose" (18:18; a rabbinic expression; the sentence is absent
from Lk), the "phylacteries and fringes" of 23:5 (passage
not found in Lk), the reference to a "sabbath day's journey"
in 24:20 (omitted by Mk and Lk in the parallel place). Towards the same conclusion points Matthew's habit of numerical grouping, a procedure practised by the Jewish rabbis to
assist memory. The number seven particularly is exploited:
the seven parables of ch. 13, seven "woes" of ch. 23, the
seven clauses of the Lord's Prayer (6:9-13), seven demons
in 12:45, seven loaves and seven baskets in 15:34-37, forgiveness "seventy-seven times seven times" (18:22). And
indeed the whole Gospel falls naturally into seven parts (cf
the circular presentation facing p.32). For the number three,

the student may find it an interesting exercise to consult:
1:17; 4:3-10; 6:1-18; 7:17-19; 7:22; 23:20-22; 23:23.

5. THE ORIGINAL LANGUAGE OF THE GOSPEL

The earliest evidence is in favour of Aramaic, the Semitic language (closely akin to Hebrew and often referred to as "Hebrew") current in Palestine in the time of Christ and spoken by Jesus himself. Thus Papias (c. 60-130), bishop of Hierapolis, Irenaeus (c. 130-200), Origen (c. 185-254).

Despite this evidence, the existence of a Semitic original is commonly denied on the ground that our Greek Matthew is manifestly not a translation. This may be so, but it is no longer claimed that our Greek Matthew *is* a translation but rather an *edition* of a Greek translation (cf the chart on p. 35), and therefore at two removes (the second of these being very significant) from the Semitic original. An important element in the controversy is the form of the frequent O.T. quotations in the present Greek Matthew which is said to betray its Greek origin by using the Greek Bible, the Septuagint. But this argument is far from conclusive because the use of the Septuagint is not uniform and, where it occurs, may be ascribed to the Greek editor. Indeed, it may be argued that the use of the O.T. by this Gospel in fact points positively to a Semitic original. The form of ten of the quotations betrays the influence of the Hebrew text, and in six of these cases (1:23; 2:6, 18; 12:18-21; 13:35: 21:5) no adequate reason can be assigned for such recourse to the Hebrew other than the fact that this, and not the Septuagint, was already used in the work which lay before the editor's eyes. The most natural explanation of such citations is that "Matthew the Apostle, writing in Aramaic, had before him the Hebrew text with which he was familiar and which he uses with a certain freedom". At times this characteristic of the original is reproduced in our Greek Matthew, at other times (especially when the quotation is paralleled in the other Synoptics) the Septuagint form is preferred.

6. THE AUTHORITY AND AUTHORSHIP OF THE FIRST GOSPEL

Early witness to its authority

Already at the end of the first century and during the first years of the second, the Gospel we know as Matthew's had won special prominence. The allusions of Clement of Rome (1 *Ep. ad Cor.*, 95 A.D.) of the *Epistle of Barnabas* (100-130 A.D.), of Ignatius of Antioch (d. 115 A.D.), of the *Didache* (c. 100 A.D.), clearly reflect the text of the first Gospel. Nor are these reflexions confined to the discourses (*logia*) of our Lord (e.g. Ignatius, *Ep. ad Smyrn.* 1:1; cf Mt 3:15). The authority of Mt's text is even underlined by the phrase "as it is written", which is technical for the canonical writings of the O.T. (*Ep. Barn.* 4:14, alluding to Mt 22:14). Though the name of the apostle is not yet used in connexion with these texts this early preference for the first Gospel, in Rome and in Antioch, does not favour a recent or obscure origin.

Early witness to Matthean authorship

From the mid-2nd cent. at least, and probably from its beginning, the title "according to Matthew" was current; there is no trace of any other name in connexion with the first Gospel. Explicit evidence comes from Irenaeus writing before the end of the 2nd cent.: he declares that Matthew not only preached to the Hebrew (i.e. Aramaic) speaking public but also produced for them a written Gospel in their own tongue. Origen (writing c. 233 A.D.), severe critic though he was, accepts the truth of the already rooted tradition that the apostle-publican Matthew wrote the first Gospel in Hebrew characters for converted Jews. This witness becomes a commonplace in the 4th cent.

The testimony of Papias

"Matthew wrote an ordered account of the oracles (*logia*) in the Hebrew tongue, and each interpreted those oracles according to his ability." This is the earliest known explicit witness to the Matthean authorship of the first Gospel. It comes from Papias, Bishop of Hierapolis, who wrote a five-volume work, *Explanation of the Lord's Discourses* (or: of the Oracles about the Lord). The date of Papias' birth was probably 60 A.D. (Chapman) or 70 (Lagrange) and his book is commonly dated c. 125. He was in touch with the immediate disciples of the Apostles (Irenaeus). The precise sense of his term *logia*, "oracles", has been much disputed, but it is becoming increasingly recognized that Papias was not attributing to Matthew merely a collection of our Lord's words (the hypothetical document originally dubbed "Q" in critical circles). It may be that Papias chooses the term *logia* because the discourses are to form the theme of his book, but it by no means follows that Papias denies to Matthew anything more than discourses. There is a growing reluctance to credit the existence of a document containing Christ's words without any factual background and, moreover, its existence was not even suspected by those who originally used Papias' evidence. "From his context it is quite clear that Eusebius took it (the term *logia*) to mean the Gospel according to St Matthew. The same is true of Irenaeus. This interpretation seems the most satisfactory one, especially as we know that the Gospel was used by Ignatius some twenty years before Papias wrote. Nor can the ascription 'according to Matthew' be later than Papias' time. Hence the presumption is that Papias by *ta logia* means our Gospel" (Kilpatrick,

The Origins of the Gospel according to St Matthew, Oxford, 1946).

For those, therefore, who deny that the apostle Matthew wrote a Gospel at all it remains only to refuse the witness of Papias. This is done on the alleged authority of internal evidence. Before we examine this internal evidence and the legitimate conclusions to be drawn from it we should do well to make some preliminary and cautionary observations. In the first place, the evidence of Papias is not the only evidence that remains to be explained away. Even granted that Irenaeus was its unwitting victim we are still faced with the conviction of the critical Origen who claims not Papias only but a whole tradition in its support; Eusebius, too, mistrustful of Papias on other points, accepts his evidence on this without question. Secondly, in questions of this kind both internal and external evidence must be respected and not manipulated. Thirdly, the historical evidence is stubborn on two points which are not necessarily connected—Matthean authorship and Aramaic original; the "critical" hypothesis must reject both, however, if its arguments are to hold; in fact it argues from the Greek to the non-apostolic authorship of the same. Here there is danger of confusing the issue because the traditional view is not tied down to the detailed identity but only to the substantial identity of the Greek translation with its apostolic, Aramaic original. Fourthly, the firm tradition insists that our Greek Matthew is not the original Gospel but derived from it. If it is right in so doing we are already in presence of a complex problem to which we might reasonably expect a complex answer. It will not therefore be wise to dismiss such an answer lightly as a "cumbersome hypothesis". We shall outline the possible solution below.

The historical tradition provides us with no clear evidence on the precise date of writing of the Synoptic Gospels. For Mark, however, the tradition indicates a date between 64-70, and quite explicitly puts the original Matthew before Mark. This original, Aramaic Matthew may be dated at 50 A.D. with some probability, perhaps even earlier.

As for our present Greek Matthew, this was certainly well established in the first years of the 2nd century: the seven letters of Ignatius of Antioch (115 A.D. or earlier) use the Gk text as we know it. On this score alone it is difficult to believe that our Greek Matthew is later than 90 A.D. The arguments for 90-100 A.D. are not compelling: the situation which our Gospel was designed to meet was already developing before the Synod of Jamnia in 90 A.D. In view of the fact that our Greek Matthew seems to contemplate the Jewish catastrophe as something still to come, a date some time before 70 A.D. is not improbable. The editor, who, as will be seen, uses a certain freedom (cf 21:39 note), would doubtless have allowed his language to be influenced by that event had it already taken place. Indeed, recent comparative studies of Matthew and Paul have suggested a date earlier than the latter's first epistles (i.e. before 51 A.D.) for a Greek translation of Aramaic Matthew. Whether this translation or one of these translations (cf the evidence of Papias) is identical with our Greek Matthew, or whether it is only the precursor and source of the same, will have to be decided on other grounds (cf pp. 33-4).

8. THE COMPOSITION OF GREEK MATTHEW

The two-source theory with varying modifications is still

accepted in most critical circles as a demonstrated thesis. Rejecting the historical evidence for an original Aramaic Gospel, it affirms two principal sources of Greek Matthew. First, the Gospel of Mark, incorporated almost *in toto*. Second, a written document containing the sayings of Jesus (document "Q") which is the supposed source of non-Marcan matter common to Mt and Lk. It is commonly held today that Q contained narrative material also, that it was an embryonic Gospel. In addition to these two sources, at least one other is postulated for those parts of Greek Matthew not found in either Mk or Lk—a source of Semitic origin.

The above conclusions are drawn from a close comparative study of the Synoptic texts. But there are other scholars who doubt that this study reveals a consistent dependence of Matthew on Mark; furthermore, they insist that the historical tradition of the priority of the work of Matthew the Apostle over that of Mark cannot be explained away or ignored. Amongst these scholars there are three differing hypotheses.

The oral tradition theory holds that the Synoptic phenomenon is sufficiently explained by the uniformity of the original spoken Gospel. This last was "a traditional outline of the life of Christ and his chief sayings, current in Jerusalem both in Aramaic and in Greek". It is claimed that the hypothesis is confirmed by the language of the Gospels themselves, which displays a colourless uniformity in sections common to the three Synoptics as opposed to the marked individuality of other passages. The tenacious oriental memory is credited with the preservation of the order of events and content of discourses found to be the same in the three Synoptics. Stress is laid on the differences which, it is said, the theory of written sources finds difficult to explain. In criticism of this hypothesis it may be said that memory is certainly an element to be reckoned with in any final solution: the rabbis and Jesus himself use mnemonic devices for the sake of their disciples. Nevertheless, the Synoptic similarity is striking and sustained, nor is it confined to discourses, and hence the majority of scholars dissatisfied with the two-source theory invoke, in addition to the part played by oral tradition, some form of mutual dependence of one written Gospel on another.

Dependence of Mark on Greek Matthew. This theory is a return to Augustine's view that Mk is, in effect, an abridgement of Gk Mt. "The Gk Mt served as Mk's chief source in sense that Peter, when preaching in Rome, had the Gk Mt before him, and adapted it in his own way to his hearers' needs." And Mark was, as it were, Peter's stenographer. In this theory, Gk Mt is considered as an independent translation of the Aramaic original, and a discussion of its "composition" lies outside the range of the Synoptic Problem.

Dependence of Greek Matthew on Mark. This hypothesis enjoys the advantage of combining the historical data with what appear to be the more assured findings of recent inquiry into the internal evidence. We adopt it here. It suggests that the source called "Q" by the critics is no other than the original Aramaic Gospel, discourse and events, of the apostle Matthew. This Gospel presented the Jerusalem catechesis which was the framework of Peter's preaching, the preaching which Mark committed to writing. Composed in Aramaic, as its Semitic flavour often suggests, it was very soon translated into Greek. There were doubtless many such translations (cf Papias). These translations were used by our three evangelists, each of whom adjusted his source to his purpose. Thus Mark, for example, omitted many sayings of Jesus, notably the opening discourse, and arranged the narrative matter in his own way. In this Luke followed him fairly closely but filled in many of his omissions of discourse. The Gk Mt completely reorganized the narrative sequence and, to some extent, the discourses—though

apparently his arrangement of five great discourses is due
to his source, the Aramaic Mt.

The vindication of this hypothesis cannot here be pursued
in detail and a few general remarks must suffice. The theory
rightly insists that the two-source position has a fatal weakness: its rejection of the distinction between our Gk Mt and
an Aramaic original vouched for by firm historical evidence.
It agrees, however, that oral tradition alone is not capable
of explaining the similarity between Mark and Gk Mt (the
latter has all of, but little more than, Mark's narrative; its
order from Mt ch. 14 is identical; 45 verses of Mk, one-
fifteenth of his Gospel, are remarkably similar in form to
their counterpart in Mt; 23 rare words are found only in
the parallel places of Mk and Gk Mt). It agrees also that
the form of narrative in Gk Mt is dependent upon Mk and
not vice-versa (its less vivid and more correct style, its signs
of transposition, its doublets, etc.). Attention is called, on
the other hand, to contrary phenomena—the Gk Mt is more
Semitic in character than Mk who also shows signs of having
abridged the Mt narrative in places. This cannot be due to
a dependence of Mk on Gk Mt, as has been shown; it must
therefore be due to Mark's dependence upon the common
source (the Aramaic catechesis). The same apparently contradictory phenomena occur in the discourses and lead to the
same conclusion; dependence of Greek Mt on Mk and
dependence of both on a common source. It is regarded as
fairly probable that Mk knew and used the catechesis not
only through the medium of Peter's preaching but also in
its written form in the original Gospel of Mt. As for the
translator of Mt, he too "knew this primitive tradition in the
Aramaic Gospel of Mt which was probably already translated. He undertook to present this Gospel more fully than
Mk, his predecessor, of whose work however he made considerable use. Employing this Gk text of Mk he adjusted it
when his prudence suggested, omitting those descriptive

details which did not further his essential purpose which was doctrinal, and at times preserving the flavour of his Aramaic original. He made use also of Mark's sequence which was, to a great extent no doubt, the sequence of Aramaic Matthew; this he sometimes followed, sometimes manipulated. From the original Gospel of Mt he took over the discourses in their entirety, even adding to them with the help of other traditions" (Benoit, *L'Evangile selon Saint Matthieu*, 1950).

As for the relationship of Gk Mt with Lk, it seems impossible to suppose any direct dependence of either upon the other in view of their notable differences (e.g. the Infancy Narratives, the genealogies, the wording of the Lord's Prayer, etc.). Their similarities are, therefore, best explained by a common written source of their non-Marcan material containing (as we have noted) not only discourses but also events. This source is the early translation, or better "translations", of the original Matthew. In addition to this source a second is postulated which Luke took bodily into his "great intercalation", Lk 9:51 — 18:14, but which the Gk Mt quarries for the structure of his great discourses. (For a schematic presentation. cf p. 35).

If this conception of the facts is approximately correct, it follows that our Gk Mt is not a mere translation of the apostle's original Aramaic Gospel; nevertheless it maintains the same fundamental structure and the same substantial teaching. Indeed any hypothesis which rejected the substantial identity of our Gk Mt with the apostolic work would collapse before the historical evidence. It is undeniable that the earliest ecclesiastical writers unanimously accepted our Gk Gospel as the reliable presentation of the apostle's Aramaic work. It may be added that they received the Greek text as sacred and canonical.

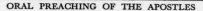

```
┌─────────────────────────────────────────────────────────────────────┐
│                ORAL PREACHING OF THE APOSTLES                        │
│ The earliest Apostolic preaching concerned primarily the redemptive  │
│ death and resurrection of our Lord (the Kerygma; cf Ac 2:14-40;      │
│ 3:12-26; 4:8-12.33; 5:29-32; 10:37-43) but would be accompanied by   │   30
│ more detailed accounts. Of these the first would be of the Passion    │
│ which, by repetition, would assume a fixed form—hence close agreement │
│ of four gospels. To this would be added episodes of our Lord's life   │
│ which threw light on his Person and mission, together with sayings    │
│ illustrating his teaching on various points of particular interest    │
│ to the early Church. Citation of Old Testament also a prominent       │
│ feature.                                                              │
└─────────────────────────────────────────────────────────────────────┘
```

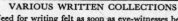

```
        ┌────────────────────────────────────────────┐
        │         VARIOUS WRITTEN COLLECTIONS         │
        │ Need for writing felt as soon as eye-       │
        │ witnesses begin to disperse: the groupings  │
        │ of incidents and sayings, small at first    │
        │ (e.g. Mk 1:16-39; 2:1-3:6), would become    │
        │ larger later.                               │
        └────────────────────────────────────────────┘
```

P
E
T
E
R

```
            ┌──────────────────────────────────────────────────┐
            │   ARAMAIC GOSPEL OF MATTHEW THE APOSTLE          │
            │ first continuous narrative of Public Ministry    │
            │ (Baptism to Resurrection) with some sayings of   │    40-50
            │ our Lord. It represents the Palestinian          │
            │ catechesis as preached by Peter.                 │
            └──────────────────────────────────────────────────┘
```

```
    ┌──────────────┐   ┌──────────────┐   ┌──────────────────────┐
    │ A GREEK      │   │ A GREEK      │   │  SAYINGS COLLECTION  │
    │ translation  │   │ translation  │   │                      │
    │ of Aram. Mt  │   │ of Aram. Mt  │   │ Further sayings of   │
    │ one of many. │   │ one of many. │   │ our Lord collected   │
    └──────────────┘   └──────────────┘   │ (in Aramaic) to      │
                                           │ supplement Aram. Mt  │
                                           └──────────────────────┘
```

```
┌──────────────────────┐   ┌──────────────┐   ┌──────────────┐
│        MARK          │   │ A GREEK      │   │ A GREEK      │
│ Using Peter's vivid  │   │ translation  │   │ translation  │
│ Roman preaching      │   │ of Sayings.  │   │ of Sayings.  │   60
│ (c.64 AD) and a      │   │ One of many. │   │ One of many. │
│ Greek translation    │   └──────────────┘   └──────────────┘
│ of Aram. Mt but      │
│ omitting or abridg-  │
│ ing many of our      │
│ Lord's sayings.      │
└──────────────────────┘
```

```
┌─────────────────────────────────────────────────────────────────────┐
│            GREEK MATTHEW (OUR PRESENT GOSPEL)                         │
│ Anonymous but inspired development of Aram. Mt. For deeds of our      │
│ Lord making use of Mark (adding only the Infancy Narrative). For      │   70
│ sayings using a Greek form of the Sayings Collection. Upon all this   │
│ the author imposes his own very careful scheme. He avails himself     │
│ also of other sources. Whether his work preceded or followed Luke's   │
│ is uncertain.                                                         │
└─────────────────────────────────────────────────────────────────────┘
```

```
┌─────────────────────────────────────────────────────────────────────┐
│                            LUKE                                      │
│ Based on Mark, closely following him in 4:31—6:19; 8:4—9:50;        │
│ 18:15—21:38. But in 9:51—18:14 embodying a great block from the      │
│ Sayings Collection in one of its Greek forms other than that used by  │
│ our Greek Matthew. Luke (like our Greek Matthew) has his own source   │
│ for his Infancy Narrative and his own source for certain material     │
│ peculiar to his gospel—e.g. parables of Prodigal, of Good Samaritan   │
│ etc. Luke and our Greek Matthew seem to be entirely independent of    │
│ each other.                                                           │
└─────────────────────────────────────────────────────────────────────┘
```

9. THE INSPIRATION OF THE GOSPEL

It seems probable that the immediate, though not necessarily exclusive, object of the Church's pronouncements relative to "sacredness and canonicity" is the Greek version, since this is the form of the Gospel in ecclesiastical use from the first century onwards, the well-known "evangelium Matthaei". If this view is exact, we possess a work inspired in its entirety and not simply an edition substantially identical with an inspired original.

10. GOSPEL INTERPRETATION: A RECENT PRONOUNCEMENT

It is folly to attempt the interpretation of any literary work without first identifying its type. A child will see in *Gulliver's Travels* no more than a story of dwarfs and giants, but unless the book is recognized as a satire on human institutions no beginning can be made with interpretation. The work written by inspired men, which we call the Bible, is not an exception to this rule. Indeed, to quote Pope Pius XII, the rule cannot be neglected "without serious detriment to exegesis". A recent Instruction of the Biblical Commission (dated 21 April 1964) explicitly notices that this principle must be applied not only to the Old Testament but also to the New.

Amongst the books of the New Testament we are concerned for the moment with the Gospels. Now the Gospel does not belong to that type of literature called "biography". It is essentially a preaching, a proclamation (*kerygma*, to use the Greek term) designed to lead men "to believe in Christ and to accept by faith the doctrine of salvation". [This quotation and those that follow are taken from the above-mentioned Instruction.] This proclamation in its four written forms aims "to furnish the Church with the foundation on which to build up faith and morals". It should not of course be concluded from this that the Gospel does not contain a variety of ways in which the proclamation is made. The Instruction mentions "catecheses, narratives, testimonies, hymns, doxologies, prayers". Kerygmatic instruction takes many shapes. Thus, for example, it does not follow that because the Passion narrative and the Infancy narrative are equally Gospel material, their interpretation is to be approached in the same way. [This example is not taken from the Instruction.]

Three stages, the Instruction continues, are to be distinguished in the development of the tradition which eventually emerges in our canonical Gospels.

The first stage is Christ's own preaching in action and in word, precisely as he performed the one and spoke the other. Here already there is an accommodation to the mentality of our Lord's contemporaries. Jesus "observed the methods of reasoning and of exposition which were in common use at the time". [We suggest the example of Mt 22:31-32, where the argument is rabbinic, see note ad loc.; and Mt 22:43 where the attribution of Ps 109 (110) to David should not be taken as a formal pronouncement on a literary question which was not raised by the contemporaries of Jesus.]

The second stage is the preaching of the Apostles. "The Apostles bearing testimony to Jesus, proclaimed first and foremost the death and resurrection of the Lord, faithfully recounting his life and words, and as regards the manner of their preaching, taking into account the circumstances of their hearers. After Jesus had risen from the dead, and when his divinity was clearly perceived, the faith of the disciples, far from blotting out the remembrance of the events that had happened, rather consolidated it, since their faith was based on what Jesus had done and taught. Nor was Jesus transformed into a 'mythical' personage, and his teaching distorted, by reason of the worship which the disciples now paid him, revering him as Lord and Son of God. *Yet it need not be denied that the apostles, when handing on to their hearers the things which in actual fact the Lord had said and done, did so in the light of that fuller understanding which they enjoyed as a result of being schooled by the glorious things accomplished in Christ, and of being illumined by the Spirit of Truth. Thus it came about that, just as Jesus himself after his resurrection had 'interpreted to them' (Lk 24:27) both the words of the Old Testament and the words which he himself had spoken, so now they in their turn interpreted his words and deeds according to the needs of their hearers."* [Italics ours.]

The third stage is that of the written Gospels. The transmission of the apostolic preaching by word of mouth and by written document (Lk 1:1) led finally to the four Gospels as we know them. The evangelists made selections and syntheses from this material according to the special purpose of each. Here, then, is the person and word of Jesus living in, and being interpreted for the community in the second half of the first century. The interpretation is authoritative because, though the voice of Jesus is no longer audible, the Spirit of Christ speaks through the community and its inspired representatives (cf Jn 14:26). One would not therefore subscribe to the sharp distinction implied in this sentence: "It is His authentic voice we would fain hear, not the mere echo of His words upon the lips even of the holiest and most devoted of His disciples" (F. C. Grant in *Form Criticism*, Harper Torchbooks, New York, 1962). The distinction has historical, but not ultimately theological, significance.

The Instruction accepts in principle and with reserves the interpretative method known as Form Criticism (a very useful summary of which will be found in the book just quoted). Form Criticism is based on the study of the oral tradition behind the Gospels. From the comparative study of the Gospels themselves (assuming the priority of Mark) it attempts to trace the direction of development of the primitive oral tradition. In addition to this, it compares the literary units within the Gospels with contemporary Jewish and Hellenistic stories and sayings. Many advantages follow from this approach: it involves a scrupulous examination of the Gospel texts, places them in a wider literary context, brings out the importance of a living community in the formation of the Gospels. For this reason the Instruction says that "in appropriate cases the interpreter is free to seek out what sound elements there are in the method of Form Criticism, and these he can duly make use of to gain a fuller understanding of the Gospels". Admirable as a literary method, Form Criticism has often been used to attack the historical value of the documents of revelation: the perfectly sound perception of selection and development on the part of the early Christian community has frequently, under the influence of philosophical or theological prejudices, become an assertion of creative invention. As the Instruction puts it: "(Certain exponents of this method) on the one hand underestimate the authority which the apostles had as witnesses of Christ, and the office and influence which they wielded in the primitive community, whilst on the other hand they overestimate the creative capacity of the community itself." After all, the denial of the possibility of miracle (a philosophical prejudice), and the notion that faith is indifferent to historical truth (a theological one), are no part of literary method, and it would be a pity if a valuable instrument of Gospel interpretation were to be discredited by its abuse.

The Text of the Gospel

Genealogy 1:1-17

1 The book of the genealogy of Jesus Christ, the son of
2 David, the son of Abraham.   Abraham was the father of
Isaac, and Isaac the father of Jacob, and Jacob the
3 father of Judah and his brothers,   and Judah the father of
Perez and Zerah by Tamar, and Perez the father of
4 Hezron, and Hezron the father of Ram,   and Ram the
father of Amminadab, and Amminadab the father of
5 Nahshon, and Nahshon the father of Salmon,   and
Salmon the father of Boaz by Rahab, and Boaz the father
6 of Obed by Ruth, and Obed the father of Jesse,   and
Jesse the father of David the king. And David was the
7 father of Solomon by the wife of Uriah,   and Solomon
the father of Rehoboam, and Rehoboam the father of
8 Abijah, and Abijah the father of Asa,   and Asa the
father of Jehoshaphat, and Jehoshaphat the father of Joram,
9 and Joram the father of Uzziah,   and Uzziah the father
of Jotham, and Jotham the father of Ahaz, and Ahaz the
10 father of Hezekiah,   and Hezekiah the father of Manasseh,
and Manasseh the father of Amos, and Amos the father
11 of Josiah,   and Josiah the father of Jechoniah and his
12 brothers, at the time of the deportation to Babylon.   And
after the deportation to Babylon: Jechoniah was the
father of Shealtiel, and Shealtiel the father of Zerubbabel,
13 and Zerubbabel the father of Abiud, and Abiud the father
14 of Eliakim, and Eliakim the father of Azor,   and Azor the
father of Zadok, and Zadok the father of Achim, and
15 Achim the father of Eliud,   and Eliud the father of
Eleazar, and Eleazar the father of Matthan, and Matthan
16 the father of Jacob,   and Jacob the father of Joseph the

Birth and Infancy of Jesus 1:1 – 2:23

Genealogy 1:1-17 (cf Lk 3:23-38)

1 – A brusque opening in headline-form. It refers perhaps to the whole Gospel (Westminster Version "book of the coming"), more probably to the genealogy only (Knox "record of the ancestry") or to the genealogy together with the conception-narrative; cf 1:18. The use of **Christ** (not "the Christ") as a proper name became common after our Lord's death (it is frequent in St Paul). The term is the Greek equivalent (*christos*) of the Aramaic *meshiha* (Gk transliteration *messias*) meaning "anointed", technical at this time for the prophesied king. The most popular title of this king, representing his basic characteristic, was **Son of David,** 2 Sam (Kg) 7:12-17; Is 11:1ff, etc. Its vindication for Jesus is the goal of Mt's genealogy. **Son of Abraham,** whether immediately qualifying "Jesus Christ" or "David", implicity presents Jesus as fulfilling in his person the Abrahamitic promise, Gen 12:3; Gal 3:16.

2 - 6a – *First Series: Abraham to David: patriarchal list*—Cf 1 Chr (Par) 1:27-2:15 where, as here, the list is incomplete since only three names occur between Perez and Nahshon to cover the period (at least 315 years) of the Egyptian sojourn.

6b - 11 – *Second series: Solomon to Jechoniah: royal list*—Cf 1 Chr (Par) 3:5-16 where, unlike here, the list is complete, placing Ahaziah, Joash, Amaziah between Joram and Uzziah (or Azariah) and naming Jehoiakim as also Zedekiah. The historical situation summarized in 11f is this: about the time of the deportation to Babylon, 598, Josiah, 638-608, was succeeded by his son Jehoahaz, 608, whose successors were Jehoiakim, brother of Jehoahaz, 608-598, Jechoniah son of Jehoiakim, 597, finally Zedekiah brother of Jehoahaz, 598-587. Jechoniah, aged 18, was taken captive to Babylon in 598 and was released 37 years later. Zerubbabel, 12f, headed the returning exiles in 537.

12-16 – *Third series (Jechoniah to Jesus): dethroned Davidic family*—For Shealtiel and Zerubbabel, cf 1 Chr (Par) 3:17-19; Ezr 3:2. From Abiud onwards Mt's source must have been family archives, carefully preserved in Jewish circles and easily challenged by hostile readers. **17** – Three series of fourteen generations are punctuated by two national crises: the inception of a divinely guaranteed Davidic dynasty in the 10th cent. and the Babylonian exile in the 6th.

Notes on the Genealogy – (a) *Purpose.* The genealogy does not prove Messiahship, but vindicates for Jesus its prerequisite condition, viz.

husband of Mary, of whom Jesus was born, who is called Christ.

17 So all the generations from Abraham to David were fourteen generations, and from David to the deportation to Babylon fourteen generations, and from the deportation to Babylon to the Christ fourteen generations.

Israelitic stock traceable to the patriarch of the whole race and, in particular, royal Davidic descent. But the singular manner of our Lord's conception, 18-25, introduced a special difficulty: though Mary was apparently of Davidic family herself (cf Rom 1:3), ancient—and particularly Jewish—genealogical usage ignored descent from the female line. Mt, therefore, gives the ancestry of Joseph, reputed and legally registered father through whom alone the Davidic descent of Jesus could be juridically established. (b) *The phrase "was father of"*. Used of mediate natural generation in e.g. v.8 ("Joram the father of Uzziah") and possibly of legal ("levirate"; 22:25 note) generation in v. 12 ("Shealtiel the father of Zerubbabel" cp. Ezr 3:2 with 1 Chr (Par) 3:19). (c) *The women in the genealogy*. Contrary to usage and therefore with a purpose four women are mentioned: Tamar, Rahab, Ruth, Bathsheba; cf Gen 38; Jos 2; Ru 1-4; 2 Sam (Kg) 11. Their common quality is apparently that of alien blood; Rahab Canaanite, Ruth Moabite, Tamar probably Canaanite, Bathsheba probably "Hittite" like her first husband. Their mention prepares us for an association of the Gentiles with God's design—an association subsequently emphasized by the incident of the Magi (ch. 2). (d) *Fourteen generations*. The number is taken from the O.T. record of the first series and deliberately, 17, applied to the second and third as a symmetrical aid to memory. It may have been a further recommendation (or happy accident?) that 14 is the first multiple of the sacred number 7 (favoured by Mt) and the numerical equivalent of the Hebrew consonants of David's name (DWD, 4+6+4). (e) *Defect of the third series*. The third series is apparently one name short unless we count Jechoniah twice—as king, 11, and as dethroned civilian, 12. Alternatively, Jechoniah need not be counted as beginning the third series if Mary be reckoned one of the fourteen; this is not improbable in view of the singular quality of her motherhood. A third solution reads Jehoiakim for Jechoniah in v. 11 (translator's carelessness?). Besides solving the numerical question, this gives point to the mention of "brothers", 11, since two of Jehoiakim's brothers reigned. (f) *The conclusion of the genealogy*. The evangelist studiously avoids the phrase "Joseph the father of Jesus": Joseph figures only as the legal husband of Mary. The text is critically certain. The Syriac variants (all careful to insert the word "virgin" with "Mary") are the result of subsequent effort to combine the legal paternity of Joseph and the virginal motherhood so clearly asserted in 18-25. The Sinaitic Syriac reads "Joseph to whom was betrothed Mary the virgin was the father of Jesus". That it intends no more than a legal paternity is clear from its care to render the Greek of 1:18 ("before they came together") by "at a time when they had not come together", thus safeguarding the antecedent virginity of Mary even more scrupulously than the Greek text.

Virginal Conception 1:18-25

18 Now the birth of Jesus Christ took place in this way.
When his mother Mary had been betrothed to Joseph,
before they came together she was found to be with child
19 of the Holy Spirit; and her husband Joseph, being a just
man and unwilling to put her to shame, resolved to
20 divorce her quietly. But as he considered this, behold,
an angel of the Lord appeared to him in a dream, saying,
"Joseph, son of David, do not fear to take Mary your
wife, for that which is conceived in her is of the Holy
21 Spirit; she will bear a son, and you shall call his name
22 Jesus, for he will save his people from their sins." All this
took place to fulfil what the Lord had spoken by the
23 prophet:

"Behold, a virgin shall conceive and bear a son,
and his name shall be called Emmanuel"

24 (which means, God with us). When Joseph woke from
sleep, he did as the angel of the Lord commanded him;
25 he took his wife, but knew her not until she had borne
a son; and he called his name Jesus.

Virginal Conception 1:18-25 (cf Lk 1:26-38)
This passage more clearly explains the situation suggested in 16. Joseph appears as witness of two things: first, of his own assumption of legal paternity (this fact alone justifies the presence of Joseph's genealogy in Mt); second, of his virginal relationship with Mary and of his heaven-sent conviction of the virginal conception. **18** – Betrothal (*qiddushin*) in Jewish law conferred the status of husband and wife (hence the terms of 19f). A child conceived during this period was regarded as legitimate unless disowned, but the marriage was regarded as incomplete until the husband formally "took possession" (the *nissuin*) of his bride by taking her to his home. This he was free to do at any time, 2 Sam (Kg) 3:14; cf Edersheim, I, 353-5. After Mary's return from her cousin's house her condition became clear (**she was found** or, in the weakened sense of the Heb. verb, "she became"). Mt adds with reverent haste what was revealed later, 20, that the child was God-begotten. **19** – That denunciation was a legal duty in the circumstances cannot be proved; nor does the text suggest that Joseph sacrificed legal scruples ("and" – not "but" – **unwilling to put her to shame,** or "to make her case public".) It suggests rather that precisely because Joseph was **just** (i.e. aware of duties to God and his neighbour, in this case to Mary) he did not place the matter before the village court. Such a course, though not necessarily involving condemnation (a woman might be pronounced blameless in such cases, Deut 23:25 f) meant publicity for Mary, unwelcome, and evidently incompatible with Joseph's "justness". Why incompatible? Presumably because ignorance of the facts coupled with knowledge of Mary's character made of mere publicity an injustice. Joseph's attitude is to be observed: there is no word of complaint or even of inquiry. The evangelist leaves us with the impression of a patient instrument of God. Another course remained open: to give Mary her freedom by a bill of divorce before two witnesses (19:7 note) without the publicity of the court. To this course Joseph was inclining. His delicacy is admirable – communicated to him, no doubt, from his knowledge of Mary. He cannot believe her blameworthy; he knows nothing of the Annunciation (Mary had been silent and absent for three months, Lk 1:39ff); he can think only of some unknown cause, perhaps supernatural, certainly consistent with Mary's character. **20** – There remained a third possibility: to celebrate the *nissuin* and thus acknowledge the child as his own. From this, evidently, Joseph shrank; perhaps because it would put him publicly in a false position. The angel reassured him. He could now without scruple adopt this third course because the child, though not his, was his more than any man's. It was the child of his betrothed. His patience and obedience make Joseph a model of Christian men; his unique relationship to the child makes him a powerful intercessor. **21** – Joseph is to assume the duties of parent (cf Lk 1:31, 63) and impose the name **Jesus** (in Heb.: *Yehoshua* or *Yeshua*). The name means

Magi 2:1-12

¹ Now when Jesus was born in Bethlehem of Judea in the
  days of Herod the king, behold, wise men from the East
² came to Jerusalem, saying,   "Where is he who has been
  born king of the Jews? For we have seen his star in the
³ East, and have come to worship him."   When Herod the

"Yahweh is salvation". The salvation is to be not from Herod nor from Rome but **from sin**. We are warned from the outset that the child's kingdom is not of this world, Jn 18:36, contrary to the popular messianic idea which Jesus was to find so difficult to eradicate. This same work is assigned to God himself in Ps 129:8 – one of many hints (e.g. v. 23 with note) preparing for a greater revelation of the child's true dignity. **22-23 – All this took place,** says Mt (for whom the Incarnation is an abiding thing) in such a way as to fulfil the prophecy of Isaiah, Is 7:14. Over seven centuries before, the prophet had announced a Davidic king to be born of a young woman (a **virgin** LXX) by divine intervention, Is 7:14. His contemporary, Micah (Mic 5:3-5) had alluded to the same event. Mt recalls this quality of the Messiah which had been allowed to fall into the background in Jewish messianic tradition (Lagrange, *Le Messianisme*, 223). The incompatibility of virgin-birth with physical descent from the Davidic male line is resolved in Mt by legal descent through Joseph's adoption. The child's name is to be Jesus, but he is to be **called** (i.e., in Semitic idiom, the true description of his mission, or even of his personality, is to be) **Emmanuel** (*immanu El:* Hebrew for "with us (is) God"). Of all the numerous O.T. theophoric names (e.g. Joshua, "Yahweh is salvation"; Johanan "Yahweh has been gracious") this name, found applied only to the Isaian child, Is 7:14; 8:8, is the one most strangely suitable to describe the real personality of Jesus. In order to bring it down to the level of other theophoric names it has to be reduced by paraphrase (though this is not impossible) to, e.g., "God is by our side to help". Mt (for his Aramaic-speaking readers) or his translator (for Greeks) interprets the Hebrew term. **24-25** – Though the *nissuin* took place very soon, perhaps on the following day, this marriage was not consummated. Mt makes this statement of the period which directly concerns him, his purpose being to safeguard the virginal nature of the conception and birth of Jesus. Of the period following the birth he says nothing. His sentence would be best paraphrased: she brought forth a son without having relations with Joseph. The Semitic turn of phrase, **not . . . until**, while denying the action for the period preceding the verb **borne** implies nothing for the period which follows it; cf Gen 8:7; 1 Tim 4:13, etc.

The Magi 2:1-12

1 – Mt's first indications of time and place are given incidentally as if already known to readers, but recalled with a view to the subsequent story. The child was born during the reign of Herod the Great, 37-4 B.C., at Bethlehem of Judea (scene of David's birth and anointing, 1 Sam (Kg) 16:13; 17:23), 6m. S of the capital. The **wise men** (Gk *magoi*) were originally a Median priestly tribe of clairvoyants who retained their functions under their Persian conquerors. The term later became general, Dan 1:10; Ac 8:9; 13:8, for astrologers, sorcerers, etc.,

king heard this, he was troubled, and all Jerusalem with
⁴ him; and assembling all the chief priests and scribes of
the people, he inquired of them where the Christ was to
⁵ be born. They told him, "In Bethlehem of Judea; for
⁶ so it is written by the prophet:
    'And you, O Bethlehem, in the land of Judah,
    are by no means least among the rulers of Judah;
    for from you shall come a ruler who will govern my
        people Israel.' "
⁷ Then Herod summoned the wise men secretly and ascer-
⁸ tained from them what time the star appeared; and he
sent them to Bethlehem, saying, "Go and search diligently
for the child, and when you have found him bring me
⁹ word, that I too may come and worship him." When
they had heard the king they went their way; and lo, the
star which they had seen in the East went before them, till
¹⁰ it came to rest over the place where the child was. When
they saw the star, they rejoiced exceedingly with great
¹¹ joy; and going into the house they saw the child with
Mary his mother, and they fell down and worshipped
him. Then, opening their treasures, they offered him gifts,
¹² gold and frankincense and myrrh. And being warned in
a dream not to return to Herod, they departed to their
own country by another way.

of all nationalities. We may translate "sages", since Mt clearly does not
intend a derogatory sense. Their homeland, **the East,** is most probably
the district just beyond Jordan and the Dead Sea, i.e. Nabataean
Arabia which at that time reached as far north as Damascus. (For this
use of "the East" cf the early Palestinian writers: Justin, Origen,
Epiphanius.) Here Jews and Arabs speaking similar dialects formed a
mixed population. The nature of their gifts confirms their Arabian origin:
Arabia was renowned for its gold, 1 Sam (Kg) 9:28, incense, Jer 6:20,
and myrrh, Pliny, *Hist. Nat.* 12, 30-5. The time of the Magi's visit is
to be put after the Purification, Lk 2:33-38, which took place forty
days after our Lord's birth, since Joseph plainly would not have taken
his charges to the capital after the warning of 13 (see note). It was
probably not more than a year after the nativity (16 note). **2** – The
appearance of a new and brilliant star in the eastern sky (*anatole* in the
sing. as in 9, not plur. as 1) sends the Magi in a westerly direction to
the Jewish capital. Evidently they were aware of the high pitch of
messianic expectation among their Jewish neighbours (witness the many
pseudo-Messiahs after Herod's death). Possibly also (though Mt is
silent) the Magi received a special revelation. The **star** (*aster*) cannot
mean a group or conjunction of planets (*astron*); this excludes Kepler's
conjunction in 7 B.C. of Saturn, Jupiter, Mars. Halley's comet, 12 B.C.,
is apparently excluded by its date. The comet-hypothesis in general is
difficult to reconcile with the description of the star's behaviour in 9
unless we grant that Mt intends no more than a popularized account
of an extraordinary but natural phenomenon. But it is preferable to
suppose that Mt, within his chosen literary form, is speaking of a
miraculous star. **3** – The common, general **trouble** no doubt takes the
form of anxiety in Herod, of excitement in the populace. **4** – The
Sanhedrin, the supreme Jewish advisory body of 71 members, was
composed of three groups in approximately equal force: the **chief
priests,** i.e the high-priest in office, the deposed high-priests and the
heads of the twenty-four priestly classes; the **scribes,** Pharisee in
persuasion, specialists in the Mosaic Code and instructors of the people;
the "ancients" or prominent laymen. Since these last are not mentioned
here, it is probably not a formal meeting of the Sanhedrin, rarely
consulted by Herod and unnecessary to his present purpose. Herod's
question does not imply his faith in the prophets, but his appreciation
of the dangers of the popular belief. Any pretender, especially with an
appearance of prophetic backing, was seen as a peril by Herod, who did
not overestimate his own popularity. **5** – The answer to the question
may not have come as promptly as appears from the brief account of
Mt. The birthplace of the Messiah was the subject of diverse opinions
(cf Jn 7:27, 42) among the people and presumably among their
teachers. In Jewish written tradition there is no evidence of the Bethlehem birthplace before the 3rd cent. A.D. The prophecy (Mic 5:1, 3)

Flight into Egypt. Massacre of the Innocents 2:13-18

13 Now when they had departed, behold, an angel of the
Lord appeared to Joseph in a dream and said, "Rise, take
the child and his mother, and flee to Egypt, and remain
there till I tell you; for Herod is about to search for the

was doubtless quoted verbatim by the scribes. Mt is content with substantial fidelity; moreover he adapts the text to the circumstances. For him Bethlehem is no longer "least among the rulers (better: 'clans') of Judah" because the Messiah has been born there; when Micah wrote, the greatness was still to come. **7-8** – Herod betrays a superstitious anxiety, though he is careful to make his further inquiries in private – there is excitement enough already, 3. He attaches importance to the time of the star's appearance, evidently presuming that it coincides (if it has any significance at all) with the time of the birth. His plans are already made, but his assumed appearance of leisure, 8, ultimately defeats its own end. **9-10** – The star reappears (cf **and lo**) – it had evidently not led the Magi to Jerusalem. It stands now in the southern sky in the direction of Bethlehem. Mt's text, literally interpreted, gives the impression of a light visibly advancing southwards (unless we translate "had gone before them"). This impression is heightened by the apparent implication that it was the star which showed the actual dwelling. If this is correct, the "star" is a luminous body in the lower atmosphere. **11** – The Magi enter the dwelling (*oikia*). This is either a new abode or possibly still the cave-stable (cf the 2nd cent. tradition recorded by Justin), not an unusual home for Orientals. Joseph though he may have been present is not mentioned; with this delicate touch, Mt recalls the virginal conception and Mary's incomparable closeness to the child. Note the similar indications of 2:13 f. The verb "adored" (*proskunein*), frequent in Mt, does not necessarily imply divine honours; yet the emphasis of the expression **fell down and worshipped** is suggestive, and the offering of incense, usually reserved to the divinity even among pagans, strengthens the suggestion. The gifts are probably products of the Magi's native land (cf Gen 43:11) – indispensable for visits to a king. The **frankincense** (i.e. "precious" incense) is, like the myrrh, a resin. **myrrh,** a perfume, Cant 3:6, was used in powdered form as a deodorant at burials, Jn 19:39, and, mixed with wine, as a narcotic, Mk 15:23 – hence its suggestion of mortality adopted in later symbolism: "gold for the king; incense for the God; myrrh for the mortal". **12** – Being warned in sleep the Magi went home not by the way they had come (probably from the direction of Moab via Jericho) but either by making for the south of the Dead Sea by way of Hebron or by effecting a crossing from its western shore at En-gedi.

Flight into Egypt. Massacre of the Innocents 2:13-18

13 – The circumstances (delay would have been fatal) and the terms (**behold** following the aorist participle and preceding the historic present, "appears" in the Greek – cf the same construction in 2:19) suggests that the flight took place very soon after the Magi's departure, probably the same night. Five or six day's travelling would take the holy family to the frontier of Egypt, now an imperial Prefecture, with a Jewish

14 child, to destroy him." And he rose and took the child
15 to Egypt, and remained there until the death of Herod.
This was to fulfil what the Lord had spoken by the
16 prophet, "Out of Egypt have I called my son." Then
Herod, when he saw that he had been tricked by the wise
men, was in a furious rage, and he sent and killed all the
male children in Bethlehem and in all that region who
were two years old or under, according to the time which
17 he had ascertained from the wise men. Then was fulfilled what was spoken by the prophet Jeremiah:
18   "A voice was heard in Ramah,
          wailing and loud lamentation,
          Rachel weeping for her children;
          she refused to be consoled,
          because they were no more."

Nazareth 2:19-23
19 But when Herod died behold, an angel of the Lord
20 appeared in a dream to Joseph in Egypt, saying, "Rise,
take the child and his mother, and go to the land of Israel,
21 for those who sought the child's life are dead." And he

population of about one million concentrated especially in Alexandria and Heliopolis. As a refuge from oppression at home Egypt was convenient and traditional, 1 (3) Kg 11:40; 2 (4) Kg 25:26. **14** – Mt's narrative, not being an edifying fable, preserves a sober silence (unlike the apocryphal gospels) on the details of the journey. There is no ancient, constant tradition relating to the new home. **15** – Mt implicitly anticipates the return, the better to space his O.T. quotations, 15, 18, 23. It might be noted here that, as in 18, rather than "the incident being made to fit the quotation" it would be less false to say that the quotation, Ho 11:1, is made to fit the incident. The original text (not LXX which reads "his (Jacob's) children" – unsuitable to Mt's purpose) refers in the strictly literal sense to the end of the Egyptian exile for Israel (God's "son", cf Ex 4:22f). The text is not a formal prophecy since the tense of the verb, faithfully preserved by Mt, is past. Mt, therefore, introduces the original situation merely as a providential rehearsal of the present event, thus calling our attention to a fuller sense of **son** than Hosea could have imagined. **16** – The sacrifice of a few **children** to the safety of his throne meant nothing to Herod; his own sons had suffered in the same cause. Bethlehem and district (the term excludes neighbouring villages) had a population of about 1,000 which, allowing for the high infant-mortality rate, would bring the number of children of two years and under to about 20. The age of the victims indicates that the star had appeared not more than two years before – probably about one year, Herod callously leaving a safety-margin on either side. **17-18** – The text, Jer 31:15, quoted here *ad sensum*, poetically presents **Rachel** (mother of Benjamin and of Joseph, the father of Ephraim) lamenting the fate of her children on their way into exile. She mourns from her tomb near Rama in Benjamin, 1 Sam (Kg) 10:2f. Rama lies 5 m. N. of Jerusalem and was the mustering place for the exiles on their way to Babylon, Jer 40:1. For Mt the circumstances are similar – the maternal lament of Rachel is echoed now in Bethlehem. Nevertheless, he does not allege a literal fulfilment of prophecy, otherwise he would have omitted **in Rama.** The quotation receives added point from another tradition (represented by what is probably an ancient but incorrect gloss in Gen 35:19) which places Rachel's tomb near Bethlehem.

Nazareth 2:19-23 (cf Lk 2:39)

19 – Herod died shortly before the Passover (12 April in that year) of 4 B.C. Archelaus (the elder of his sons by Malthace) was assigned Judea and Samaria and named king in Herod's will, being saluted as such on his father's death, Jos., *Ant.* 17, 8, 2. He had to wait perhaps six months for the confirmation of Augustus who granted him the title of ethnarch only. The length of the Egyptian sojourn during the period between the Magi's visit and the accession of Archelaus was probably

rose and took the child and his mother, and went to the
22 land of Israel. But when he heard that Archelaus
reigned over Judea in place of his father Herod, he was
afraid to go there, and being warned in a dream he with-
23 drew to the district of Galilee. And he went and dwelt
in a city called Nazareth, that what was spoken by the
prophets might be fulfilled, "He shall be called a
Nazarene."

at least six months, because at the time of the Magi's visit there is as yet no sign (cf 2:8) of Herod's fatal illness contracted probably in Sept. of 5 B.C. That the sojourn was not prolonged after Herod's death seems clear from 19 (cf 2:13) and perhaps accounts for the use of **reigned** in v. 22, which possibly suggests that Archelaus's title of "king" had not yet been formally reduced to that of "ethnarch". **20** – The word **those** (though possibly a plural of generalization) is perhaps best explained as a deliberate reference to the similar situation of Moses in Ex 4:19f. **21-22** – Joseph evidently intended to return to Bethlehem, if not to settle there at least to order his affairs. He was doubtless on the coast-road (Egypt-Gaza-Azotus) when he heard of the accession of Archelaus who had a bad reputation, not undeserved. Judea was still no place for a messianic claimant, and Joseph proceeded to his old home in Galilee. **23** – This was Nazareth, Lk 2:4, lying in the hills on the northern fringe of the plain of Esdraelon, c. 20m. W. of Tiberias. The insignificant village, mentioned neither in Josephus nor Talmud, was known to Julius Africanus (160-240 A.D.). Nazareth was to be the scene of Christ's childhood and youth. The term **Nazarene** (*Nazoraios*) might be more exactly transcribed "Nazoree". Its termination thus suggests a member of a sect (cf Pharisee, Sadducee) rather than an indication of origin; cf Magdalene, i.e. of Magdala. It is probable that the term "Nazoree" was first applied to the disciples after our Lord's death, Ac 24:5, with a measure of contempt for the provincial origin (cf Jn 1:46) of the founder of the sect. When the word became common its hostile sense would diminish (cf "Quaker") and it might well have become synonymous with the strictly geographical term Nazarene originally used of Jesus himself – hence its use throughout Mt, Ac, Jn (Mk uses Nazarene). Nevertheless, it was always possible to recall the original, contemptuous flavour of the expression, and it is probable that this is Mt's intention here. If this is so, he wishes to say that the obscurity of his Master's home, though now a subject of derision, should not be unexpected to those who knew the prophets. These, rightly read, had spoken of a Messiah humanly inglorious, Is 53, Ps 21. It is perhaps less probable that the term "Nazoree" contains a verbal reference to the "sapling" (*neser*, "branch") from the Davidic root, Is 11:1. This would make the "prophecy" little more than a punning coincidence and would scarcely justify Mt's plural **prophets.**

John the Baptist 3:1-12

¹ In those days came John the Baptist, preaching in the
² wilderness of Judea, "Repent, for the kingdom of
³ heaven is at hand." For this is he who was spoken of
by the prophet Isaiah when he said,

"The voice of one crying in the wilderness:
Prepare the way of the Lord,
make his paths straight."

⁴ Now John wore a garment of camel's hair, and a leather
girdle around his waist; and his food was locusts and wild
⁵ honey. Then went out to him Jerusalem and all Judea
⁶ and all the region about the Jordan, and they were baptized by him in the river Jordan, confessing their sins.
⁷ But when he saw many of the Pharisees and Sadducees
coming for baptism, he said to them, "You brood of vipers!
⁸ Who warned you to flee from the wrath to come? Bear
⁹ fruit that befits repentance, and do not presume to say
to yourselves, 'We have Abraham as our father'; for I
tell you, God is able from these stones to raise up children
¹⁰ to Abraham. Even now the axe is laid to the root of the
trees; every tree therefore that does not bear good fruit
¹¹ is cut down and thrown into the fire. "I baptize you
with water for repentance, but he who is coming after me
is mightier than I, whose sandals I am not worthy to carry;
he will baptize you with the Holy Spirit and with fire.

The Kingdom Proclaimed 3:1 – 7:29

I

Narrative: Introductory 3:1 – 4:25

John the Baptist 3:1-12 (Mk 1:1-8; Lk 3:1-18)

1-6 – "In those days" (Mt's vague formula is given precision in Lk 3:1) an ascetic who achieved fame and respect among his compatriots (Jos., *Ant.* 18, 5, 2; 21, 2, 6) inaugurated his penitential message in the mountainous, arid district east of the Jerusalem-Hebron road. He demanded repentance (*metanoia*, lit. change of mind) as the necessary disposition for receiving an imminent divine gift – **the kingdom of heaven** (or "of God" throughout Mk and Lk, but Mt's form is probably the Baptist's and our Lord's). This realm and rule of God is the goal of messianic prophecy. **John** preached repentance preparatory to the kingdom because he was the divinely appointed herald to the king. He personified the disembodied voice, Is 40:3, that heralded the return from pagan Babylon and the establishment of the new religious era of Judaism, itself a foretaste of, and preparation for, the new era declared by John. **4-6** – The garb suggests the prophet. John's outer garment is woven of camelhair; cf. Zec 13:4. He wears a loincloth of skin, cf Elijah, 2 (4) Kg 1:8. His food is of the simplest: the easily caught **locust** (a winged insect some two inches long, eaten still by Bedouin) and the insipid tree-gum (perhaps of the tamarisk, common on the Jordan banks). He baptizes in the **Jordan** near Jericho, of easy access from the capital. It was his impressive proclamation of the kingdom that drew the crowds, Jos., *Ant.* 18, 5, 2. His baptism was not the Jewish ceremonial bath removing Gentile defilement, a rite too narrow for John's horizon (cf 9); nor had it the *ipso facto* efficacy of Christ's sacramental baptism. It held a place between the two, characteristic of its period which was one of transition from "ceremonial washings" to the "better times" of inner, sacramental re-birth; cf Heb 9:10. By accepting it the Jews acknowledged, in formal ritual fashion, their conviction that the kingdom was at hand and their willingness to admit and (implicitly) to remedy past guilt. Thus they became subjects of the era of preparation announced by John and this act of willing submission would earn God's grace. **7-10** – Mt, having given, 2, the two themes of John's preaching, now proceeds to expand them in the Baptist's own words. The first theme, repentance, is urged against the **Pharisees**

[12] His winnowing fork is in his hand, and he will clear his threshing floor and gather his wheat into the granary, but the chaff he will burn with unquenchable fire."

and Sadducees. Neither of these two parties could afford to ignore the popular religious movement. The Pharisees (i.e. Separatists – from the common herd by reason of their legalistic punctilio) stood for the Law and for the traditions that had accrued to it. They held no official religious or political position in the Jewish State; as professional and orthodox "holy men" their influence with the people was enormous. The Sadducees (i.e. "sons of Zadok", representative of the priestly line; cf. 1 (3) Kg 2:35; 1 Chr (Par) 6:8-15; Ezr 3:2, Ez 40:46) were the rationalists of the day, Mt 22:23, and, as such, unpopular. Nevertheless, almost all members of the priestly families, including the high priest himself, were Sadducees. Both parties were concerned in the Jewish governing body, the Sanhedrin (more powerful now than under Herod). The high priests were members of that assembly and the Pharisees exercised a strong influence in it through the scribes (see on 2:4). The Pharisees, though loathing the occupying power, prudently repressed their nationalism; the more cynical Sadducees were indifferent to any regime provided it left them in office. The Pharisees were, perhaps, more concerned with the religious aspect of the Baptist's movement but, like the Sadducees, they would fear its taking a political turn disastrous alike to the State and to their own interests. They come, therefore, as spies, not as devotees; and John knows it. He ironically asks: Who can have taught the Teachers? They have clearly come with subtle and venomous intent (**vipers,** cf Ps 13:3). They cannot escape the coming **wrath** of the messianic judgment without a profound change of heart with its appropriate change of life: **fruit that befits repentance.** Provoked, evidently, by their pompous attitude, the Baptist interjects: "Do not wear the appearance of those inwardly saying 'We are the sons of Abraham!' " They are priding themselves on a divine gift in receiving which they were as passive as the stones on the river bank. He then, **10,** resumes the invitation of 8. The axe of the messianic judgment already threatens the fruitless trees, but there is still a short time for repentance. The **fire** that awaits the felled trees is not explicitly the fire of hell but a metaphor indicating in general the punishment reserved for those who do not take the present opportunity. **11-12** – John now turns to address the crowd (cf Lk 3:15f) who conjecture his Messiahship, to assure them that he and his baptism will not bear comparison with the real Messiah and the baptism to come. John is less than a slave, unworthy to carry his sandals. His baptism is only an expression of, and stimulus to, repentance; the **baptism** of the coming Messiah will be a steeping in the Holy Spirit, a profoundly purifying fire (cf the messianic purification of Mal 3:2f), not merely touching the surface like water. **and with fire,** better "and fire" (the preposition is not in the Greek), is explanatory of **Holy Spirit.** John thus foretells the outpouring of the Holy Spirit, Ac 2:3, of which the sacrament of baptism is one means. This purifying action on the individual soul produces a

Jesus is baptized 3:13-17

13 Then Jesus came from Galilee to the Jordan to John, to
14 be baptized by him.   John would have prevented him,
saying, "I need to be baptized by you, and do you come to
15 me?"   But Jesus answered him, "Let it be so now; for
thus it is fitting for us to fulfil all righteousness." Then he
16 consented.   And when Jesus was baptized, he went up
immediately from the water, and behold, the heavens
were opened and he saw the Spirit of God descending
17 like a dove, and alighting on him;   and lo, a voice from
heaven, saying, "This is my beloved son, with whom I
am well pleased."

distinction between those who accept and those who refuse it. Hence the messianic action is like a winnowing fan (or fork): the grain is thrown into the air and the wind carries off the light chaff. The perspective is final: those not purified by the fire of the Spirit will be consumed by the fire of the wrath of God, Is 66:24.

Jesus is baptized 3:13-17 (Mk 1:9-11: Lk 3:21-22)

Jesus comes from Nazareth, 2:23, to associate himself by baptism with all who thus expressed their readiness for the messianic era. As his kinsman, Lk 1:36, John very probably knew him personally. He is evidently aware of the sanctity of Jesus and (as Mt suggests, cp. 11, 14) of his Messiahship. Of this last, however, John was not formally assured until after the baptism, Jn 1:33. The strange inversion of roles shocks John (Mt only), but our Lord assures him that for this occasion it must be accepted since it is the divine will (**righteousness,** "justice" in Douay Version), means the observance of the due order established by God). "Why had the institutor of the new baptism to receive the old?" This is precisely the question that Mt answers and the one that lies at the root of his Gospel. It is not by a coincidence that this same evangelist has here, **15,** used **fulfil** as in 2:15, 17, 23; 5:17. Jesus did not come as a revolutionary innovator, he came to perfect the old order. Just as he submitted himself to the Law, so he accepted the conditions preparatory to the messianic age—the principal condition appearing as a baptism of repentance. It was God's design for a "period of transition", Lagrange. **16-17** – Where others had delayed in order to confess their sins, 6, the innocent Christ does not, but, being baptized, "immediately" leaves the water. The heavens (the clouds?) were torn apart, Mk 1:10, like a veil before him to give passage to the descending and approaching Spirit. The shape of a dove is fitting for the brooding and creative Spirit (Gen 1:2). Its appearance at this decisive moment in conjunction with the voice of the Father and the person of the Son would symbolize, for a Christian writer familiar with baptism and its formula, the second creation – the re-birth through water and the Holy Ghost. Whether the dove was seen and the voice heard by the bystanders is not clear, but the Baptist's function as herald of the Messiah and his own words, Jn 1:32-34, suggest at least that it was John alone who saw the full significance of both. The words of the voice, cf Is 42:1 but note the significant substitution of "Son" for "Servant", do not imply that the divine sonship of Jesus dates from the baptism. Had this been Mk's intention he would aptly have completed his echo of Ps 2:7 ("Thou art my son") with its following words: "This day I have begotten thee". It is the voice of the Father testifying to John (and the bystanders?) and at the same time encouraging his incarnate Son with a new expression of his love. The descent of the Spirit is the Son's investiture for his heroic office; cf Is 42:1; 61:1; Lk 4:18.

Jesus is tempted 4:1-11

¹ Then Jesus was led up by the Spirit into the wilderness
² to be tempted by the devil.   And he fasted forty days
³ and forty nights, and afterward he was hungry.   And the
tempter came and said to him, "If you are the Son of God,
⁴ command these stones to become loaves of bread."   But
he answered, "It is written,

'Man shall not live by bread alone, but by every word
that proceeds from the mouth of God.' "

⁵ Then the devil took him to the holy city, and set him on
⁶ the pinnacle of the temple,   and said to him, "If you are
the Son of God, throw yourself down; for it is written,

'He will give his angels charge of you,'

and

'On their hands they will bear you up, lest you strike
your foot against a stone.' "

⁷ Jesus said to him, "Again it is written, 'You shall not
⁸ tempt the Lord your God.' "   Again, the devil took him
to a very high mountain, and showed him all the king-
⁹ doms of the world and the glory of them;   and he said to
him, "All these I will give you, if you will fall down and
¹⁰ worship me."   Then Jesus said to him, "Begone, Satan!
for it is written,

'You shall worship the Lord your God
and him only shall you serve.' "

¹¹ Then the devil left him, and behold, angels came and
ministered to him.

Jesus is tempted 4:1-11 (Mk 1: 12-13; Lk 4:1-13)

1-2 – The Spirit who had appeared at the baptism now leads Jesus to his encounter with the personal power of evil, naturally hostile to the messianic plan. The single combat is to be engaged on the devil's own ground – the desert; cf 12:43. According to a tradition dating back to the 5th cent. this is the lonely, barren, mountainous district between Jerusalem and Jericho. **3-4** – *First Temptation.* Christ's unbroken fast of forty days (model of our Lenten fast, and cf Moses in Ex 34:28; Elijah in 1 (3) Kg 19:8) provides the occasion for the first temptation. The devil had evidently heard the voice, 3:17, because he echoes its phrase: Son of God. His words **If you are the Son of God,** though perhaps only half-understood, are only an affectation of doubt. They seek to goad Jesus to a self-assertive and unnecessary (11) display of power. The word "tempt" (lit. "to put to the test") is therefore here to be understood in its usual sense of stimulating to evil rather than in the possible sense of seeking information, 22:35 note. Our Lord, who later was to create bread for the multitudes, refuses to work such a miracle in his own interest and declines to demonstrate his powers to the devil. He is content with a quotation from Holy Writ, Deut 8:3, to show his perfect detachment from everything but God's will. The text in its original setting declares that the manna had shown that God could dispense with the ordinary means of sustenance when necessary; its basic lesson is calm trust in God. Jesus refuses to anticipate God's providence and later, 11, his trust is amply vindicated. In the circumstances, his retort, unlike the dictum of Jn 4:34, refers rather to physical life than to the life of the spirit. **5-7** – *Second Temptation.* The devil now takes Jesus to Jerusalem, c. 20 m. from the traditional site of the first and third temptations. He causes him to stand on a projection of the temple roof – probably on the S.E. corner of the outer temple about 300 feet above the valley of the Kidron. Jesus has already used a scriptural text to express his confidence in God; the devil adroitly joins issue on this very point. But the situation (**throw yourself down**) would turn the confidence of the psalm quoted, 91 (90): 11, into presumption. Our Lord counters with a quotation (Deut 6:16 referring to the incident of Ex 17:7) which supposes that the Son will not thus seek to wrench a miracle from the Father. Miracles must not be the condition of our trust in God: such an attitude is "tempting" God, i.e. "putting him to the test". **8-11** – *Third Temptation.* Satan stakes all. The traditional scene is Djebel Qarantal, a few miles N.W. of Jericho. This mountain, walling-in the plain of Jericho, looks eastwards across Jordan to the hills of Moab. The devil now appeals to earthly ambition, and his boast of political power (cf 2 Cor 4:4) does not today appear empty. **10** – But this is the only power he can offer and Jesus refuses it. His kingdom is not of this world. He names the devil for what he is – **Satan.** (In Heb. *satan* – rendered *diabolos* in Gk – means an enemy, 1 Sam (Kg) 29:4, or legal accuser, Ps 108:6, and in post-exilic literature the arch-enemy of man, 1 Chr (Par) 21:1, and his accuser before God, Job 1:6 – 2:7). Jesus quotes the great principle of Hebrew monotheism, Deut 6:13, anticipating his own declaration that it is impossible to serve two masters, Mt 6:24. Satan leaves him "for a time", Lk, to return in other guise, Mt 16:22f, Lk 22:3, 53. The "ministry" of the angels appears in Mk 1:13 ("were ministering" Westminster Version) to extend over the forty days' fast. It is evidently not a ministering of food. In Mt also it is possible that the service (*diakonia*) is to be taken in the more general sense, 25:44, of a support which rendered food unnecessary.

Notes on the Temptations. (a) *Messianic significance.* – There are three occasions of temptation, but the underlying suggestions are one: to take the crown without the cross. But since this is directly opposed to the divine plan (cf Is 53:2-12; Zec 12:10ff) the crown can only be an earthly one. The devil, fully aware of the messianic atmosphere, seeks to make the approaching attack on his kingdom harmless. Experience had taught him all he had to lose when men took the hard way, and the prophets had pointed this way to the establishment of the messianic kingdom. It was for him to urge the easy and deceptive way. There is a crescendo in his temptations. He suggests first the reasonable satisfaction of bodily needs (certainly not gluttony after forty days' fast) by means of a miracle before one witness only. The second is an invitation to a more spectacular display of power. The choice of the distant temple for the scene of the second temptation evidently has point: it suggests the achievement of popular messianic acclaim by means of a public prodigy worked in the sacred precincts. In each case Jesus is called upon for an unwarranted provocation of God's power. The instinct of the tempter is sound: he probes for the defects which normally accompany human qualities, assuming that where he finds great trust in God he will find presumption. Having failed, in the first two temptations, to reveal presumption he begins to suspect the strength of the quality of which this is usually the defect. The third temptation, therefore, attacks the quality of trust. It invites to total apostasy from God and reliance upon Satan himself. (b) *Mode of the temptations.* The evangelists no doubt present the temptations in dramatic form, and it is possible that the action of this drama took place entirely within the mind of Christ. (On literary forms in the Gospel, cf p. 33). The importance of the incident lies, in any case, not in the dramatic presentation but in the doctrine thus conveyed, namely that the popular idea of an entirely "glorious Messiah" was, despite its attractions, rejected by Jesus, and rejected at the very outset. (c) *Nature and further purpose of the temptations.* By reason of the hypostatic union our Lord was incapable of sin nor, being without original sin, could he be tempted from within by concupiscence (i.e. by the inordinate desire consequent upon original sin). He could be tempted, therefore, not by the lower nature itself, but only by the exterior suggestion of the Enemy. The devil's proposition could be presented to Christ's senses or imagination and so to his judgement. But, in virtue of the hypostatic union, the judgement being affected by no intrinsic unbalance would unerringly perceive, and the will inflexibly reject, the inordinate suggestion. In allowing even this satanic approach Jesus warns us that the holiest may be tempted but leaves us a model of firmness in dealing with Satan. Lastly, he draws as near to our condition as his sinlessness would permit so that, through human experience, he could "sympathize" with us, Heb 4:15.

He returns to Galilee 4:12-17

¹² Now when he heard that John had been arrested, he
¹³ withdrew into Galilee;   and leaving Nazareth he went
and dwelt in Capernaum by the sea, in the territory
¹⁴ of Zebulun and Naphtali,   that what was spoken by
¹⁵ the prophet Isaiah might be fulfilled: "The land of
Zebulun and the land of Naphtali,
toward the sea, across the Jordan,
Galilee of the Gentiles—
¹⁶   the people who sat in darkness
have seen a great light,
and for those who sat in the region and shadow of death
light has dawned."
¹⁷ From that time Jesus began to preach, saying, "Repent,
for the kingdom of heaven is at hand."

Call of the first four disciples 4:18-22

¹⁸ As he walked by the Sea of Galilee, he saw two brothers,
Simon who is called Peter and Andrew his brother, cast-
¹⁹ ing a net into the sea; for they were fishermen.   And he
said to them, "Follow me, and I will make you fishers of
²⁰ men."   Immediately they left their nets and followed him.
²¹ And going on from there he saw two other brothers, James
the son of Zebedee and John his brother, in the boat
with Zebedee their father, mending their nets, and he
²² called them.   Immediately they left the boat and their
father, and followed him.

He returns to Galilee 4:12-17 (Mk 1:14-15; Lk 4:14-15)

Mt briefly introduces us to the public ministry with a glance at its first scene, 4:12-17, its first collaborators, 4:18-22, its first acts and initial effect, 4:23-25. The temptations had followed immediately upon the baptism, but some months now elapse (for the events of this interval, cf Jn 1:19 – 3:36) at the end of which Jesus withdrew from Judea to Galilee. The immediate occasion of this withdrawal was the arrest of the Baptist (cf 14:3-13); the silenced herald is succeeded by his Master and the work of the kingdom goes on. **13** – By way of Samaria, Jn 4:3ff, and Cana, Jn 4:46ff, Jesus went back home to secluded Nazareth; cf Lk 4:16ff. He soon left there to make his headquarters in Capernaum (Tell-Hum on the north-west shore of the "sea" of Galilee) a busy little market-town on the Damascus-Egypt highway and situated in the old tribal district of Naphtali which bordered on that of Zebulun; both districts lie north and west of the lake. **14-16** – Mt solemnly announces the advent of the messianic age. He calls attention to the messianic (Emmanuel) section of Isaiah from which he has already quoted, 1:22f. The text, Is 8:23 – 9:1, contrasts the Assyrian devastation of northern Palestine, in 734 B.C., with the future messianic deliverance. **toward the sea:** lit. "on the way of the sea", perhaps better "on the sea-road" (Knox) probably describes, in the text of Isaiah, the district of Zebulun and Naphtali through which the road (the "Via Maris" of the Crusaders) passes from Damascus to the Mediterranean Sea at Acre. For Mt, however, thinking of Capernaum-on-Sea (*porathalassia*, 13), the "sea-road" is apparently that which runs along the west coast of the "sea" of Galilee. The district called **across the Jordan** is doubtless the province of Gilead on the east side of Jordan facing Zebulun and Naphtali; this too was overrun by the Assyrians. **Galilee of the Gentiles** (the Isaian *gelil*, i.e. "district", of the Gentiles had become a proper name) probably refers to a non-Jewish district of western Galilee. These precisions are of Isaiah rather than of Mt who quotes the prophecy as a whole, content to see it broadly verified in the fact that Christ's ministry opens formally in Galilee. **17** – The messianic age (Jesus uses the same words as the Baptist in 3:2) has passed from prophecy to fulfilment. It is **at hand** – a phrase probably equivalent in itself (as certainly in the context, cf Mk 1:15 "the time is fulfilled") to "is here".

Call of the first four disciples 4:18-22 (Mk 1:16-20)

Mt here (though cf 8:14-17) passes over the first miracles, Mk 1:23-34, being content with a general reference, 23f. But he evidently regards the call of the four (introduced parenthetically) as a necessary part of his summary introduction to the Galilean ministry. The ready obedience of the four is more easily explained if we bear in mind their previous familiarity with Jesus, Jn 1:35ff. For the detail, cf Mk 1:16-20 notes.

Jesus preaches and heals the sick 4:23-25

²³ And he went about all Galilee, teaching in their synagogues and preaching the gospel of the kingdom and
healing every disease and every infirmity among the
²⁴ people.   So his fame spread throughout all Syria, and
they brought him all the sick, those afflicted with various
diseases and pains, demoniacs, epileptics, and paralytics,
²⁵ and he healed them.   And great crowds followed him
from Galilee and the Decapolis and Jerusalem and Judea
and from beyond the Jordan.

Jesus preaches and heals the sick 4:23-25 (Mk 1:39)

These verses are a summing-up, and in part an anticipation, of Christ's missionary activity before the evangelist proceeds to present the great charter of the new kingdom, 5:1 – 7:29, and the power of its founder, 8:1 – 9:34. **23** – repeated almost exactly in 9:35, appears to prelude the personal work of Jesus as 9:35 introduces the mission of the apostles. His activity, doctrinal and miraculous, spreads from Capernaum throughout Galilee and his reputation as a wonder-worker beyond the borders of Israel ("Syria" – probably the non-Jewish district to the south of Hermon). The preaching is the good news ("gospel", *euaggelion*) of the kingdom. The **miracles** were of all kinds: too numerous and too varied to be explained by faith-healing. It is incredible that all the sick laid in the streets were neurotic patients. Attempts to ascribe the miracle-narratives to the pious inventive genius of the later Christian community are not only gratuitous, but overlook the fact that the miracle-narratives formed part of the very earliest Christian teaching, e.g. Ac 10:38. **25** – By way of immediate introduction to the Sermon Mt suggests the audience. Crowds follow Jesus; they come not only from Galilee, but from the Ten Towns ("Decapolis"). This last was a confederation of Greek-speaking cities, all east of Jordan facing Galilee except Scythopolis. They come also from Judea, even from its capital, and from the district (Perea) which faces it across Jordan.

II

Discourse: Inaugural 5:1 – 7:29

Structure and Content

The discourse, four times as long in Mt as in Lk, appears to have been expanded by the evangelist's habit of synthesis (cf p. 19). But Mt has not been haphazard: though the connexion in some places be loose, the discourse as it stands is a connected whole and Mt proposes it as such. According to Lagrange the imported passages are as follows: 5:13-16 (Lk 14:34f; 11:3); 5:18 (Lk 16:17); 5:25-26 (Lk 12:57-59); 6:7-15 (Lk 11:2-4); 6:19-34 (Lk 12:33f; 11:34-36; 16:13; 12:22-32); 7:7-11 (Lk 11:9-13); 7:22-23 (Lk 13:26f). The Sermon, pronounced in substance in the first few months of the Galilean ministry, sounds the keynote of the new age which our Lord has come to introduce. The new spirit (and with this our Lord is chiefly concerned) is to be gentle, 5:3-12, generous, 5:21-24, 38-47, thorough, 5:27-30, simple, 5:33-37, and above all sincere, 6:1-6, 16-18. It must not be arrogantly censorious, 7:1-5, but rather mistrustful of self, 7:13-14, yet sober, prudent, discriminating, 7:15-20, and, finally, energetic, 7:21-27. In short, the spirit of one always consciously imitating his perfect and watchful Father, 5:48. Since this fatherhood of God pervades the discourse, 6:4, 9, 15, 18, 26, 32; 7:11, implicit appeal is made throughout to filial love. Love is to be the mainspring of the new era – and love can ask more than fear can command. God, through his prophets, demanded less of a people that had to be mastered by awe; when the time was ripe he, through his Son, asked more of those who were made free by love; cf St Augustine. The new spirit is thus at variance with the Pharisaic ideal by reason of the emphasis laid upon the spirit at the expense of the letter of the Mosaic Code and of the casuistry that had gathered about it. The Law does not pass, on the contrary its moral commands remain, but the fullness of time demands a new perspective. The Law, of its nature, could not go deep enough into the heart of man; its Pharisaic interpretations had spread too widely over his external actions. Hitherto there has been a wrong emphasis and an imperfect law.

Analysis

(1) *The New Spirit.* The selfless outlook, having little to attract externally, must first be presented with prospect of heavenly reward (beatitudes). 13-16 are a parenthetical warning to the preachers of the new spirit. (2) *The New Spirit and the Old Law: perfecting, not opposing,* 5:17-48. (i) The principle laid down, 5:17-20. (ii) The principle explained by examples, 5:21-48. (a) Murder and "internal" murder (anger), 5:21-26. (b) Adultery and "internal" adultery (impure

73

The Beatitudes 5:1-12

1 Seeing the crowds, he went up on the mountain, and when
2 he sat down his disciples came to him.   And he opened
3 his mouth and taught them, saying: "Blessed are the poor
4 in spirit, for theirs is the kingdom of heaven.   Blessed
  are those who mourn, for they shall be comforted.
5 Blessed are the meek, for they shall inherit the earth.
6 Blessed are those who hunger and thirst for righteousness,
7 for they shall be satisfied.   Blessed are the merciful, for
8 they shall obtain mercy.   Blessed are the pure in heart,
9 for they shall see God.   Blessed are the peacemakers, for
10 they shall be called sons of God.   Blessed are those who
  are persecuted for righteousness' sake, for theirs is the
11 kingdom of heaven.   Blessed are you when men revile
  you and persecute you and utter all kinds of evil against
12 you falsely on my account.   Rejoice and be glad, for
  your reward is great in heaven, for so men persecuted
  the prophets who were before you."

thoughts etc.), 5:27f. (c) Divorce once restricted now abrogated, 5:31-32.
(d) Oaths once regulated now declared unnecessary, 5:33-37. (e) Strict
justice gives way to mercy, 5:38-42. (f) Limited charity to break its old
bounds, 5:43-47. (3) *The New Spirit and Hypocrisy*, 6:1-6, 16-18. (i)
Example taken from almsgiving, 6:2-4. (ii) From prayer, 6:5-6;
followed, 6:7-15, by a development on the subject of prayer. (iii)
From fasting, 6:16-18. (4) *Interlude on the Demands of the New Spirit*,
6:19-34. These verses occupy a central place in Mt's arrangement.
They describe the outlook that the new spirit demands – the single heart
and the will confidently surrendered to the Father. (5) *The New Spirit
in Action*, 7:1-27. (i) Its social manifestation (charity, prudence), 7:1-6,
12. (ii) Its difficulties and unpopularity, 7:13-14. (iii) Its opponents,
7:15-20. (iv) Its true possessors, 7:21-23. (v) Reward of action; penalty
of lethargy, 7:24-27. Note: 7:7-11, absent from Lk's sermon, on the
efficacy of prayer, have no clear connexion with the context.

The Beatitudes 5:1-12 (Lk 6:20-23)

1-2 – The "mountain" which served as our Lord's pulpit was evidently a hill near Capernaum (cf 4:13; 8:1, 5) dominating the plain
of Genesar. It is perhaps near et-Tabgha, about half an hour's walk
from Capernaum. Among the audience were many beside his more
regular followers, 7:28. **3-12** – The sermon opens with a series of magisterial pronouncements which, in rhythmic prose, describe and approve
the new spirit that Jesus is to preach. The form chosen ("blessed", Latin:
"beati"; hence **beatitudes**) is biblical; Ps 1:1; 112 (111):1; Prov
3:13 etc. The qualities mentioned are so clearly the product of one
consistent, spiritual outlook ("many facets of one diamond") that the
shades of difference are at times very faint. The **number** of beatitudes
is reckoned variously as 7 (by elimination of 4), 8 (retaining 4), 9
(reckoning *all* the "beati" formulae, even that of 11), 10 (as a new
"decalogue"). The last is the least probable and the choice probably
lies between 7 and 8. **3** – The **poor in spirit** of Mt (i.e. lowly in their
own estimation) renders the sense of Lk's "poor" (probably the original
form of the dictum) since "poor" in biblical language indicates all in
adversity (rich and poor) who humbly turn to God. It is for such that
the kingdom, even now awaiting them in heaven, is designed; cf Is 61:1.
4 – The second blessing (reckoned in the third place by many authorities,
and cf Douay Version) is for those who have cause to lament (without
complaint, as is clear). It is a challenge and an answer to the problem
of suffering. The promised "comfort", as the atmosphere of the promises
shows, far exceeds the sorrow, Jn 16:20. **5** – The term **meek** in its O.T.
background seems to imply much the same as "poor". The reward in
its original setting (Ps 37 (36):11, almost verbatim) is of prosperity in
Palestine, the land of promise. In this context, however, the land
(rendered **earth** in the text) is a reward as spiritual as the **kingdom of**

Salt of the earth; light of the world 5:13-16

13 "You are the salt of the earth; but if salt has lost its taste,
how shall its saltness be restored? It is no longer good for
anything except to be thrown out and trodden under foot
14 by men.   You are the light of the world. A city set on a
15 hill cannot be hid.   Nor do men light a lamp and put
it under a bushel, but on a stand, and it gives light to all
16 in the house.   Let your light so shine before men, that
they may see your good works and give glory to your
Father who is in heaven."

heaven, 3, or the vision of God, 8, and indeed the qualities Jesus demands (meekness etc.) are unlikely to win political success. **6** – The eager desire for **righteousness** will be more than satisfied. This righteousness may be the state of the soul described in the Sermon or possibly the restoration of the right order of things when God is to reward the poor, the meek, the afflicted. **7** – The **merciful** (i.e. forgiving, sympathetic, etc. to others) will obtain God's pardon which, to meet man's needs, must be and is infinitely greater than man's; cf 18:23-25. **8** – From the **heart** come (in Heb. metaphor) thought, plans, memory, affections; its "cleanness" (cf Ps 24 (23):4) means, therefore, a freedom from blemished purpose. This purpose is, as the reward shows, the search for God. Nothing short of the direct vision of God will be its recompense, envisaged already in the O.T., Ps 15 (14), more clearly in the New, 1 Cor 13:12; 1 Jn 3:12. **9** – The **peacemakers** are those who by patience and, if necessary, by judicious intervention spread their own inward peace about them. These **shall be called** (i.e. "shall be", in Heb. idiom) **sons of God** – made in the likeness of the God of peace, I Thess 5:23, whose Son by nature is "the Lord of peace", 2 Thess 3:16. **10** – Persecution endured for the sake of the religion of which Jesus is the founder and object (cf Lk 6:22, "for the Son of Man's sake") is pronounced a blessing (cf Ac 5:41) because it establishes a claim to **the kingdom of heaven.** This last phrase (10b) echoes that of 3b; if this is the Semitic literary device known as "inclusion" (the ending of a discourse as it began, cf 15:2-20; 16:6-11; 18:10-14; 19:4-8; 19:13-15), it is probable that the beatitudes finish here. **11-12** – An expansion of the last beatitude with the warmth and appeal of personal address and the added consolation of suffering with God's chosen prophets.

Salt of the earth; light of the world 5:13-16 (cf Mk 9:50; Lk 14:34-35; 11:33)

Dealing with the responsibilities arising from the world importance of Christian discipleship (cf Mk 4:21; 9:50; Lk 14:34-35; 8:16; 11:33) these verses have no close connexion with the context. The world (the **earth**) is henceforth dependent for its moral well-being on the preservative influence of the Christian disciple. If this **salt** becomes insipid (as the impure salt of common Palestinian usage could), there is nothing in the world to restore its savour. It is so much rubbish to be cast out into the street (the oriental refuse-bin). Even the world as it passes spurns the disciple who has lost his fervour. The comparison changes to **light**, like salt a necessity of life. The disciples have the social obligation (not incompatible with personal humility, cf 6:1, 5, 16) of lighting the way to the Father by their example for a world in darkness. If they shirk this responsibility they thwart their public purpose; they will be useless as a lamp hidden behind the flour-bin

Fulfilment of the Law 5:17-19

[17] "Think not that I have come to abolish the law and the
prophets; I have come not to abolish them but to fulfil
[18] them.   For truly, I say to you, till heaven and earth pass
away, not an iota, not a dot, will pass from the law until
[19] all is accomplished.   Whoever then relaxes one of the
least of these commandments and teaches men so, shall
be called least in the kingdom of heaven; but he who does
them and teaches them shall be called great in the kingdom
of heaven."

The new righteousness surpasses the old 5:20-48

[20] "For I tell you, unless your righteousness exceeds that of
the scribes and Pharisees, you will never enter the kingdom of heaven.
[21] "You have heard that it was said to the men of old, 'You
shall not kill; and whoever kills shall be liable to judg-
[22] ment.'   But I say to you that every one who is angry with
his brother shall be liable to judgment; whoever insults
his brother shall be liable to the council, and whoever
[23] says, 'You fool!' shall be liable to the hell of fire.   So if

(**bushel**: the Greek word actually means one peck in dry measure; here used for the jar that contains it). The comparison of the hill-town is surprising here and may be a separate saying of Jesus inserted in this place for convenience. The image recalls Mt 16:18.

Fulfilment of the Law 5:17-19

17 – The solemnity of Christ's opening pronouncements and his clear intention of inaugurating a new religious movement make it necessary for him to explain his position with regard to the Mosaic Law. He has not come to abrogate it but to bring it to perfection, i.e. to reveal the full intention of the divine legislator (cf 22:40 note). The sense of this "fulfilling" will become apparent from the few samples he chooses, 21-48; the object of it is the total expression of God's will in the old order (**the law and the prophets**). Here as the context shows, the emphasis is rather on the moral life in the new kingdom than on the fulfilment of prophecy in the person of its founder. **18** – Far from dying (our Lord proceeds, in this parenthetical verse) the old moral order is to rise to a new life, infused with a new spirit. Not its tiniest letter (the letter *yod = i*, in the square alphabet of our Lord's time) nor "flourish" (Knox) of a letter (narrowly distinguishing letters like *kaph* and *beth*) is to pass away. It is as durable as the heavens and the earth themselves (cf Lk 16:17). **19** – This verse, pursuing the statement of 17 (cf **then**), insists that this re-born Law will be enforced with no less rigour. The Christian disciple is perforce always a teacher by his example, 13-16: neglect even of the minutiae will be noticed and will do damage. The new order is to be distinguished by the perfection of its inward spirit, 21-48, but it will not dispense with external works. By its exacting standards the careless disciple will be accounted less than his more scrupulous brother. The **kingdom** in this and the following verse would appear to be the new kingdom of Christ on earth in which the Law and the Prophets find their goal and their deepest sense.

The new righteousness surpasses the old 5:20-48 (cf Lk 12:57-59; Mk 10:11-12; Lk 16:18; 6:27-36)

20 – Membership of this kingdom imperatively demands a sanctity more generous than that of the leading exponents of the Mosaic Law because its ideals are higher and its spirit more profound. **21** – For the prohibition cf Ex 20:13; Deut 5:17 and, for its sanction, Ex 21:12; Lev 24:17. The old law, being a law, could control effectively only external acts. The new spirit reaches down to the innermost part of man and its sanctions are of the spiritual order. This double truth is expressed in Semitic fashion by Jesus in three parallel and synonymous sentences without crescendo, but with cumulative effect. **22** – For internal anger or a sharp, angry word man is to be accountable before the tribunal of God (**judgment . . . council**) and thus liable to divine punishment

you are offering your gift at the altar, and there remember
24 that your brother has something against you, leave your
gift there before the altar and go; first be reconciled to
25 your brother, and then come and offer your gift. Make
friends quickly with your accuser, while you are going
with him to court, lest your accuser hand you over to the
judge, and the judge to the guard, and you be put in
26 prison; truly, I say to you, you will never get out till you
have paid the last penny.

27 "You have heard that it was said, 'You shall not commit
28 adultery'. But I say to you that every one who looks at
a woman lustfully has already committed adultery with
29 her in his heart. If your right eye causes you to sin,
pluck it out and throw it away; it is better that you lose
one of your members than that your whole body be
30 thrown into hell. And if your right hand causes you to
sin, cut it off and throw it away; it is better that you lose
one of your members than that your whole body go into
hell.

31 "It was also said, 'Whoever divorces his wife, let him give
32 her a certificate of divorce.' But I say to you that every
one who divorces his wife, except on the grounds of unchastity, makes her an adulteress; and whoever marries
a divorced woman commits adultery.

33 "Again you have heard that it was said to the men of old,
'You shall not swear falsely, but shall perform to the Lord
34 what you have sworn.' But I say to you, Do not swear
at all, either by heaven, for it is the throne of God, or by
35 the earth, for it is his footstool, or by Jerusalem, for it is
36 the city of the great King. And do not swear by your
head, for you cannot make one hair white or black.
37 Let what you say be simple 'Yes' or 'No'; anything more
than this comes from evil.

(the hell of fire). The tribunals mentioned, the judgment and the council, i.e. Sanhedrin – perhaps respectively local and central courts – are terms symbolic of God's judgment, as the last sanction (hell-fire) shows and as the context demands. The phrase translated insults is literally "says Raca to" the Aramaic word Raca (reka or "empty-head") means much the same as the "fool" of the later part of the verse. The Aramaic Gehinnam, (hell) i.e. "Valley of Hinnom", a ravine touching Jerusalem on the south, was the ever smouldering rubbish dump (cf 2 Sam (Kg) 23:10) of the city. In some pre-Christian Jewish writings it becomes the place of punishment for the wicked. Used symbolically, it is opposed to eternal life by Jesus himself, 18:19. The shock of the phrase in our context is lessened if we remember that our Lord is simply saying in striking language that the smallest faults of enmity are matter of accusation before a divine tribunal in whose competence lies even the extreme spiritual penalty. Naturally the tribunal will judge of greater or less. Nevertheless Jesus seems to imply that even internal anger can be murderous and so of mortal guilt. The virtue of charity, therefore, comes before all ceremonial pieties, even that of sacrifice (gift). 25-26 – It is a matter of spiritual prudence, too, as Jesus parabolically explains (cf Lk 12:58-59). We owe a debt of charity; the prudent debtor will attempt an amicable arrangement before the matter comes to court, and so to imprisonment. The solemnity of Christ's warning suggests the spiritual application of the parable.

27-30 – The prohibition (Ex 20:14; Deut 5:15; cf Lev 20:10; Deut 22:22) in the polygamous society of Moses' day attached to the wife but not to the husband (over whom none of the wives had exclusive rights) – unless, of course, he sinned with the wife of another. Hence the punishment of Lev 20:10; Deut 22:22 is appointed only for a wife and her accomplice. Our Lord who is directly addressing men, again condemns the internal act even if unaccompanied by external effect. He is the first to point this out (the Rabbis quoted in this connexion are post-Christian). The energetic language in which Jesus warns against the occasion of sin must not be taken literally, such language has its freedom: the left eye, for instance, is not less a danger than the right. Right eye and right hand clearly mean all we hold most dear. If these cause to sin (lit. "are a scandal", i.e. stumbling block in the moral path) they must be put aside.

31-32 – Deut 24:1-4 mitigated the evils of divorce by demanding of the husband a formal renunciation of rights in the interest of the dismissed wife. Jesus, attacking the matter radically, roundly denounces divorce itself as incompatible with the new spirit. The whole tone of the Sermon and the magisterial But I say to you lead us to expect a fundamental reform. Clearly Jesus is not simply taking sides in a rabbinic dispute. Rather is he robbing those disputes of meaning. (See 19:3-12).

33-37 – The Old Law, Ex 20:7; Deut 23:21; Num 30:3, forbade

³⁸ "You have heard that it was said, 'An eye for an eye and
³⁹ a tooth for a tooth.' But I say to you, Do not resist one
who is evil. But if any one strikes you on the right cheek,
⁴⁰ turn to him the other also; and if any one would sue you
⁴¹ and take your coat, let him have your cloak as well;
and if any one forces you to go one mile, go with him
⁴² two miles. Give to him who begs from you and do not
refuse him who would borrow from you.

⁴³ "You have heard that it was said, 'You shall love your
⁴⁴ neighbour and hate your enemy.' But I say to you,
⁴⁵ Love your enemies and pray for those who persecute you,
so that you may be sons of your Father who is in heaven;
for he makes his sun rise on the evil and on the good, and
⁴⁶ sends rain on the just and on the unjust. For if you love
those who love you, what reward have you? Do not even
⁴⁷ the tax collectors do the same? And if you salute only
your brethren, what more are you doing than others?
⁴⁸ Do not even the Gentiles do the same? You, therefore,
must be perfect, as your heavenly Father is perfect."

perjury and infidelity to solemn vows made to the Lord. This was good so far as it went, but such external vehemence should be unnecessary in the new regime of inward sincerity of mind and honesty of purpose. Henceforth, therefore, it will involve a disrespectful use of God's name amounting to a usurpation of what belongs to God. The disrespect is no less if the name be casuistically avoided, as when the Pharisees swore by heaven and by the temple. They even sustained the validity of oaths made to the detriment of justice as when, e.g., a husband vowed to deprive his wife of conjugal rights. (This last practice was so common that it may account for the juxtaposition of divorce and oaths in the Sermon.) Man, therefore, has no right to pledge what is God's. He must not swear even by his own body, for over this, too, God has dominion, not man: the youth cannot make his dark hair grey, nor the old man his white hairs black. Jesus asks for a simplicity of speech that reflects the equable spirit: **Let what you say be simply "Yes" or "No"** (cf Jas 5:12). Extravagant vehemence proceeds from a disordered state of human relations (**comes from evil**) and has no place in the new order. In this, it should be noted, our Lord is giving a general rule of Christian life; moreover, his clear-cut phrases must be interpreted with the finesse that all aphorisms demand. Thus, for example, it was no less clear to him than it is to us that some answers cannot be "Yes" or "No" without misleading. Thus, also, he is not attacking juridical procedure in which oaths are calmly and respectfully taken. Yet even here the necessity for such oaths issues from a defect which, though characteristic of human societies, should be absent from the kingdom whose charter Jesus defines.

38-42 – The Mosaic code (Lev 24:19f) sanctioned the existing practice of vendetta, but restrained it by the principle known in Roman Law as *talio* (cf Lat. "talis", Eng. "retaliation"): the compensation was not to exceed the damage. This principle of personal vindication, effective in primitive conditions and the unpoliced state, had probably taken the shape of pecuniary compensation in Gospel times. **39** – Jesus, again speaking for the individual Christian soul and not for governments, subordinates strict justice to generous charity. Four little examples illustrate his point. Here again allowance must be made for the vigour of his language: he himself did not literally "turn the other cheek", Jn 18:23, but his prayer, "Father forgive them", Lk 23:34, shows what he means. **40** – The second picture is of the law-court where a man is sued for his under-garment – **Let him have your cloak as well. 41** – The third is of a man (or his beast) temporarily requisitioned for State service by way of errand or transport ("force" is technical in this sense). Let such a one overcome his natural resentment by doing more than he is forced to do. As for the borrower (the fourth picture, **42**), Jesus recommends neither the worldly prudence of a Polonius nor (for the whole context would protest) the investments of a Shylock.

Almsgiving in secret 6:1-4

[1] "Beware of practising your piety before men in order to be seen by them; for then you will have no reward from [2] your Father who is in heaven. Thus, when you give alms, sound no trumpet before you, as the hypocrites do in the synagogues and in the streets, that they may be praised by men. Truly, I say to you, they have their [3] reward. But when you give alms, do not let your left [4] hand know what your right hand is doing, so that your alms may be in secret; and your Father who sees in secret will reward you."

43-47 – Only the first half of the quotation in **43** is found in the O.T., Lev 19:18. Bearing in mind the sharp Semitic antithesis, the occasional Heb. use of the word **hate,** Gen. 29:31; Mal 1:2f, and the hint of "permission" often contained in the future tense, we may thus render the second half of the sentence: "but need not love your enemy". The old law, addressed primarily to a nation, secondarily to individuals, was perforce at war with pagan foreigners 'inasmuch as they were a menace to the purity of race and religion, Deut 23:6. Moreover, by the *lex talionis*, cf v. 38, it committed to individuals the punishment of enemies ("hate" in the juridical order). For the O.T. and the rabbis the "neighbour" is the Israelite. For Jesus (cf Lk 10:36) the word admits of no exception. **44** – Jesus was the first to teach mankind to regard everyone as a neighbour and to love him. Christ recommends not tolerance but positive beneficence: **Love your enemies and pray for those who persecute you! 45** – In this we shall be in the likeness of God – demonstrably his children – because he, with his sun and rain, feeds the lands of friends and enemy alike. **46** – If we refuse this, in what are we superior to the despised publicans (9:9 note) or the pagans? If we salute only those of our clique, *what generosity is this?* (perhaps preferable to "what reward have you?").

48 – By way of conclusion to his programme of the new perfection Jesus refuses to set bounds to the ideal. The children are asked to aim at the completeness of their spiritual capacity. When, in their measure, they achieve this they will be like their Father who possesses (though he eternally and of necessity) the fullness of his being.

Almsgiving in secret 6:1-4

The essential inwardness of the new era does not exclude the practice of external works with their danger of ostentation. Jesus, therefore, warns his followers: Do not perform your acts of piety with a view to admiration. This intention robs the act of its spiritual value. For illustration Jesus takes three practices – alms, prayer, fasting – characteristic of Jewish piety, Tob 12:8. Each illustration is constructed on the same clearly marked plan: the practice, its abuse, condemnation of the abuse, advice; 2-4; 5-6; 16-18. 7-15, a self-contained instruction on prayer, break the sequence of these illustrations and have apparently been drawn into this place by the mention of prayer in 5-6. This hypothesis is confirmed by the fact that they are grouped about the Lord's Prayer which is elsewhere in Lk 11:1-4.

2 – The hypocrite (*hupokrites*, actor) has many subtle ways of publishing his philanthropy ("sounding a trumpet" is metaphorical). Such conduct assumes the character of a mere transaction: he has bought public admiration; the business is finished; he has "signed the receipt for his pay" (the common technical sense of the Greek); he can expect no more. **3** – The striking and original picture of secrecy (the right

Prayer in secret 6:5-6

5 "And when you pray, you must not be like the hypocrites; for they love to stand and pray in the synagogues and at the street corners, that they may be seen by men. Truly,
6 I say to you, they have their reward.   But when you pray, go into your room and shut the door and pray to your Father who is in secret; and your Father who sees in secret will reward you."

The Lord's Prayer 6:7-15

7 "And in praying do not heap up empty phrases as the Gentiles do; for they think that they will be heard for
8 their many words.   Do not be like them, for your Father
9 knows what you need before you ask him.   Pray then like this:

Our Father who art in heaven,
Hallowed by thy name.
10   Thy kingdom come,
Thy will be done,
On earth as it is in heaven.
11   Give us this day our daily bread;
12   And forgive us our debts,
As we also have forgiven our debtors;
13   And lead us not into temptation,
But deliver us from evil.

14 For if you forgive men their trespasses, your heavenly
15 Father also will forgive you;   but if you do not forgive men their trespasses, neither will your Father forgive your trespasses."

hand hiding its beneficence from the left) even suggests the unhealthiness of reflecting upon one's own good deeds. **4** – But nothing goes unseen by the Father (**sees in secret,** i.e. sees what is secretly done) and the reward will come.

Prayer in secret 6:5-6

Jesus does not condemn the practice of praying in public assemblies, Lk 18:10 – the words of **6** are as hyperbolic as those of **3.** Nor does he condemn the practice (in use among the Moslems) of praying in the streets, but of deliberately striking a pious attitude for public notice.

The Lord's Prayer 6:7-15 (Lk 11:2-4)

First a warning, 7-8, then the ideal prayer, 9-13. **7-8** – There must be no gabbling over empty formulae. This is superstition like that of the pagans who feared to omit from their prayer the name of one god or the mention of one request. The Christian is not forbidden to lay his needs before God (though he already knows them) but he should do so in simple, general terms, and in a trustful spirit. If we use repetition it must not be to secure God's attention, but to sustain our own. **9-13** – Mt's text of the Lord's Prayer is longer than Lk's. There are three prayers for the glory of God ("hallowed be thy name, thy kingdom come, thy will be done") with an expansion ("On earth as it is in heaven") and three personal requests: for food, forgiveness, freedom from temptation, with an expansion of this last ("But deliver us from evil"). Lk has neither of the expansions and omits "Thy will be done". The Jewish colouring of Mt's text (obscured in Lk's), and its semitic balance, powerfully suggest that Mt represents the original form of the prayer, abbreviated and simplified by Lk. Lk, however, has probably given the prayer its exact chronological setting. Most of the phrases of the prayer are to be found in Jewish sources, but its simple brevity and the deliberate exclusion of the spirit of Jewish nationalism (markedly present, e.g. in the great Jewish prayer, the *Tephillah* or *Shemoneh Esre*) prove that though the body may be Jewish, the soul is Christian. **9** – The tenderness and trust of the whole prayer are revealed in the bold word **Father.** The phrase "**our** Father" draws the followers of Jesus together as children of one family. It is fitting that the first ejaculations should be addressed to the Father's honour which, however, is always inseparable from man's benefit. The Christian prays that the holiness of the divine **name,** (i.e. in Semitic expression, the person as known and revealed) may be recognized. Since this "holiness" is not only God's sacred remoteness, Lev 10:3 etc., but his absolute moral perfection, Ez 36:21ff, the recognition means man's practical acceptance of his Father's commands. **10** – The second petition implies the same recognition, but, this time, rather of God's kingship establishing itself increasingly in the hearts of men. The third, **thy will be done,** declares

Fasting in secret 6:16-18

16 "And when you fast, do not look dismal, like the hypocrites, for they disfigure their faces that their fasting may be seen by men. Truly, I say to you, they have their re- 17 ward.   But when you fast, anoint your head and wash 18 your face,   that your fasting may not be seen by men but by your Father who is in secret; and your Father who sees in secret will reward you."

True treasures 6:19-21

19 "Do not lay up for yourselves treasures on earth,   where

clearly what is latent in the first two: effective acknowledgment of God as Father and king is accomplished by filial and loyal subjection. May this be as perfect as that of the angels! (Ps 103 (102) 19ff). **11** – The second half of the prayer also has three members which, unlike those of the first half, are direct petitions for our needs. Of these, the first is a request for the simple necessaries of life, embraced in the term **bread.** The word translated **daily** (*epiousios* in the Greek) is rare and obscure. Etymologically it means either "necessary for subsistence" (*epi+ousia =* for substance) or "for the day that lies before us" (*epi+iousa =* for the coming [day], cf Prov 27:1, LXX). This interpretation, however, makes the phrase **this day** redundant. It may therefore be preferable to accept another explanation and read "Give us our bread *day by day*" as a more exact rendering of an Aramaic idiom (wrongly translated in the Gk) which runs literally "of today and the following day". **12** – The next petition is for forgiveness of sins, called **debts** in Mt and in common Jewish parlance (Lk has simplified to "sins"). We ask forgiveness on conditions that must make us reflect on our own conduct towards those who have injured us (cf 14 and 18:32-35). **13** – Is probably one petition put negatively and positively (the latter being omitted by Lk). It asks that our Father should not **lead** us into temptation. Since God tempts no man, Jas 1:13, the phrase "lead us not" may be understood "permit us not to go" (in the Semitic manner). Nor does the word **temptation** necessarily imply a direct invitation to sin; it may indicate circumstances which, for us, prove to be an occasion of sin. The prayer ends with a final cry for deliverance from all moral **evil** (probably – in view of Mt's usual sense of the Greek word – not "from the evil one"). The liturgical addition found in some MSS ("for thine is the kingdom and the power and the glory, forever, Amen") was probably made to avoid ending the prayer with the word "evil". **14-15** – explain and underline in antithetic parallelism the condition of divine forgiveness implied in the petition of v. 12.

Fasting in secret 6:16-18

The last of three illustrations contrasting true with merely professional piety. The time will come when the disciples of Jesus will, like the Pharisees, form a compact body of religious men. Like the Pharisees they will fast, 9:15. Our Lord warns them against the faults into which many of the Pharisees fell. Far from wearing gloomy looks and pulling long faces (the Greek verb means "to disfigure", or possibly "to hide" with a veil as in certain Jewish fasts) the disciple should take the greatest care to disguise his piety. The image used by Jesus even suggests the appearance of one on his way to a banquet!

True treasures 6:19-21 (Lk 12:33-34)

It is not improbable that Mt has gathered to the section 6:19-34

moth and rust consume and where thieves break in and
20 steal, but lay up for yourselves treasures in heaven,
where neither moth nor rust consumes and where thieves
21 do not break in and steal. For where your treasure is,
there will your heart be also."

The eye, lamp of the body 6:22-23

22 "The eye is the lamp of the body. So, if your eye is sound,
23 your whole body will be full of light; but if your eye is
not sound, your whole body will be full of darkness. If
then the light in you is darkness, how great is the darkness!"

God and money 6:24

24 "No one can serve two masters; for either he will hate the
one and love the other, or he will be devoted to the one
and despise the other. You cannot serve God and mammon."

Trust in Providence 6:25-34

25 "Therefore I tell you, do not be anxious about your life,
what you shall eat or what you shall drink, nor about
your body, what you shall put on. Is not life more than
26 food, and the body more than clothing? Look at the
birds of the air: they neither sow nor reap nor gather into
barns, and yet your heavenly Father feeds them. Are you
27 not of more value than they? And which of you by being
28 anxious can add one cubit to his span of life? And why
are you anxious about clothing? Consider the lilies of the
29 field, how they grow; they neither toil nor spin; yet I
tell you, even Solomon in all his glory was not arrayed like
30 one of these. But if God so clothes the grass of the field,
which today is alive and tomorrow is thrown into the
oven, will he not much more clothe you, O men of little
31 faith? Therefore do not be anxious, saying, 'What shall

various sayings of our Lord. Nevertheless they constitute here a compact discourse pervaded by the one ideal: abandonment to the Father and the futility of all else. Experience shows the uselessness of trust in worldly goods. Hoarded stuffs are the prey of **moth and rust** (*brosis*, lit. an "eating"; more probably a variety of moth, or possibly "decay"); hoarded valuables are the prey of thieves. Not so (continues our Lord with elaborate Semitic antithesis) the treasure earned on earth, banked in heaven – real though intangible. Why not amass material goods? Because such conduct shows that the heart is not set on God alone. The reasoning assumes Christ's hearers recognize this last duty at least.

The eye, lamp of the body 6:22-23 (Lk 11:34-36)
This sense of due proportion comes from a sound mind ("heart"; cf 5:8 note) which guides morally just as the sound eye, like a lamp, shows a man his way. But if the eye itself be diseased, then **how great is the darkness.**

God and money 6:24 (Lk 16:13)
It has already been implied, 21, that exclusive choice must be made between God and gold. Each is a jealous master. The slave of two masters is in an impossible position. Their interests are sure to clash: he will have to declare openly for one or the other (**hate, love**), or, at least consult the interests of one (for the Greek verb used, cf 1 Thess 5:14) and slight the other.

Trust in Providence 6:25-34 (Lk 12:22-31)
Because this divided service is impossible, we must renounce not only the anxious pursuit of wealth as an insurance against future need, but also anxiety about our present wants, for even this divides the heart. The central idea of the passage is therefore freedom from anxiety (a word which keeps recurring, 25, 27, 28, 31, 34). **Mammon,** more accurately *mamon*, is a Greek transliteration of the Aramaic *mamona*, meaning wealth. This Semitic form has been left untranslated possibly to bring out the personification of this "master" better. **25** – The two primary needs are **food** and **clothing.** Food keeps the life in the body, clothing protects the body itself. The argument is briefly expressed. It implies that, since soul and body are "greater gifts" (Knox) than their necessities, God who gave the gifts can and will surely sustain them by providing for their needs. Naturally, this does not exclude placing our needs trustfully before God; cf 6:11; 7:11. Jesus goes on to demonstrate his point from God's conduct towards even his lesser creatures – the birds (proving the "food" point; 27 belongs to this little section) and the flowers ("clothing"; 28-30). **26** – Even animals make prudent provision; this is not condemned, but only worry – an exclusively human failing and inexcusable because man alone is conscious of a Father in

[32] we eat?' or 'What shall we drink?' or 'What shall we wear?' For the Gentiles seek all these things; and your heavenly Father knows that you need them all. But seek [33] first his kingdom and his righteousness, and all these [34] things shall be yours as well. Therefore do not be anxious about tomorrow, for tomorrow will be anxious for itself. Let the day's own trouble be sufficient for the day."

Judgment of others 7:1-5

[1] "Judge not, that you be not judged. For with the judg- [2] ment you pronounce you will be judged, and the measure [3] you give will be the measure you get. Why do you see the speck that is in your brother's eye, but do not notice [4] the log that is in your own eye? Or how can you say to your brother, 'Let me take the speck out of your eye,' [5] when there is the log in your own eye? You hypocrite, first take the log out of your own eye, and then you will see clearly to take the speck out of your brother's eye."

heaven and of his own rank in the creator's order. **27** – If this argument does not convince, appeal may be made to the obvious uselessness of being anxious. This will not lengthen life (or "stature", the Greek word being ambiguous) by one cubit (Hebrew measure, about 1½ ft.). If we translate **span of life**, the word **cubit** is used metaphorically; cf Ps 38:6. "Span of life" is certainly more probable in the parallel place in Lk 12:25 by reason of the preceding parable, Lk 12:16-20; it is perhaps more probable here also (cf 25) especially as length of life, not of figure, is the common anxiety. **28-30** – The "lily of the field" (called "grass" or "herb" in 30) is a simple flower (not, therefore, the gladiolus etc.). It is possibly the wild narcissus or the mayweed with its daisy-like flower (anthemis). These are more beautiful in their God-given simplicity than Israel's richest potentate in his man-made splendour; 1 (3) Kg 10. If the creator so cares for his creature, how much more the Father for his children! Man's years outlast the season of the flowers and, at the end, he is to be gathered into the granary of eternity, 13:30, whereas the dead herb is destined only to serve man's humbler needs. The inference is obvious: only those (so many!) with less than a modicum of trust could fail to see it. **31-33** – Bringing to a close his attack on these daily anxieties Jesus tells his Jewish audience that such preoccupation reduces them to the level of heathens and, moreover, insults the providence and love of the Father. The **kingdom and its righteousness** must be the first object of daily care. The kingdom in this connexion is the way of life God requires of his subjects – a way that Jesus has been explaining; cf 5:20. Provided (and this is understood) man calmly pursues his labour, God will provide. **34** – Do not add today's anxiety to the morrow's sum of worry; the morrow will have anxieties of its own (Westminster Version). Providence allows a daily measure of difficulty; the prudent proportion should not be upset. Since 34 speaks of difficulties in general (**trouble**), and not merely of anxieties; since also it speaks not of the present but of the morrow, it has a viewpoint rather different from 25-33. This, plus its omission by Lk, possibly indicates that the words were originally spoken in another context.

Judgment of others 7:1-5 (Lk 6:37-38, 41-42)

Before the concluding exhortation to action, 13-27, Jesus gives two pieces of advice for those to whom he has explained the new spirit. The first, 1-6, concerns the relationship of the Christian with his fellows; the second, 7-11, of the Christian with God by prayer. There is no clear connexion of the sections within the chapter nor of this chapter with the preceding.

Condemnation of our neighbour (like forgiveness, 6:12) brings a like answer from God. In this sense (but cf Lk 6:38 note) the rabbinic saying "measure for measure" is true. But even on the human plane such procedure is unjust and absurd. By a remark involuntarily echoed

Profaning sacred things 7:6

⁶ "Do not give dogs what is holy; and do not throw your
pearls before swine, lest they trample them under foot
and turn to attack you."

Effective prayer 7:7-11

⁷ "Ask, and it will be given you; seek, and you will find;
⁸ knock, and it will be opened to you. For every one who
asks receives, and he who seeks finds, and to him who
⁹ knocks it will be opened. Or what man of you, if his
¹⁰ son asks him for bread, will give him a stone? Or if he
¹¹ asks for a fish, will give him a serpent? If you then, who
are evil, know how to give good gifts to your children,
how much more will your Father who is in heaven give
good things to those who ask him!"

in our own conscience our Lord shows it. Psychologically we are quick to see (and to magnify) our own faults in others ("lynx to our neighbours, mole to ourselves"). We see the **speck** (*karphos*, a dry particle of sawn wood) in his eye and miss the plank (or **log**) in our own – this is the true proportion and it escapes us. Yet we kindly (and hypocritically) offer to remove what we are too blind to see.

Profaning sacred things 7:6

Yet a discreet assessment of our fellow's dispositions is sometimes necessary as when, for instance, there is danger of sacrilegious profanation. Indiscretion in such matters may turn indifference to malevolence, thus uselessly harming our neighbour, injuring ourselves, wasting what is precious and sacred. Jesus speaks, as it seems, of prudence in expounding the mysteries of the kingdom; he himself later, 13:10-15, shows the example. The principle was applied in the early Church to the question of non-admission of the unbaptized to the Holy Eucharist. Our Lord compares the indiscretion to that of offering sacred (sacrificial meat?) or precious things to mere brutes which turn on the giver with disappointed ferocity. The comparison is a general one. We should not seek therefore to identify the **swine**, e.g. with pagans, nor the **dogs** with lapsed Christians, nor to regard the terms as a pointed insult. The animals together represent the religiously inappreciative: their distinction is merely graphic and stylistic in the manner of Semitic parallelism. This parallelism will be all the more marked if we accept the not improbable suggestion that the Aramaic has been mistranslated or subjected to interpretations, and originally read: "Give not a precious ring (Aram. *qedasha*) to dogs". Our present text (**what is holy**), supposes an original Aramaic *qudsha*.

Effective prayer 7:7-11 (Lk 11:9-13)

In Lk this passage is not included in the Sermon, and it is unexpected in this place in Mt, though it would aptly follow 6:33. **7-8** – It is a constant divine law that prayer is never unanswered. Provided we pray as Jesus taught his disciples, 6:9-13, a door will be opened to us (by God, as in the similar use of the impersonal in 2, 19). **9-11** – To doubt this would be to insult our Father. Even human fathers, with all their imperfections, are capable of perfect paternal love. How much more the heavenly Father who is perfection itself! He will not disappoint the hungry children with a stone that looks like bread nor with a serpent (equally useless for food) which has perchance been netted with the fish. The **serpent** may be identified with the *tropidonotus tesselatus*, sometimes hooked, and presumably netted, in the lake of Galilee. Hence (in the absence of any similarity, comparable to the bread-stone similarity, between the "serpent" and any known Galilean fish) the fish-serpent juxtaposition.

The golden rule 7:12

12 "So whatever you wish that men would do to you, do so to them; for this is the law and the prophets."

The two ways 7:13-14

13 "Enter by the narrow gate; for the gate is wide and the way is easy, that leads to destruction, and those who enter
14 by it are many.   For the gate is narrow and the way is hard, that leads to life, and those who find it are few."

False prophets 7:15-20

15 "Beware of false prophets, who come to you in sheep's
16 clothing but inwardly are ravenous wolves.   You will know them by their fruits. Are grapes gathered from
17 thorns, or figs from thistles?   So, every sound tree bears

The golden rule 7:12 (Lk 6:31)

The whole message of the ancient scriptures which Christ had come to fulfil (5:17 note) is summed up: In all things that concern our fellows (practical charity, forgiveness, kindly judgments, etc.) our best available standard of conduct is the treatment we should like to receive (though perhaps do not) from him. This eliminates the interest we have in ourselves or rather shares it with our neighbour, thus restoring the balance. Mt evidently takes this love of neighbour to include the love of God which is its true motive, 22:34-40. For a negative form of the golden rule cf Tob 4:16. The original setting of the maxim is perhaps, as in Lk 6:31, after the "retaliation" section, 5:38-42, though it would as suitably follow the "Judge not" passage, 7:1-5. The falling cadence at the end of the verse and the echo of 5:17 give the impression that the Sermon proper is now at an end. This prepares us for the concluding exhortation to serious action (7:13-27).

The two ways 7:13-14 (Lk 13:23-24)

The Christian must not follow the majority, 13-14, nor run after every specious teacher, 15-20, nor be content with mere professions of loyalty or even with the grace of miracle-working, 21-23. He must do the will of the Father as declared by the Son, otherwise his efforts are wasted, 24-27, 13-14 (Lk 13:23f). Jesus does not minimize the difficulty of the Christian way of life, but laments the fewness of those who in fact follow it. He uses images familiar to Jewish teachers.

13 – The **gate** (of the city), or possibly the "defile", through which we enter upon the way is as narrow as the path is hard to which it leads. That there are few who walk this way is a fact of experience. It does not follow that only these reach the goal – who can calculate the mercy of God? Jesus does not intend to define the number of the "elect" – a question which he refuses to answer in Lk 13:23f. It is the practical solution that counts: strive to enter by the narrow door, Lk 13:24. The answer to the theoretical question is not useful to man; God reserves the knowledge to himself. We know that "God wishes all men to be saved", 1 Tim 2:4, and this is solid foundation for our hope.

False prophets 7:15-20 (Lk 6:43-45)

Again there is no close connexion with what precedes, but the passage has been drawn into this place by the idea of finding the right way, 14. Jesus here deals not with the personal morals of those who falsely claim to bear a message from God (**false prophets**), but with the damaging effects of their teaching. Doubtless he has the Pharisees in mind, but he is providing for the more distant future, too. **15** – These false teachers will bear the appearance of belonging to the flock of Christ, hence the danger. Heresies live on their modicum of truth. But underneath that skin, error devours the duped victim. **16-18** – Yet how recognize the

[18] good fruit, but the bad tree bears evil fruit.   A sound tree cannot bear evil fruit, nor can a bad tree bear good fruit. [19] Every tree that does not bear good fruit is cut down and [20] thrown into the fire.   Thus you will know them by their fruits.''

The true disciple 7:21-27

[21] "Not every one who says to me, 'Lord, Lord,' shall enter the kingdom of heaven, but he who does the will of my [22] Father who is in heaven.   On that day many will say to me, 'Lord, Lord, did we not prophesy in your name, and cast out demons in your name, and do many mighty [23] works in your name?'   And then I will declare to them, [24] 'I never knew you; depart from me, you evildoers.'   Every one then who hears these words of mine and does them will [25] be like a wise man who built his house upon the rock;   and the rain fell, and the floods came, and the winds blew and beat upon that house, but it did not fall, because it had [26] been founded on the rock.   And every one who hears these words of mine and does not do them will be like a foolish [27] man who built his house upon the sand;   and the rain fell, and the floods came, and the winds blew and beat against that house, and it fell; and great was the fall of it.''

Amazement of the crowds 7:28-29

[28] And when Jesus finished these sayings, the crowds were [29] astonished at his teaching, for he taught them as one who had authority, and not as their scribes.

false teacher? A little patience and the effect of their work (**fruit,** by an abrupt change of metaphor) will betray them. That grapes and figs do not appear on thorns and thistles is a commonplace of experience. And so indeed it is with any tree. It does not, **17,** and cannot, **18,** produce fruit alien to its nature. The **bad,** or rotten tree, (*sarpos,* decayed, or corrupt in the moral sense cf Eph 4:22) will bring forth **evil** (*poneros,* wicked) fruit. The adjectives, which are susceptible of a moral interpretation, have been chosen with a view to the application of the comparison. **19** – Parenthetically Mt prophesies the punishment of these false teachers (or possibly the certain elimination of their teaching) in the words of the Baptist, 3:10; cf Lk 3:9. **20** – The passage closes as it began (cf 16a), summing-up what has been said ("inclusion").

The true disciple 7:21-27 (cf Lk 6:46; 13:26-27; 6:47-49)

Jesus now passes to his concluding appeal for serious action. He has just spoken, 15-20, of false teachers; he speaks now of the danger of self-deception – the danger of presuming upon the privilege of belonging officially to the fellowship of Jesus. **21** – The gates of heaven do not open to the urgent cry **Lord, Lord!** (cf 25:11 note) but to those who do **the will** (good pleasure) of God. Jesus, with quiet assurance, uses the phrase **my Father,** as again in 26:39, 42. He teaches the disciples to say "*our* Father", 6:9, but studiously avoids the phrase himself – his sonship is not of the common sort. **22-23** – (Lk 13:25, 27). Not even preaching on the authority ("in the name") of Jesus, nor exorcism nor miracles worked through that same authority will, in themselves, qualify preacher or wonder-worker for entrance when he comes to stand at heaven's gate. Unless such a one also "does the will of the Father", Jesus will openly declare that even while working these prodigies the man was never truly of his company. Christ himself significantly assumes the power of expulsion from the kingdom of those who, ignoring the will of the Father, have worked nothing but evil (cf Ps 6:9). **24-27** – A concluding appeal in the form of two parables in elaborate antithesis. The man who hears and acts upon our Lord's teaching has a firm dwelling. The torrential winter rains, the streams in flood, high winds will not disturb it. Not so the man who builds on thin, crumbling earth (*ammos*).

Amazement of the crowds 7:28-29

Mt rounds off the Sermon with the formula he reserves for the end of his five great groups of discourse, 11:1; 13:53; 19:1; 26:1. All were amazed at the matter of the discourse and the manner of the Teacher. They were used to the Scribes and Pharisees who repeatedly appealed to the authority of scripture and of the teachers of repute who had preceded them. But Jesus had interpreted, even modified, the scriptures, 5:21-47, and this without appeal to any authority but his own.

The Kingdom Preached 8:1–10:42

I

Narrative: Opening of Christ's Ministry. Ten Miracles 8:1 – 9:38

The light that dawned on Galilee, 4:15f, with the teaching of Jesus, ch. 5—7, now shines also through his works, ch. 8—9. Mt selects as samples ten miracles. He recounts them in one group though (after the first three) with significant interruptions. Between the leper, 8:2-4, the son of the centurion, 5-13, Peter's mother-in-law, 14f, there is no pause in the narrative. Mt then makes general mention of many miracles, 16f, and tells of the sobering demands made by Jesus of two enthusiastic would-be followers, 19-22. Our Lord and his disciples then cross to the east side of the lake, 23, and three more miracles are narrated: the calming of the storm, 24-27, the Gadarene exorcisms, 28-34, and (back in Capernaum) the paralytic, 9:1-2. This last is followed by the disputes on forgiveness of sins, 3-8, and, after Matthew's call, 9, on our Lord's association with sinners, 10-13, and finally, on the fasting question, 14-17. The last four miracles: Jairus's daughter, 18-19, 23-25, the issue of blood, 20-22, the blind men of Capernaum, 27-30, the dumb demoniac, 32-33, are interrupted only by comments on the effect of Christ's miracles, 26, 31, 33-34. Mt, indeed, makes a point of noting the human reactions to this prodigious display of power. The confidence of those in trouble, 8:2, 8, 16; 9:2, 18, 21, 28, the astonishment of the multitudes, 8:27; 9:8, 26, 31, 33, and, on the other hand, the cavils of some, 9:3, 11, 24, culminating in blind hostility, 9:34. In this section therefore, we have not merely a list of miracles arranged systematically, to prove Christ's powers. The miracles are narrated not, as it were, statically, but with a view to the dynamic development of the ministry in itself and in its impact upon the public. As for the exact placing of the events in time, Mt's general procedure and the fact that he is here selecting only samples of Christ's miracles forbid us to expect rigid chronological sequence. This last, however, is not entirely ignored. Matthew's vocation, for example, is doubtless placed in its actual setting. The order of events is vastly different from Mk's. For more ample historical detail on the miracles of ch 8—9 cf Jones, *The Gospel according to St Mark* (London and New York, 1963).

The leper 8:1-4

¹ When he came down from the mountain, great crowds
² followed him; and behold, a leper came to him and
knelt before him, saying, "Lord, if you will, you can make
³ me clean." And he stretched out his hand and touched
him, saying, "I will: be clean." And immediately his
⁴ leprosy was cleansed. And Jesus said to him, "See that
you say nothing to any one; but go, show yourself to the
priest, and offer the gift that Moses commanded, for a
proof to the people."

The centurion's servant 8:5-13

⁵ As he entered Capernaum, a centurion came forward to
⁶ him, beseeching him and saying, "Lord, my servant is
⁷ lying paralysed at home, in terrible distress." And he
⁸ said to him, "I will come and heal him." But the
centurion answered him, "Lord, I am not worthy to have
you come under my roof; but only say the word, and my
⁹ servant will be healed. For I am a man under authority,
with soldiers under me; and I say to one, 'Go,' and he
goes, and to another, 'Come,' and he comes, and to my

The leper 8:1-4 (Mk 1:40-45; Lk 5:12-16)

By placing the miracle of the leper in this setting (after the Sermon) Mt illustrates the power of Jesus, and at the same time his respect for the Law; cf 5:17. **1** – This verse may perhaps be reckoned as part of the conclusion of the preceding account of the Sermon. In any case, it implies no close chronological connexion with the miracle, which took place probably before the Sermon. **2** – The term "leprosy" was used of skin diseases of many degrees, some of which were curable, though the cure had to be certified by the priests, Lev 13:2ff. For description and distinction of various forms of "leprosy" cf Lev 13-14. One variety was incurable, eating away the extremities and covering the body with running sores until eventually the flesh rotted away. Thus acute leprosy may be suggested by Luke's "full of leprosy", Lk 5:13. The leper had no right to approach: the precautions of the Law require that he live apart and never appear in public without warning. **3** – Our Lord's pity overlooks the legal fault. Moved by the man's faith he touches the repulsive body. Aware of his own authority and of his power to heal, he fears neither legal contamination, Lev 15:7, nor physical. The cure is immediate. **4** – Careful as ever, 9:30; 16:20; 17:9, to preclude popular excitement, Jesus binds the man to silence; vainly however, Mk 1:45. The injunction does not necessarily exclude the presence of the "crowds" (8:1, though see note) who may have been at some distance; or possibly Jesus forbids only a formal declaration made before the priests had pronounced. Indeed, though the man was cured he was not legally pure before such pronouncement. The Law must be respected: first, medical examination by the priests of Jerusalem, then the complicated ritual of purification. The **gift** (sacrifice) was, for the poor, of one lamb or two turtle-doves; cf Lev 14:1-32. The purpose of this last command is to afford to the official representatives of Judaism the opportunity of recognizing both the power of Jesus and his scrupulous respect for the Law.

The centurion's servant 8:5-13 (Lk 7:1-10)

Mt tells in summary fashion the more detailed story of Lk. The incident took place after the Sermon; cf Lk 7:1-2. **5** – The **centurion** (commander of one hundred men, approximately "sergeant-major") though not a Jew, 10-12, was well-disposed to Judaism and had contributed to the building of a synagogue in Capernaum, Lk 7:5. He was an officer, perhaps, of a Roman garrison at Capernaum or possibly of the army of Herod Antipas, tetrarch of Galilee and Perea. **6-8** – A valued servant had been struck with paralysis (a general term covering, e.g., arthritis, meningitis). Having heard of the miracles of Jesus (cf 4:23) the centurion enlists Jewish friends to ask him to visit the sick man (Lk; Mt's account is shorter). Repenting his own action with its appearance of a brusque summons he hastens to forestall the visit and (through

¹⁰ slave, 'Do this,' and he does it." When Jesus heard him, he marvelled, and said to those who followed him, "Truly, I say to you, not even in Israel have I found such faith.
¹¹ I tell you, many will come from east and west and sit at table with Abraham, Isaac, and Jacob in the kingdom of
¹² heaven while the sons of the kingdom will be thrown into the outer darkness; there men will weep and gnash
¹³ their teeth." And to the centurion Jesus said, "Go; be it done for you as you have believed." And the servant was healed at that very moment.

Peter's mother-in-law 8:14-15
¹⁴ And when Jesus entered Peter's house, he saw his mother-
¹⁵ in-law lying sick with a fever; he touched her hand, and the fever left her, and she rose and served him.

his friends; Lk) professes his unworthiness. The humble words of the pagan soldier are used now in the Christian liturgy. **9** – The soldier knows what discipline is: he takes orders and gives them, and obedience is unquestioned (a man **under authority,** one used to the atmosphere of military discipline). It is possible, however, that the original Aramaic read less awkwardly "I am a man who has authority, and soldiers are under my charge". **10** – Jesus was capable of surprise: "although nothing was hidden from Christ yet a thing could come freshly to his experiential human knowledge and so produce wonder" (Aquinas). Israelites had shown their faith in him, 4:24, but the centurion's quiet conviction of his power to heal at a distance was a new experience. **11-13** – Cf Lk 13:28f. The faith of this Gentile recalls to Mt the words of Jesus (used probably on the occasion assigned to them by Lk) lamenting the fate of **the sons of the kingdom,** of those who would naturally be expected to inherit the blessings of the messianic age. The images of the banquet and of the darkness are familiar in Jewish descriptions of the world to come. Nevertheless, Mt's formula "kingdom of the heavens" (i.e. "of God") does not exclude the kingdom on earth; nor does it appear to do so in this place – especially as there is an allusion to those **from east and west** who, Mal 1:11, are to become subjects of a kingdom of God on earth. Many of the Gentiles will inherit the promises made to the patriarchs and finally share their reward. Ironically the very children of the patriarchs will, as a body, be excluded. In the darkness that lies outside the kingdom shall be despair and fear: the weeping and the chattering of teeth (i.e. from fear, rather than "gnashing" from disappointed rage) spoken of in the Jewish eschatological literature. Though, in that literature, the phrases are used in connexion with a future, entirely transcendent order, we are not thereby forced to restrict Christ's thought to the same limits. For him the "kingdom" inherited by the Gentiles is the kingdom of which he is the centre here and hereafter.

Peter's mother-in-law 8:14-15 (Mk 1:29-31; Lk 4:38-39)
In the interests of his logical plan Mt, unlike Mk and Lk, ignores details of time and circumstance. Actually the miracle preceded those of the leper and the centurion's servant. Simon (Mk; Lk) called "Peter" (Mt; cf 4:18), though a native of Bethsaida, Jn 1:44, lived with his brother Andrew (Mk) in Capernaum. The brothers invited Jesus (with James and John; cf Mk) to take refreshment in their home. The woman, cured in the height of fever (Lk), prepares a meal for him. This detail is mentioned in Mt's summary account not as a picturesque circumstance, but to prove that the cure was instantaneous and complete.

Various cures 8:16-17

¹⁶ That evening they brought to him many who were
possessed with demons; and he cast out the spirits with a
¹⁷ word, and healed all who were sick.   This was to fulfil
what was spoken by the prophet Isaiah, "He took our
infirmities and bore our diseases."

The apostolic calling and its demands 8:18-22

¹⁸ Now when Jesus saw great crowds around him, he gave
¹⁹ orders to go over to the other side.   And a scribe came
up and said to him, "Teacher, I will follow you wherever
²⁰ you go."   And Jesus said to him, "Foxes have holes, and
birds of the air have nests: but the Son of man has nowhere
²¹ to lay his head."   Another of the disciples said to him,
²² "Lord, let me first go and bury my father."   But Jesus
said to him, "Follow me, and leave the dead to bury their
own dead."

Various cures 8:16-17 (Mk 1:32-34; Lk 4:40-41)

After sunset, as soon as the Sabbath with its enforced rest was over (Mk; Lk), the people flocked thither with their sick. The miracle at Peter's house was soon known in the village. Christ's exorcisms, unlike the elaborate Jewish ceremonies, were worked by a simple command. Of the "Servant of God" who was to suffer the prophet had said: He has taken our sufferings upon himself and has burdened himself with our sorrows, Is 53:4. Mt (who quotes here from the Heb. text and not from LXX) applies the words, as the context clearly shows, to the removal of human sufferings. It is not clear that Mt means that Jesus undertook to endure these sufferings himself, since the text as used here might be satisfied by our Lord's taking it upon himself to annihilate the suffering. Yet the Isaian prophecy means that the Servant himself assumed the suffering due to others (thus expiating human sin) and this sense would not escape the Christian reader fully aware of the Passion and its spiritual significance. Under the obvious sense of the quotation in this passage there lies, therefore, a profound dogmatic sense.

The apostolic calling and its demands 8:18-22 (Lk 9:57-60)

The date of the departure across the lake and of the two miracles, 8:23-27, 28-34, is uncertain but it is placed much later in the ministry by Mk and Lk. The incident of the two would-be disciples, 19-22, is perhaps correctly placed in Lk 9:57-60. **18** – The **great crowds** surrounding Jesus are not necessarily the people of 16. Indeed, there is a ring of finality in 17 and, in any case, Mt does not mention the time of departure for the eastern side of the lake. **19-20** – On the way to the boat (Peter's?) a scribe (cf 2:4 note) enthusiastically offers himself as a permanent disciple. Our Lord while not rejecting the offer warns him of the consequences of discipleship. It means sharing the homeless existence that Jesus is now embarking on. Even the marauding fox and the wandering bird have their headquarters. Not so **the Son of man.** This is Mt's first use of this strange title; he uses it 33 times in all. The expression (cf Ps 8:5 where "a son of man" means "a mere human being") is used by Jesus on about 40 occasions to emphasize his humanity and at the same time to surround it with a mysterious dignity. Its messianic implication will appear only when it is placed in the setting of Daniel's prophecy; cf 26:64 note. Probably Jesus took the expression from Daniel (where "one like a son of man" is the symbol of the coming kingdom), giving it definition ("*the* Son of man"). It is possible, too, that he chose this title because he perceived the last consequences of the messianic synthesis of lowly Servant, Is 53, and glorious Son of Man, Dan 7:13f, thus accepting what Judaism in its retrospect upon its own prophetic history had refused to see or failed to grasp. Of the scribe's reaction to Christ's words we know nothing.

The storm 8:23-27

²³ And when he got into the boat, his disciples followed him.
²⁴ And behold, there arose a great storm on the sea, so that
the boat was being swamped by the waves; but he was
²⁵ asleep. And they went and woke him, saying, "Save,
²⁶ Lord; we are perishing." And he said to them, "Why
are you afraid, O men of little faith?" Then he rose and
rebuked the winds and the sea; and there was a great
²⁷ calm. And the men marvelled, saying, "What sort of
man is this, that even winds and sea obey him?"

The Gadarene demoniacs 8:28-34

²⁸ And when he came to the other side, to the country of
the Gadarenes, two demoniacs met him, coming out of
²⁹ the tombs, so fierce that no one could pass that way. And
behold, they cried out, "What have you to do with us,
O Son of God? Have you come here to torment us before
³⁰ the time?" Now a herd of many swine was feeding at
³¹ some distance from them. And the demons begged him,
"If you cast us out, send us away into the herd of swine."
³² And he said to them, "Go." So they came out and went
into the swine; and behold, the whole herd rushed down
the steep bank into the sea, and perished in the waters.
³³ The herdsmen fled, and going into the city they told
everything, and what had happened to the demoniacs.
³⁴ And behold, all the city came out to meet Jesus; and when
they saw him, they begged him to leave their neighbourhood.

21 – Another of the disciples (perhaps better, "another person, one of his disciples", and therefore expected to accompany Jesus on his journey) asks leave to stay and bury his father. The respite he asks is evidently short, since in Palestine burial follows very soon after death. **22** – But when God calls, neither comfort must be considered, 19-20, nor even the most sacred human ties: Leave the burial of the dead to those who are not alive to the greater interests of God.

The storm 8:23-27 (Mk 4:35-41; Lk 8:22-25)

Storms come suddenly on the lake of Galilee. Itself more than 600 ft below sea-level, it is surrounded by high hills. The differences of temperature produce sudden, high winds from the north-west. The boat was being swamped, but Jesus, taking the opportunity of a brief rest, was undisturbed. When the frightened disciples awakened him, he first (Mt) calmly rebuked the lack of faith shown in the cry "We are perishing!" They should have known they were safe with him, awake or asleep. Erect on the pitching boat he rebuked winds and sea as if they were unruly servants. **27 – the men** is a strange expression to use of the disciples (though in Hebrew use "the men" often means simply "they"). It is possible, therefore, that Mt is rounding-off his account of the miracle, as in 9:8, 26, by noting its effect on the general public who would be informed by the disciples. Mt is more systematic and less picturesque throughout than Mk. For details, therefore, cf Mk 4:36-41.

The Gadarene demoniacs 8:28-34 (Mk 5:1-20; Lk 8:26-39)

They disembark in the district of Gadara (Mt **of the Gadarenes**; Mk "Gerasenes"; Lk "Gergesenes"), a town of the Decapolis on a height c. 6 m. S.E. of the lake (now *Um Qeis*). It was a well-known town, even called "the metropolis of Perea" by Josephus, and perhaps for this reason Mt (or his translator) uses the name to indicate vaguely the place of disembarkation on the "lakeside". This place was probably at a spot called *Moqa Edlo* where, after thirty yards of shore, the bank rises sharply to hills in which are natural caves possibly once used as tombs, 28. A mile or two to the north lies the deserted hamlet of Chorsia (*el-Korsi*) doubtless the "city" of 33f. It lies on the east side of the lake facing Magdala; its name probably accounts for Mk's "country of the Gerasenes". **28** – Mk (followed by Lk) mentions only one demoniac, presumably the more violent of the two and around whom the account, as Mk received it, had centred. Mt had evidently an independent source of information. **29** – The devils resent the pressure of the power that confronts them (Mk; Lk). They complain that Jesus has invaded their territory before **the time** of their final expulsion to hell. Meanwhile they claimed the right to exercise their malignity on earth without interruption (cf the Jewish apocalyptic writings, e.g. Book of

The paralytic 9:1-8

¹ And getting into a boat he crossed over and came to his
² own city.   And behold, they brought to him a paralytic,
lying on his bed; and when Jesus saw their faith he said to
the paralytic, "Take heart, my son; your sins are for-
³ given."   And behold, some of the scribes said to them-
⁴ selves, "This man is blaspheming."   But Jesus, knowing
their thoughts, said, "Why do you think evil in your
⁵ hearts?   For which is easier, to say, 'Your sins are for-
⁶ given,' or to say, 'Rise and walk'?   But that you may
know that the Son of man has authority on earth to
forgive sins"—he then said to the paralytic—"Rise, take
⁷ up your bed and go home."   And he rose and went
⁸ home.   When the crowds saw it, they were afraid, and
they glorified God, who had given such authority to men.

Jubilees, 10:8; Henoch 10:12-14). **30-31** – In this predominantly pagan district the Talmudic prohibition against the rearing of pigs would be, as elsewhere, ignored. In any case, it is not said that their owners (much less their consumers) were Jews. For lack of a nobler object of their essential malevolence the spirits ask to be sent into (or possibly "among") the herd (2,000, Mk) of swine. **32** – Jesus worked no second miracle to restrain the devils from the pigs. He was concerned with the salvation of human beings. Moreover, his rights over property were sovereign and the demoniac action, which he at least tolerated, was calculated to emphasize both the blind malignance of evil and his own mastery of it. These lessons, had they been learned, were more precious to the inhabitants than all their pigs. **33-34** – But the lessons were not learned, though the scared herdsmen took the story straight to the village. Fear (Lk) lost the villages their great chance, and they asked our Lord to go. Here again Mt's account is summary. He has not the vivid description of the demoniac's violence, Mk 5:3b-5, nor the subsequent history of the exorcized, Mk 5:15-20. He is concerned with the fact of the miracle and with its effect upon the public.

The paralytic 9:1-8 (Mk 2:1-12; Lk 5:17-26)

The series of miracles is continued and Mt still notes the wonder of the people, 8, 26, 31, 33. Yet a discordant note is now struck – the opposition of the Jewish religious leaders, 3, 11, 34. Mt, like Mk, connects the three incidents that follow (the paralytic, the call of Matthew, the fasting-question) but, unlike Mk, Mt's scheme is not chronological; moreover he is, as usual, less detailed than Mk. For his dogmatic purpose he tells only the essentials. **1** – Jesus *re*-enters the boat and *again* sails across the lake back to **his own city,** Capernaum, which he has chosen as his centre (cf 4:13) on the western shore. **2** – The house is packed (Mk) and the bearers of the paralytic are forced to carry him up the outside staircase onto the flat roof. Part of this they remove, lowering the man through the gap (cf Mk. 2:4). Jesus is touched by the faith of the paralytic and his friends. This faith, manifested by their extraordinary conduct, is more obvious in Mk than in Mt who omits the "roof" incident. It seems from Christ's first words that the paralytic's hopeful courage is failing him at the thought of his unworthiness. The belief probably prevailed then (as later, Jn 9:2) that sin was the cause of disease and that pardon must therefore precede cure. **3-4** – The declaration that the man's sins are even now being forgiven, or are forgiven from this moment, is actually a remission (cf 3, Mk 2:7). The thoughts of the scribes (and of the Pharisees; Lk) are not merely troubled by Christ's words, but actively and spontaneously hostile (**evil**). His words, they consider, do an injury to God (**blaspheming**) since only the offended can forgive the offence (Mk). That Jesus reads their thoughts is only the beginning of their discomfiture.

Call of Matthew 9:9

⁹ As Jesus passed on from there, he saw a man called Matthew sitting at the tax office; and he said to him, "Follow me". And he rose and followed him.

Note that whereas "Pharisee" is the term for a school of thought, "scribe" is that of the profession of students and teachers of the Mosaic Law. Not all the scribes were Pharisees (some were Sadducees) not all the Pharisees scribes. From the time of the Babylonian exile (6th cent. B.C.) the study of the Law intensified, and the profession of scribe grew steadily in importance. With the Law as his textbook he expounded what we should call dogmatic and moral theology (*haggadah* and *halakah*). The scribe was not fully-fledged until, after study from childhood, he attained his fortieth year. He received the title of "rabbi" and his authority was said to be greater than that of the Law itself. The qualified scribe had his disciples who acted as preachers, instructors, etc. in the smaller towns. **5-7** – The scribes were thinking that it was easy to use a formula whose effectiveness no one could either verify or contest. It was impossible to prove that the sins were in fact forgiven; Jesus, therefore, proves that, where results can be checked, his formulae are not empty. Hence he deserves credence as God's envoy even when he speaks of the invisible world. He concedes that to pronounce one formula (forgiveness) is as easy as pronouncing the other (physical cure) but defies their incredulity in the first case by confronting it with startling results in the second. He claims the power to forgive sins without saying whether it is in his own name or in God's. Yet he does not say that he has received the power, but simply that he has competent authority. The most natural conclusion is, therefore, that he claims a divine prerogative. The term **Son of man** (8:18 note) clearly does not mean in this place: man (i.e. mankind in general, cf Aramaic: *bar nasha*) since Jesus is vindicating a special prerogative for himself, just as his miracle of healing is a special prerogative. Nor is it, of itself, a messianic title. Used in this context it means that Jesus though *a man among men*, claims to exercise on earth the very authority that God wields from heaven. It is already a hint of the doctrine of the Incarnation. **8 – saw it:** The people are impressed by the miracle not by the invisible remission of sin. Filled with reverential awe they praise God for this miraculous power given to a "son of man" like themselves. Unlike the scribes, 3, they forget the more significant part of the episode – the claim to remit sin.

Call of Matthew 9:9 (Mk 2:13-14; Lk 5:27-28)

9 – Capernaum lay at the place on the Damascus road where the province of Herod Antipas touched on his brother Philip's – hence the custom-house near the lakeside (Mk). Here were collected the tolls and dues. The tax collectors (*portitores*) were agents of the proprietors of tax-collecting firms (*publicani*); these firms bought from the state (in this case, from Herod) the right to collect taxes. The demands of their masters and their own greed caused the agents to exploit the opportunities offered by ill-defined taxation and the ignorance of their

Eating with sinners 9:10-13

10 And as he sat at table in the house, behold, many tax collectors and sinners came and sat down with Jesus and 11 his disciples.   And when the Pharisees saw this, they said to his disciples, "Why does your teacher eat with tax 12 collectors and sinners?"   But when he heard it, he said, "Those who are well have no need of a physician, but those 13 who are sick.   Go and learn what this means, 'I desire mercy, and not sacrifice.' For I came not to call the righteous, but sinners."

Discussion on fasting 9:14-17

14 Then the disciples of John came to him, saying, "Why do we and the Pharisees fast, but your disciples do not 15 fast?"   And Jesus said to them, "Can the wedding guests mourn as long as the bridegroom is with them? The days will come, when the bridegroom is taken away from them, 16 and then they will fast.   And no one puts a piece of unshrunk cloth on an old garment, for the patch tears 17 away from the garment, and a worse tear is made.   Neither is new wine put into old wineskins; if it is, the skins burst, and the wine is spilled, and the skins are destroyed; but new wine is put into fresh wineskins, and so both are preserved."

victims. This conduct together with their professional association with Gentiles explains the common Gospel phrase "publicans – more exactly *portitores* – and sinners". **Matthew** (Heb. Mattai, prob. abbreviated from Mattatiah or "gift of God") appears in the lists of apostles (Mt adds "the tax collector"; cf 10:3 note). There is no doubt that he is to be identified with the "Levi" of the parallel places in Mk, Lk. Two names for one person (even two Semitic names, like "Matthew" and "Levi") were not uncommon (e.g. 1 Mac 2:2-5). The evangelist is not ashamed to make open reference to his old profession, but Mk (followed by Lk) uses the less-known name.

Eating with sinners 9:10-13 (Mk 2:15-17; Lk 5:29-32)

10 – Probably to celebrate the occasion Matthew invites his new master to a banquet (Lk) together with many business-fellows and **sinners,** careless livers, at least in the eyes of the legalist Pharisees. **11** – The Pharisees were certainly not sitting at table. It is possible that, in the fashion of the country, they stood at the door and watched; or perhaps they had the facts only on hearsay and their objections were put some time after. They did not venture (cf 9:3-8!) to attack Jesus directly, but addressed their rabbinical scruples to the disciples. **12-13** – Our Lord's answer was in proverb-form. Others may fear the contagion of legal or spiritual "disease" – not so the One who had come (i.e. into the world – a hint of pre-existence?) to cure it. "Read and comprehend the prophet", he says: "It is devotion I desire and not sacrifice". The quotation (Ho 6:6; from the Heb. as in 12:7 where it recurs more aptly) is used to emphasize God's overwhelming preference for true inward devotion over the external observances even of the Law. The argument is the more cogent in that the prohibition of eating with Gentiles is found not in the Law, but in Pharisaic practice. The appreciation of this text should make them understand how much closer to God's mind is the conduct of Jesus than their own ungenerous cavils.

Discussion on fasting 9:14-17 (Mk 2:18-22; Lk 5:33-39)

14 – It is not clear that the incident followed immediately upon the preceding (cf Mt's usual vague **then**) though it is aptly mentioned in this place. The prime movers are, doubtless, the Pharisees (cf Mk), but **the disciples of John** also take part. That our Lord's disciples do not fast is an opportunity of attack for the Pharisees; for the disciples of the Baptist it is perhaps only a difficulty. The question has a Semitic form (e.g. Is 5:4) better rendered "How is it that your disciples do not fast when we and the Pharisees fast so often?" **15** – Jesus answers that fasting, which bears the aspect of sorrow, ill becomes the joy the disciples feel in the presence of their master. Time enough for fasting (the first hint of the Passion) when the Master has been taken away from them (verb is a compound of that used in Is 53:8. LXX). The image Jesus

The woman with the issue of blood. Jairus's daughter 9:18-26

18 While he was thus speaking to them, behold, a ruler came in and knelt before him, saying, "My daughter has just died; but come and lay your hand on her, and she will 19 live." And Jesus rose and followed him, with his disciples. 20 And behold, a woman who had suffered from a hemorrhage for twelve years came up behind him and touched 21 the fringe of his garment; for she said to herself, "If I 22 only touch his garment, I shall be made well." Jesus turned, and seeing her he said, "Take heart, daughter; your faith has made you well." And instantly the woman 23 was made well. And when Jesus came to the ruler's house, and saw the flute players, and the crowd making a 24 tumult, he said, "Depart; for the girl is not dead but 25 sleeping." And they laughed at him. But when the crowd had been put outside, he went in and took her by 26 the hand, and the girl arose. And the report of this went through all that district.

uses is that of a wedding-feast; cf 22:2 note. The idea of the bridegroom would recall the Baptist's words, Jn 3:29, to the Baptist's disciples. The **wedding guests** (lit. the children of the bridal-chamber) (in this case our Lord's disciples) are more precisely the *bene hahuppah* or friends of the groom charged with the supervision of the celebrations. **16-17** – Our Lord's defence of his disciples is driven home by two comparisons. Both point to the one conclusion, namely, the imprudence and impossibility of uniting incompatibles: the new and the old. The patch of undressed cloth tears away from the cloak. Wine that is not completely fermented bursts the wineskins (of sheep or goat hide) rubbed thin by long use. In either case the imprudence is disastrous to both new and old. This dictum of Jesus is loaded with consequences, gradually appreciated by the apostles when the time came for the definitive break with Judaism. For the present, however, the principle has immediate application only to the Pharisees' fasting observance.

The woman with the issue of blood. Jairus's daughter 9:18-26 (Mk 5:21-43; Lk 8:40-56)

Mt uses a transitional formula (18; cf 12:46) not to be taken as deliberately indicative of chronological sequence. The incidents in this section are (Mk, Lk) to be placed immediately after 9:1*b*. **18-19** – A prominent official of the Capernaum synagogue (Mt **a ruler**; Mk and Lk: a ruler of the synagogue) named Jairus (Mk, Lk) went on his knees before Jesus asking a cure for his daughter, who was on the point of death (Mk, Lk) or (Mt – a celebrated difficulty) **has just died.** Jesus and his disciples set out for Jairus's house. On the way (Mk and Lk only) news was brought that the girl had died, but Jesus reassured the father. Mt, according to his custom, telescopes the whole incident. This explains his divergence from Mk-Lk in reporting the words of Jairus. He is content to sum up the successive thought, fear, faith of the father in one sentence which he puts on Jairus's lips. Augustine: "It is in the interests of brevity that Mt makes Jairus ask the Lord to do what in fact he did . . . The two (Mk and Lk) give what Jairus actually said, Matthew what he wished and thought . . . From examples of this kind we deduce a most useful and absolutely indispensable principle (of interpretation), viz . . . that (a writer) does not lie if he makes a person say what that person wishes rather than what he actually said." **20-22** – Meanwhile, before news is brought of the child's death, a woman with a chronic haemorrhage, Lk 8:43, comes stealthily and timidly, but with great faith, to touch our Lord's cloak.   To escape embarrassing notice, partly too because the malady conveyed a legal impurity, Lev 15:25-27, she touches the very edge of his outer garment – one of the multi-coloured tassels (*sisit*) worn by pious Jews at the four corners of the cloak (Num 15:37-41; on our Lord's dress cf Edersheim, 1, 620-6). She is immediately cured (Mk; Lk); not mere physical contact

The two blind men 9:27-31

27 And as Jesus passed on from there, two blind men followed
   him, crying aloud, "Have mercy on us, Son of David."
28 When he entered the house, the blind men came to him;
   and Jesus said to them, "Do you believe that I am able
29 to do this?" They said to him, "Yes, Lord." Then he
   touched their eyes saying, "According to your faith be
30 it done to you." And their eyes were opened. And Jesus
31 sternly charged them, "See that no one knows it." But
   they went away and spread his fame through all that
   district.

The dumb demoniac 9:32-34

32 As they were going away, behold, a dumb demoniac was
33 brought to him. And when the demon had been cast out,
   the dumb man spoke; and the crowds marvelled, saying,
34 "Never was anything like this seen in Israel." But the
   Pharisees said, "He casts out demons by the prince of
   demons."

but her faith had already merited the miracle (Mt). But she has not escaped notice. Jesus knows what has happened, Mk 5:30; Lk 8:45, though Mt does not suggest that this knowledge is supernatural. **23** – With Peter, James and John (Mk; Lk) he enters the house of the dead girl and encounters the confused noise of the wailing sympathizers and the dismal music of professional flute-players (indispensable at Jewish funerals). **24** – He dismisses all this apparatus as useless. There is no cause for mourning; the girl is only asleep. Jesus was to use a similar phrase of Lazarus, Jn 11:11. In each case he avoids the term "dead" because neither the girl nor Lazarus was irreparably dead. That she is not still alive, however, is perfectly clear, Mk 5:35; hence the mocking incredulity. **25** – When at last the mourners are persuaded to leave Jesus, in the presence of the father and mother and of his favoured three (Mk), takes the dead child by the hand (Mt; Mk; Lk). **26** – Our Lord has taken precautions against undue publicity (24f and Mk 5:43) possibly because such a miracle might have provoked a messianic crisis; yet, as Mt is accustomed to note, the report spread through the district.

The two blind men 9:27-31 (cf Mt 20:29-34; Mk 10:46-52; Lk 18:35-43)
The episode has, of its nature, certain similarities with that of the blind men of Jericho, 20:29-34, with which it is too confidently identified. The one common element that might be thought significant is the "Son of David" cry which (if it be not imported from 20:31) is natural enough at a time when miracles were inducing messianic atmosphere. **27** – As Jesus leaves the house of Jairus, two blind men (two for mutual support – a not uncommon sight in Palestine) hail him as **Son of David,** i.e. as Messiah; cf 1:1 note. **28** – It is perhaps for this very reason that Jesus does not acknowledge their cry (cf note to 26) but waits until he reaches **the house** (probably Matthew's; cf 9-10) before he speaks to them. The **mercy** they have asked of the Son of David is clearly the gift of sight and Jesus asks only if they believe in his power to heal. They answer **yes,** adding a term of profound respect (**Lord**; Gk: *kurie;* Aramaic: *mari*). **29** – The cure proves they have not lied. It will be noticed, however, that the faith though perfect did not work the miracle, but was our Lord's required condition. **30** – Jesus most strictly enjoins secrecy – the more strictly, no doubt, because they had already openly proclaimed his messianic character. But Mt notes (again!) that they could not resist the temptation.

The dumb demoniac 9:32-34
When the two cured of blindness had left the house, a man was brought in whom diabolic possession had made dumb. The exorcism was effortless (contrast the Jewish exorcisms; Edersheim, 2, 770-86). The remark of all: **Never was anything like this seen in Israel,** is the result of this last of a series of miracles. It makes a fitting and

Jesus and the crowds 9:35-38

35 And Jesus went about all the cities and villages, teaching
in their synagogues and preaching the gospel of the king-
36 dom, and healing every disease and every infirmity.   When
he saw the crowds, he had compassion for them, because
they were harassed and helpless, like sheep without a
37 shepherd.   Then he said to his disciples, "The harvest
38 is plentiful, but the labourers are few;   pray therefore the
Lord of the harvest to send out labourers into his harvest."

characteristic epilogue to ch. 8—9, yet Mt is forced also to note the wicked obstinacy of the spiritual leaders of the people. Their remark, too, is doubtless typical of their attitude to all the preceding miracles and Jesus later exposes its intellectual dishonesty (12:22-37, see notes).

Jesus and the crowds 9:35-38 (Mk 6:6, 34; Lk 10:1-2)
From our Lord's work amongst the people Mt is now passing to his preparation of the apostles. The twelve had already been chosen before the Sermon (cf Lk 6:12ff) and had witnessed the work of Jesus among the people – too much for a single human being. **35-36** – Experience in Galilee (and beyond?) showed the desperate case of the people. Jesus was deeply moved, for they were harried and abject like shepherdless sheep, cf 18:12-14. Their spiritual pastors had failed them. **37-38** – The metaphor changes (cf Lk 10:2 which perhaps retains the words in their true chronological place) but, shepherds or harvesters, men are needed for the work. Otherwise the sheep will perish and the harvest rot where it stands. As with his other gifts, so with this: God will provide if we ask. By the Incarnation the divine Son accepted certain human limitations. The world has a duty to pray for men to help our Saviour. It is his own command.

Mission of the Twelve 10:1-16

¹ And he called to him his twelve disciples and gave them
authority over unclean spirits, to cast them out, and to
² heal every disease and every infirmity. The names of
.the twelve apostles are these: first Simon, who is called
Peter, and Andrew his brother; James the son of Zebedee,
³ and John is brother; Philip and Bartholomew; Thomas
and Matthew the tax collector; James the son of Alphaeus,
⁴ and Thaddaeus: Simon the Cananaean, and Judas
⁵ Iscariot, who betrayed him.   These twelve Jesus sent out,
charging them, "Go nowhere among the Gentiles, and
⁶ enter no town of the Samaritans, but go rather to the
⁷ lost sheep of the house of Israel.   And preach as you go,
⁸ saying, 'The kingdom of heaven is at hand.'   Heal the
sick, raise the dead, cleanse lepers, cast out demons. You
⁹ received without pay, give without pay.   Take no gold,
¹⁰ nor silver, nor copper in your belts, no bag for your
journey, nor two tunics, nor sandals, nor a staff; for the
¹¹ labourer deserves his food.   And whatever town or village
you enter, find out who is worthy in it, and stay with him
¹² until you depart. As you enter the house, salute it.

II

Discourse: Instruction for Apostles' Ministry 10:1-42

Jesus calls together the chosen twelve, 1-4, to regulate their conduct on their first and local missionary journey, 5-16; 40-42. Further instructions, 17-19, relate to a more distant future and a wider mission where they will meet not contempt only but inexorable and universal persecution, 17-23. Conscious of the Son's example and of the Father's loving vigilance the disciple must not capitulate, 24-33; his old life may be torn up by the roots, but he will find a new, 34-39. Mt's well-knit discourse is probably a synthesis of our Lord's missionary instructions given on different occasions.

Mission of the Twelve 10:1-16 (Mk 6:7; 3:13-19; Lk 9:1; 6:13-16; 10:1-2; Ac 1:13)

1-4 – Mt does not narrate the call of the Twelve (cf Mk 6:7; Lk 9:1) but presupposes it and mentions their names in passing. The section is but a summary introduction to the discourse. Here alone Mt calls them "apostles" (i.e "envoys"), elsewhere "the Twelve". The number is chosen evidently because it suits our Lord's plan of campaign but it has the further advantage of symbolizing the twelve patriarchs of the new Israel. All four lists of the apostles (Mt; Mk; Lk; Ac) agree in placing Simon, Philip, James ("the Less") at the head of each group of four. The members of each group are the same in each list, but within the group the names are interchanged in the various lists. Mt gives the names in pairs (cf Lk), suggesting that this was the order of their sending. Mt (only) describes Simon Peter as "the first" – a phrase unnecessary at the head of a list unless it indicates pre-eminence of dignity. The name **Peter** (cf 16:18 note) was probably conferred and explained on this occasion: cf Mk 3:16. **Andrew** (like Philip) bears a completely Greek name, evidently not an uncommon custom in "Galilee of the Gentiles" where Greek was freely spoken. Had other considerations not intervened, Andrew should have appeared at the head of the list because he was the first to come to Jesus, Jn 1:40. **James** and John both bear Hebrew names. James (Jacob) "the Greater" was martyred under Agrippa I in A.D. 44, Ac 12:1*f*; **John** ("the beloved disciple") lived to write the fourth Gospel towards the end of the century. **Philip,** like Peter and Andrew, was a native of Bethsaida, Jn 1:44. **Bartholomew** (Bar-Tolmai, i.e. son of T.) is commonly identified with the Nathanael of Jn 1:45 on the grounds that Nathanael is associated there (as Bartholomew here) with Philip and because Nathanael is grouped

¹³ And if the house is worthy, let your peace come upon it;
¹⁴ but if it is not worthy, let your peace return to you.   And if any one will not receive you or listen to your words, shake off the dust from your feet as you leave that house
¹⁵ or town.   Truly, I say to you, it shall be more tolerable on the day of judgment for the land of Sodom and
¹⁶ Gomorrah than for that town.   "Behold, I send you out as sheep in the midst of wolves; so be wise as serpents and innocent as doves."

with the apostles in Jn 21:2. **Thomas** (Aramaic: *teoma;* Greek: *didumos,*
Jn 11:16, "the twin") precedes Matthew (unlike Mk; Lk) possibly
for politeness' sake; modesty may account, too, for Mt's insertion of
"the tax collector" (and see note to 9:9). **James of Alphaeus** (possibly
James, son of Cleophas, cf Jn 19:25) is called "the Less" or "the Small",
Mk 15:40, to distinguish him from James, son of Zebedee. He is probably
to be identified with the apostle, "brother of the Lord", first bishop
of Jerusalem (cf Gal 1:19; Ac 15:13). **Thaddaeus** is apparently an
Aramaic name ("stout"?) and another name for Jude (brother) of
James, Lk 6:16. The surname Thaddaeus (Mt: Mk) or the addition
"of James" (Lk) distinguishes him from Judas the traitor. **Simon the
Cananaean,** better "the Zealous" (Aramaic: *qanana*) or possibly "the
Zealot" (Westminster Version), i.e. former member of the active Jewish
nationalist party. **Judas Iscariot,** i.e. "man of Qeriyoth", a soubriquet
derived from his father, Jn 6:71. Qeriyoth is an unidentified village of
Judah, Jos 15:25. Judas himself probably lived in Galilee like the other
apostles.

5-6 – Among the Gentiles: Israel was to be first beneficiary of the
messianic offer, Rom 1:16; so the apostles are not yet to walk the roads
leading to non-Jewish districts – neither northwards to pagan Syria
nor south to Samaria, mixed in population and diluted in Yahwism
since the Assyrian colonization of the 8th cent.; cf Jn 4:7. The mission
is confined to Galilean territory. Mk and Lk, writing for Gentile readers,
delicately omit the prohibition. **7-8** – The theme of the preaching is
summed up in a sentence. It is the Baptist's theme (3:2 note) and
our Lord's, 4:17. Miracles will guarantee the genuineness of their
message. Their missionary purpose must not be obscured or defeated
by the passing of money; the power of miracle and doctrine had cost
the apostles nothing. **9-10** – Our Lord's advice for the journey is not
"practical" in the usual sense, but consists in a complete reliance on
Providence. No need for gold, silver, copper in their girdle-pouches
(**belts**), nor food-satchel (**bag**), nor warm clothing (cf Mk 6:9) but
barefoot and unarmed (**nor a staff**). Mk, 6:8-9, allows shoes and
a staff; evidently the general sense, and not the actual words, is preserved
by each evangelist. Thus Mt's atmosphere is of complete detachment,
Mk is more practical; the substance of each is the same, viz. no undue
anxiety but reliance upon Providence. The supernatural powers of the
apostles cannot be sold or bought, 8, but for the labour involved in
their exercise, and in the preaching of the Gospel they deserve their
upkeep (cf Lk 10:7; 1 Tim 5:17-18; Gal 6:6; 1 Cor 9:13-14). Providence
will see that this is provided. **11-15** – Arrived at his destination the
apostle having found a respectable (**worthy**) house should lodge there
until he leaves the town lest he appears restless or fickle or over-par-
ticular in material things. **peace:** (*shalom*) is the common oriental
greeting, but on apostolic lips it takes a religious significance; it is

Persecution foretold for missionaries 10:17-25

17 "Beware of men; for they will deliver you up to councils,
18 and flog you in their synagogues, and you will be
dragged before governors and kings for my sake, to bear
19 testimony before them and the Gentiles. When they
deliver you up, do not be anxious how you are to speak
or what you are to say; for what you are to say will be
20 given to you in that hour; for it is not you who speak, but
21 the Spirit of your Father speaking through you. Brother
will deliver up brother to death, and the father his child,
and children will rise against parents and have them put
22 to death; and you will be hated by all for my name's
23 sake. But he who endures to the end will be saved. When
they persecute you in one town, flee to the next; for truly,
I say to you, you will not have gone through all the towns
24 of Israel, before the Son of man comes. A disciple is not

efficacious if its recipients be worthy. In biblical writings, "peace" is the sum of all blessings. This apostolic blessing (like God's own word, cf Is 55:11) cannot be robbed of its intrinsic power by the unworthiness of the person addressed; it returns to the giver that he may confer the rejected benefit on some worthy house. The despised blessing even becomes a curse: the last Judgment will show that such rejection of the good news of the kingdom is a crime greater even than the typical wickedness of "the cities of the plain", Gen 19. Meanwhile, the apostle will show symbolically that the unworthy house, though evidently Jewish, is no better than pagan territory. **shake the dust from your feet:** exclusively Jewish gesture, practised on return to the Holy Land after journeys on the "impure" soil of paganism. It is ironical that the gesture should be turned against Jews (cf also Paul in Ac 13:51); the Holy Land itself is not proof against uncleanliness. It becomes clear that the old order of a confident national religion is passing; cf 3:9. **16** – The sombre possibility of rejection leads, through this transitional verse, to the prospect of active persecution. Good is not violent; evil is (the opposition is brought out symbolically by **sheep** and **wolves**); the only defence of the good, therefore, is the prudence of the serpent quick to perceive attack and to elude it, together with the moral armour of innocence (of which the dove is symbol) which robs the attacking evil of its pretexts.

Persecution foretold for missionaries 10:17-25 (cf Mt 24:9; Mk 13:9; Lk 21:12-13)

The horizon widens and darkens, and the tone of the passage suggests that Mk and Lk (as even Mt in summary fashion, 24:9, 13) have rightly placed its delivery at the end of Christ's life. **17-20 – kings, governors, testimony before the Gentiles:** though possibly explainable of Jewish territory (cf 10:5), these terms hint at a wider field. Parenthetically, 19-20, the apostles are assured that they may still rely on providence in their official defence of the Gospel message. No anxious thought (cf 6:27) will be necessary; the Spirit of Father will suggest their line of defence. The readiness of the apostles to face trial with courage will be a guarantee of their doctrine. We should notice how, in the remainder of this chapter, Jesus presents himself as the focus of devotion; cf **for my sake** etc., 18, 22, 32f, 37f, 39. The emphasis would be unique and intolerable in the mouth of a merely human prophet. **21-23** – Domestic dissension (not the formal overthrow of the old authorities spoken of in 10:35 where Mic 7:6 is quoted) will result, because it is a new and practical religion with a defined rallying-point ("for my name's sake") that is to be preached, not merely a philosophical system. Perfect endurance (cf 24:13 note) will alone secure salvation: hence the preacher must persevere though hounded from town to town. He need not fear that he will exhaust the towns, his

²⁵ above his teacher, nor a servant above his master;   it is
enough for the disciple to be like his teacher, and the
servant like his master. If they have called the master
of the house Beelzebul, how much more will they malign
those of his household."

Open and fearless speech 10:26-33

²⁶ "So have no fear of them; for nothing is covered that will
²⁷ not be revealed, or hidden that will not be known.   What
I tell you in the dark, utter in the light; and what you
²⁸ hear whispered, proclaim upon the housetops.   And do
not fear those who kill the body but cannot kill the soul;
rather fear him who can destroy both soul and body in
²⁹ hell.   Are not two sparrows sold for a penny? And not
one of them will fall to the ground without your Father's
³⁰ will.   But even the hairs of your head are all numbered.
³¹ Fear not, therefore; you are of more value than many
³² sparrows.   So every one who acknowledges me before
men, I also will acknowledge before my Father who is in
³³ heaven;   but whoever denies me before men, I also will
deny before my Father who is in heaven."

places of refuge, before the **Son of man** intervenes on his behalf; cf 16:28 note. **24-25** – A short parable, lightly ironical, warns the disciples that they may expect no better treatment than their teacher. They should be satisfied with the same. Indeed, lacking their master's personal dignity, the slaves may expect worse – he had already been accused of alliance with "the prince of demons", 9:34, here named **Beelzebul** (Douay Version reads Beelzebub, identifying the Beelzebul of the Gk text with the name of Baalzebub the god of Ekron, 2 (4) Kg 1:2f; 6:16. Baalzebub is probably the Heb. form of the Assyrian *bel dababi* – an opponent in a process of law. The name was chosen by the Philistines perhaps because this god was adored, in placatory fashion, as man's adversary – Heb. *satan* – in the final judgment.) The correct reading of all the Gk N.T. texts is "Bee(l)zebul" which appears to be related to the *B'lzbl* (actually *Zbl-B'l*) of the Ras-Shamra-Ugarit texts, i.e. the prince-god (prince, Ugaritic *zbl*, cf Gen 30:20; god, *b'l*). Since the pagan gods are reckoned as demons, I Cor 10:20, the term Beelzebul becomes equivalent to "the prince of demons" (cf 9:34; 12:24; Mk 3:22; Lk 11:15). The name is therefore apt for the arch-enemy of the true God.

Open and fearless speech 10:26-33 (Lk 12:2-9)

Fear of death must not deter the confessors of Christ. (The tenor of the words suggests that they concern the period after our Lord's death.) Repeated calumny may lead to self-doubt which, however, is excluded in this case by the knowledge that the perfect master was thus attacked. Another reason for confidence in these circumstances is that the truth will prevail either when the Gospel message triumphs on earth or at least in the final account, 32f. With this for comfort let the knowledge of the kingdom, confided in the intimacy of the apostolic circle (cf 13:11) be boldly and publicly declared! **28-31** – God alone, not the devil (cf Jas 4:7) is to be feared, for only with his permission can both soul and body be consigned to perdition (preferable to **destroy,** i.e. to annihilate, since the idea of the annihilation of the soul would be strange to Jewish theology). The apparent harshness of 28b is due to the vigour of Semitic expression which does not distinguish the permissive from the positive will of God; cf 13:15 note. A second consideration to cast out fear is that the disciple is not lonely and abandoned among his enemies — he who creates and cares for the sparrows is his Father and cares for every fibre of his being. If the persecutor triumphs over the body (his only sphere, cf 28) it is only because the Father permits it; such treatment is only a mysterious form of the Father's care. **32-33** – By way of conclusion to the gist of the discourse (enduring loyalty to the Son and to his teaching, 17-31) our Lord sounds a personal note. On the basis of fidelity to his own person (a point of considerable theological importance) he is to be counsel for

Jesus the cause of dissension 10:34-36

³⁴ "Do not think that I have come to bring peace on earth;
³⁵ I have not come to bring peace, but a sword.   For I have
come to set a man against his father, and a daughter
against her mother, and a daughter-in-law against her
³⁶ mother-in-law;   and a man's foes will be those of his
own household."

Renouncing self to follow Jesus 10:37-39

³⁷ "He who loves father or mother more than me is not
worthy of me; and he who loves son or daughter more
³⁸ than me is not worthy of me;   and he who does not take
³⁹ his cross and follow me is not worthy of me.   He who finds
his life will lose it, and he who loses his life for my sake
will find it."

Reward for welcoming apostles 10:40-42

⁴⁰ "He who receives you receives me, and he who receives
⁴¹ me receives him who sent me.   He who receives a prophet
because he is a prophet shall receive a prophet's reward,
and he who receives a righteous man because he is a
⁴² righteous man shall receive a righteous man's reward. And
whoever gives to one of these little ones even a cup of
cold water because he is a disciple, truly, I say to you, he
shall not lose his reward."

the defence or prosecution before the Father-Judge who, with the Son, will be watching from heaven.

Jesus the cause of dissension 10:34-36 (Lk 12:51-53)

Jesus introduces an important modification into the current hope oi messianic days: the peace he brings is between God and man, not between man and man, as the world might give, Jn 14:27, and as the Jews expected. The dividing sword is his doctrine (cf Heb 4:12); its supernatural edge cuts, if necessary, through the natural domestic loyalties (cf Mic 7:6 where the words are a lament for the chaotic state of Samaria).

Renouncing self to follow Jesus 10:37-39 (Lk 14:26-27; 17:33)

37 – For himself personally, not for his Father only, our Lord boldly claims man's whole heart – it is the claim of God. Even the grim prospect of crucifixion (all too familiar in Galilee since the ruthless suppression of the recent outbreaks, cf Jos, *Ant.* 17, 10, 10) must be faced. But again (cf 23, 32) the section closes with a word of comfort (in paradoxical form due to the epigrammatic omission of distinctions): he who finds (i.e. secures, procures) his (natural) life will lose his (supernatural) life: he who loses his (natural) life for my sake – not through any other considerations as a Stoic might sacrifice it – will find a supernatural one.

Reward for welcoming apostles 10:40-42

These concluding vv. follow naturally upon 14: the "reception" (cf 14) is not so much a material welcome (cf 42) as a docility to the apostolic message (cf Lk 10:16; "he who hears you") which is that of Christ and his Father. It is a meritorious reception of one who speaks on behalf of God (**prophet**) if it is accorded not from merely natural politeness but from a supernatural motive recognizing God's truth or God's sanctity in the person of his ministers ("in the name of", i.e. precisely as, because he is). **42** – Even material help given with the same motive to an insignificant and weary apostle will associate the giver with the work and therefore with the reward of the apostle.

The Baptist's question 11:1-15

¹ And when Jesus had finished instructing his twelve
disciples, he went on from there to teach and preach in
their cities.

² Now when John heard in prison about the deeds of the
³ Christ, he sent word by his disciples and said to him,
"Are you he who is to come, or shall we look for another?"
⁴ And Jesus answered them, "Go and tell John what you
⁵ hear and see: the blind receive their sight and the lame
walk, lepers are cleansed and the deaf hear, and the dead
are raised up, and the poor have good news preached
⁶ to them.   And blessed is he who takes no offence at me "
⁷ As they went away, Jesus began to speak to the crowds
concerning John: "What did you go out into the wilder-
⁸ ness to behold? A reed shaken by the wind?   Why then
did you go out? To see a man clothed in soft raiment?
Behold, those who wear soft raiment are in king's houses.
⁹ Why then did you go out?   To see a prophet?   Yes, I

The Mystery of the Kingdom 11:1–13:52

I

Narrative: Opposition to the Kingdom 11:1 – 12:50

The message of the Baptist occasions his eulogy as usher of the kingdom, though neither he nor his master could please the demonstrably ill-disposed, 16-19. This last thought makes Mt place here, 20-24, the denunciation of the sophisticated who scorned the preaching of the kingdom. The same thought leads by contrast to the praise of the wisdom which chose to reveal the mystery of the kingdom to the simple by means of the omniscient Son, 25-27. To all such the Son addresses his appeal.

The Baptist's question 11:1-15 (Lk 7:18-28; 16:16)
The usual formula (cf 7:28, 13:53; 19:1; 26:1) closes the discourse of ch 10, and the Baptist's question serves to introduce the theme of ch 11. John's arrest (cf 14:3ff) had been the signal for our Lord's preaching of the kingdom, 4:12; it was the end of the old order. Word had come to John of our Lord's Galilean activity and it is important to notice (in view of the interpretation of what follows) that it is this activity which provokes the Baptist's question. This question is put through the medium of two, Lk 7:19, disciples. **3** – These ask if he is **the one who is to come.** It is not clear from either N.T. or rabbis that the phrase in this form was a common messianic title, but the Baptist had already referred, 3:11, to Christ as "the one coming after me" and had indicated him as the Messiah. He certainly does not begin to doubt this now; he is no "reed shaken by the wind"; nor, evidently, is he suspecting for the first time that Jesus may be the Messiah. It remains either that the Baptist is hinting at the need for more incisive messianic action (as, for instance, the outspoken denunciations of Mt 23) in accordance with John's own zealous messianism (cf 3:10-12) or that, himself content with our Lord's gentle method, he sends his disciples for their own instruction. This last view is somewhat forced: it is not to the discredit of the Baptist that he, like the apostles (e.g. Lk 9:55), should still have to learn what Jesus meant by messiahship. **5** – The disciples are privileged

¹⁰ tell you, and more than a prophet. This is he of whom it is written,

> 'Behold, I send my messenger before thy face,
> who shall prepare thy way before thee.'

¹¹ Truly, I say to you, among those born of women there has risen no one greater than John the Baptist; yet he who is least in the kingdom of heaven is greater than he. ¹² From the days of John the Baptist until now the kingdom of heaven has suffered violence, and men of violence take ¹³ it by force. For all the prophets and the law prophesied ¹⁴ until John; and if you are willing to accept it, he is ¹⁵ Elijah who is to come. He who has ears to hear, let him hear."

to witness miracles, Lk 7:21, which Jesus himself significantly sums up in Isaian messianic terms; cf Is 26:19, 29:18f; 35:5f. That the poor (i.e. the simple and docile cf 5:3 note) have the good news (the *euaggelion*) announced to them is another sign that the "acceptable year" of the Lord has indeed come, Is 61:1f; cf Lk 4:18f. The Messiah is in their midst; there is no room for John's disciples to doubt it or for the Baptist to urge a more explicit messianic declaration. **6** – Christ's person and procedure, therefore, are justified in advance by prophecy; to those of goodwill (which sharpens understanding) they are no snare (cause for offence) in the way of faith.

The Baptist is now praised not so much for his personal sanctity as for the part he has so faithfully played in the divine scheme. He is the strong bridge between the old and the new order. It is through no fault of his incorruptible temper and unassailable integrity that that bridge has not been used. **7-8** – Galilee itself had been stirred by the Baptist's preaching (he had baptized as far north as Salim; cf Jn 3:23) and Galileans like Andrew and Simon had been among his disciples, Jn 1:40. All knew well enough that John was an envoy of God, otherwise they would not have sought the desert scenes of his activity; clearly they did not go to admire the waving reeds of the Jordan banks – a feature of the scenery happily chosen to suggest, by contrast, the Baptist himself imprisoned now for inflexible principle. They sought a man, then? Yes, but they could not have done so for any human dignity in him – otherwise, why the "**wilderness**" and not the palace? **9-11a** – They knew him, therefore, for one with a supernatural message, but they did not suspect, as Jesus now assures them, that of all the prophets John was the greatest, or indeed something greater than a prophet: a herald who proclaims the present king. John is the **messenger** ("angel" Douay Version) of the messianic age: the messenger announced by the last of the prophets (Mal 3:1; "a commonplace of messianic prophecy"; and cf Edersheim 2, 736f). The Lord's words in Malachi's text run: "Behold I send my messenger to prepare the way before *me*." By changing the pronoun Jesus significantly identifies his own coming with that of "the Lord" in Malachi. In the order of prophetic preparation for the messianic kingdom none had such pre-eminence as John. That the Baptist worthily fulfilled the function is supposed throughout, but Jesus is not speaking directly of his personal sanctity. Nonetheless – still in the order of dignity and not of sanctity – the members of the kingdom (already in existence on earth as 11*b* certainly implies) are more highly privileged. **12** – From the time of John's arrest (his **days** are the days of his unhindered preaching) when Jesus began to proclaim the kingdom, up to the present moment of Christ's speaking, these members have been and are occupying the kingdom. And this by dint of earnest effort (**violence**) for indeed it is a kingdom which yields only to attack by storm. It is possible to understand the "violence" and the taking

Jesus condemns his contemporaries 11:16-19

16 "But to what shall I compare this generation? It is like children sitting in the market places and calling to their playmates,

17   'We piped to you, and you did not dance;
        we wailed, and you did not mourn.'

18 For John came neither eating nor drinking, and they say,

19 'He has a demon'; the Son of man came eating and drinking, and they say, 'Behold, a glutton and a drunkard, a friend of tax collectors and sinners!' Yet wisdom is justified by her deeds."

Jesus condemns the lake towns 11:20-24

20 Then he began to upbraid the cities where most of his mighty works had been done, because they did not repent.

21 "Woe to you, Chorazin! woe to you, Bethsaida! for if the mighty works done in you had been done in Tyre and Sidon, they would have repented long ago in sackcloth

22 and ashes. But I tell you, it shall be more tolerable on

23 the day of judgment for Tyre and Sidon than for you. And

by force in a hostile sense. The verse then becomes a denunciation of the Pharisaic opposition which seizes upon the kingdom and bars its entrance to the simple folk who would come to it. Yet such an image is strained and the thought foreign to the context which is concerned with the praise of John's work. The interpretation would compel 12 to be read as a parenthesis since the idea of opposition does not enter until v. 16. **13** – This is happening before their eyes since the time for prophecy has ended (the "days" of the Baptist, now over, were its last stage) and the prophesied kingdom is now a reality. **14** – This being so, the audience is asked to give a docile assent to the surprising proposition that the **Elijah,** herald of the kingdom in Mal 4:5f, is none other than the Baptist; see on 17:11ff. **15** – This passing of one epoch into another is mysterious: the crisis must be attentively studied to be appreciated.

Jesus condemns his contemporaries 11:16-19 (Lk 7:31-35)
The discourse on the Baptist and the kingdom suggests a reference to the Baptist's reception and to that of the kingdom, i.e. of Jesus its representative. The reception of each by the élite of the nation was unfavourable (cf Lk 7:29f; Mt 9:10f) and the attitude of Christ's contemporaries, **this generation** reminds him of petulant children who refuse to join in any game of "pretend" no matter how wide the choice offered – grave or gay. The comparison is adroitly chosen since the game of "funerals" recalls the stern Baptist while the merrier game suggests the less unbending conduct of Jesus; cf 9:10-15. **19** – Divine wisdom, effecting the design of salvation through both John and Jesus, is vindicated by its result (**deeds,** not "children" as in Douay Version – probably a harmonization with Lk 7:35). Its effect is to demonstrate the insincerity of the opposition. The same message was delivered by John and Jesus, each using a different approach; the rejection of their contrasting methods showed that it was the message itself that was rejected. Childish obstinacy had clearly been at work, but the loving wisdom of God had done all that was possible; it stood vindicated by the manifest ill-will of its opponents.

Jesus condemns the lake towns 11:20-24 (Lk 10:13-15)
The chronological place of this discourse is doubtless towards the end of the Galilean ministry, but logically it follows admirably the attack made upon those who had rejected Wisdom's offer and introduces a description of those who accept that offer. **20** – Matthew's vague **then** introduces the condemnation. The towns are not attacked for their immorality (in the narrow sense of the word) as their unfavourable comparison with Sodom, Tyre, Sidon, shows. Their crime is spiritual obstinacy. God's offer, so clearly supported by signs, had brought no change of heart ("repentance", cf 3:2 note). **21** – **Chorazin** and Bethsaida, towns of the lakeside, had seen much of Jesus. The ruins

you, Capernaum, will you be exalted to heaven? You
shall be brought down to Hades. For if the mighty works
done in you had been done in Sodom, it would have re-
24 mained until this day.   But I tell you that it shall be
more tolerable on the day of judgment for the land of
Sodom than for you."

The Gospel revealed to the simple. The Father and the Son 11:25-27
25 At that time Jesus declared, "I thank thee, Father, Lord
of heaven and earth, that thou hast hidden these things
from the wise and understanding and revealed them to
26 babes;   yea Father, for such was thy gracious will.   All
27 things have been delivered to me by my Father; and no
one knows the Son except the Father, and no one knows the
Father except the Son and any one to whom the Son
chooses to reveal him."

of the former (*Khirbet Kerazeh*) lie, very difficult to find on the slopes, c. 2 m N. of lakeside Capernaum; **Bethsaida** (et-Tell) was near the lakeside on the east bank of the Jordan as it enters the lake. On the question of two "Bethsaidas" cf Mk 6:45 and Abel, *Géographie de la Palestine*, 2, 279-80. Our Lord's miracles were signs of the imminence of the kingdom, 11:4-6, and the necessary preparation for the kingdom was penance, 4:17. The kingdom (and, therefore, the miracles) were first offered to Israel, but Israel refused the penance. **Tyre and Sidon** themselves, coastal cities of pagan Phoenicia and typical of those beyond the pale, would not have so refused. **22** – In the final assessment of guilt, therefore, rejection of a divine invitation will turn the scale. It is clear how far Jesus is from the national messianism of his contemporaries and how exactly the apostle of the Gentiles interpreted him. **23** – **Capernaum,** privileged to be the adopted home of the Messiah, 4:13, earns a separate condemnation and the most opprobrious comparison (Sodom). Its pride (cf e.g. Ob 1:4) is as high as its fall will be abysmal (cf Is 14:13, 15). Yet this is not so much a prophecy of destruction, material and spiritual, as a declaration of exact and public assessment of worth when the time comes – the term **Hades** (the underworld of all the dead), is here, like **heaven** metaphorical.

The Gospel revealed to the simple. The Father and the Son 11:25-27 (Lk 10:21-22)

The Son thanks his Father that the revelation is given to **babes** 25-26. The essence of this revelation is the knowledge of the Father through the Son, 27. The Son, therefore, appeals for simple trust in himself, 28-30. The framework of the section recalls the more elaborate appeal for the wisdom of the Law in Ecclus 51:1-17 (prayer of thanksgiving), cf Mt 11:25-26; Ecclus 51:18-30 (the wisdom of the Law), cf the knowledge of the Father in Mt 11:27; Ecclus 51:31-38 (the appeal), cf Mt 11:28-30. Nevertheless, the wisdom Jesus asks for does not come from study, however sacred, but from personal abandonment to the Son who reveals more than the Law could ever give. The passage fits excellently into the context of the whole chapter, though Lk probably gives it its historical place after the return of the seventy-two (perhaps nine months after the Baptist's embassy). Certainly Mt's vague **at that time** contrasts with Lk's precise "at that moment".

25-26 – Jesus thanks (better "acknowledges", "praises"?) his Father as the overruling providence of the great plan now shown to be in action. The praise is not for the "hiding" but for the "revealing" (in the Semitic manner; e.g. Is 12:1). The object of the revelation, **these things,** is, in the context of Mt, not of Lk, the mystery of the kingdom (13:11). Simplicity has earned the disciples (the **babes,** cf 10:42), an intuition from God denied to the sophisticated Pharisees and scribes; cf 1 Cor 1:19-31. **27** – This verse has the tone of Christ's words as

Christ the gentle master 11:28-30

28 "Come to me, all who labour and are heavy laden, and
29 I will give you rest.   Take my yoke upon you, and learn
    from me; for I am gentle and lowly in heart, and you will
30 find rest for your souls.   For my yoke is easy, and my
    burden is light."

Sabbath question: ears of corn 12:1-8

1 At that time Jesus went through the grainfields on the
   sabbath; his disciples were hungry, and they began to
2 pluck ears of grain and to eat.   But when the Pharisees
   saw it, they said to him, "Look, your disciples are doing
3 what is not lawful to do on the sabbath."   He said to
   them, "Have you not read what David did, when he was
4 hungry, and those who were with him: how he entered
   the house of God and ate the bread of the Presence, which
   it was not lawful for him to eat nor for those who were
5 with him, but only for the priests?   Or have you not

reported by the fourth Evangelist and has therefore been called "the Johannine aerolite"; its undoubted authenticity is valuable confirmation of John's fidelity in reporting the substance of Christ's discourses. That the sentence is found also in Lk shows that it has strong roots in the Christian tradition, and its content is in complete accord with Mt's Christology. If we add the fact that a similar use of the Son—the Father occurs in Mk 13:32, this usage as a traditional saying of Christ is as strongly supported as any saying in the Gospels. The dogmatic force of the passage can hardly be overstated, especially if we remember that Jesus is implicitly identifying himself with the Wisdom of God (cf his use of Ecclus 51). The Son possesses the fullness of the Father's knowledge (**all things have been delivered** seems to mean this in the context). The bold statement that only the Father is adequate to know the Son puts both on the same transcendent plane. Moreover, the Son alone knows the Father and uses his absolute discretion in making the Father known according to the capacity of his hearers.

Christ the gentle master 11:28-30
The Son asks for devotion to his own person and acceptance of his yoke as of his comfort. This is not the language of a prophet, but of the Son who holds unique relationship with the Father, 27. **29** – The **yoke** (current metaphor for the Law; cf Jer 5:5; Ecclus 51:34; Ac 15:10) is that of the New Legislator. It is easeful (*chrestos*: suitable, easy to wear) because he perfects the Law, 5:17, making outward observance subservient to inward spirit and thus developing a law of love, available and attractive to all of goodwill, 5:3ff. Being *his* yoke it brings, too, the gift of his help. He asks for obedient disciples – **learn from me** – because he is the perfect master – not over-bearing nor of an exclusive caste (unlike the Pharisees) but gentle and of a lowly condition willingly embraced.

Sabbath question: ears of corn 12:1-8 (Mk 2:23-28; Lk 6:1-5)
Matthew now uses four incidents, 1-8, 9-14, 22-37, 38-45, to show the wisdom of the teacher in action against the "wisdom" of this world; cf 11:25-27. They show how simple and kind is the one, how tortuous and ruthless the other.

1-2 – To judge by the order of Mk and Lk (Mt uses his vague **at that time,** cf 11:25; 14:1) the first incident occurred shortly after the call of Matthew. Jesus and his disciples take a short Sabbath walk (about half a mile) through the fields. Reaping and threshing were two of the thirty-nine works forbidden on the sabbath. Later rabbinic casuistry regarded plucking the ears as reaping, and rubbing between the hands (Lk) as threshing (Edersheim 2, 56, 783). The watchful Pharisees were already of this persuasion. **3-4** – Refusing to enter into casuistical discussion Jesus solves the question on the principle that necessity

read in the law how on the sabbath the priests in the
6 temple profane the sabbath, and are guiltless?   I tell you,
7 something greater than the temple is here.   And if you
had known what this means, 'I desire mercy, and not
sacrifice,' you would not have condemned the guiltless.
8 For the Son of man is lord of the sabbath."

Sabbath question: the withered hand 12:9-14
9 And he went on from there, and entered their synagogue.
10 And behold, there was a man with a withered hand.
And they asked him, "Is it lawful to heal on the sabbath?"
11 so that they might accuse him.   He said to them, "What
man of you, if he has one sheep and it falls into a pit on
12 the sabbath, will not lay hold of it and lift it out?   Of how
much more value is a man than a sheep! So it is lawful
13 to do good on the sabbath."   Then he said to the man,
"Stretch out your hand." And the man stretched it out,
14 and it was restored, whole like the other.   But the Pharisees went out and took counsel against him, how to
destroy him.

excuses from such "positive" law. He makes this principle irrefutable for his audience by citing the example of the great David, 1 Sam (Kg) 21:1-6. From the anger of Saul, David had fled to Nob of Benjamin where the Tabernacle then was. Ahimelech the high priest allowed him to eat of the twelve loaves called often "of the face" (because placed in God's presence in the sanctuary) or "of proposition" i.e. "placed before" (cf Lev 24:5-9). This offering was renewed weekly, the withdrawn loaves being eaten (by reason of their sacred character) by the priests. Yet David's necessity prevailed over this positive law and the exception had the high priest's sanction. **5-6** – Jesus adds (Mt only) that the temple sacrifice offered on the Sabbath, Lev 23:25; 24:8-9; Num 28:9, is a literal infringement of the sabbath rest. This remark invited the obvious retort: the temple service stands alone and clearly transcends all other duties; but the retort is boldly anticipated: there is something greater than the temple here. The presence of Jesus turns the field into a sanctuary. The saying opens up limitless horizons: In conjunction with other sayings (notably Jn 2:19) it offers the person of Jesus as the great substitute for the old sanctuary – a substitution already hinted in messianic prophecy (e.g. Is 28:7-22; Mic 3:12—5:1; Ez 11:16: Dan 9:23-27; cf notes to Mt 24:30). **7** – (Mt only). The quotation is telling (Ho 6:6; cf note on 9:12-13, where it has been used already). These Pharisees have not penetrated the spirit even of the old Law. Otherwise they would not have allowed their legal scruples to oust prudent and charitable judgment of the guiltless disciples. **8** – Why guiltless? Because their master, the Son of man (8:20 note), is lord (*kurios*) of the divinely instituted sabbath and can dispense at will. Taken in the light of the preceding verses this claim to be **lord of the sabbath**, like so much else in the Gospel, cannot adequately be explained by anything short of Christ's divinity (Westminster Version).

Sabbath question: the withered hand 12:9-14 (Mk 3:1-6; Lk 6:6-11)
    On another sabbath (Lk) in the synagogue (prob. of Capernaum, cf Mk 1:21; 3:1) a man with a withered hand was present, probably asking a cure. The scribes and Pharisees (Lk) are there to trap Jesus in act (Mk, Lk) and speech (Mt). In their eyes only danger of death could excuse the administration of extraordinary remedies on the sabbath (Edersheim 2, 59-60). **11-13** – (Mt only) Christ's reply (as so often in the rabbinic fashion of counter-question with brief parable) is not explicitly abstract and final (unlike 8) but primarily practical and deterrent. It halts the Pharisees by making them see their scruples in due perspective. In the case of a beast, their own property, no sabbath scruples; in the case of a man, a mere individual to them, a singular delicacy of conscience! Underlying the argument however (and explicitly in Mk 3:4) there is also the principle that a good act is permissible at any time. Jesus, far from condemning the procedure in favour of a sheep,

Jesus the Servant of God 12:15-21

15 Jesus, aware of this, withdrew from there. And many
16 followed him, and he healed them all,   and ordered them
17 to make him known.   This was to fulfil what was spoken
by the prophet Isaiah:

18   "Behold, my servant whom I have chosen,
        my beloved with whom my soul is well pleased.
    I will put my Spirit upon him,
        and he shall proclaim justice to the Gentiles.
19   He will not wrangle or cry aloud,
        nor will any one hear his voice in the streets;
20   he will not break a bruised reed
        or quench a smouldering wick,
    till he brings justice to victory;
21   and in his name will the Gentiles hope."

Beelzebul accusation 12:22-32

22 Then a blind and dumb demoniac was brought to him,
and he healed him, so that the dumb man spoke and saw.
23 And all the people were amazed, and said, "Can this be

implicitly approves it as a dictate of common prudence. It is a frontal attack upon sabbath casuistry; for which in general cf Edersheim 2, 777-87. On Christ's sorrow and anger on this occasion cf Mk 3:5.**14** – For the Pharisees this act of defiance following on the others (cf 9:4ff; 9:11f; 12:2ff) was the last straw. Already decided on our Lord's death, they are now concerned only with procedure. This they discuss with the supporters of Herod Antipas, tetrarch of Galilee, who were equally anxious to avoid anything which might appear to threaten political stability.

Jesus the Servant of God 12:15-21

15 – Knowing the murderous intentions of his enemies, Jesus withdraws to the country districts. When the appointed time came he would deliberately walk into the enemy camp (Mt 20:17-19; Lk 13:22, 33; Jn 11:16); meanwhile there was work to do; cf 10:23. He did not intend that he should be "made known" as the Messiah and popularly so acclaimed. He was no demagogue but the gentle "Servant of God" described by Isaiah, Is 42:1-4; 41:9. **18-21** – In the form of this quotation Mt is influenced partly by the text, partly by LXX, partly by his own purpose. **my beloved** ("my chosen one" Hebrew text, LXX) recalls the "beloved son" of the baptism; cf. 3:16-17 where the **Spirit** also appears. **He will not wrangle** is a reasonable adjustment ("shout aloud", Heb., LXX) to fit the withdrawal of Jesus (15) from unseemly and useless dispute with the Pharisees. The **Gentiles** of 21 (lit. "nations", as in LXX) replace the "islands" (i.e. "distant lands") of Heb. text; an equivalent but more suitable expression for a Gospel which is to close with the words "make disciples of all nations". The general sense of the passage here, as in Isaiah, is that the "Servant of God" will expound God's integral truth, **proclaim justice,** to the nations outside Israel ("justice" in vv. 18, 20, renders the Heb. *mishpat,* a word which here embraces the whole revelation of God to his people). **19** – The triumph of this "Servant's" mission will come not by noisy propaganda, 19, nor by harsh measures, 20. On the contrary, he will be tender with the (spiritually) weak, and prudent with the souls in which the divine light is flickering out – the **bruised reed** and the **smouldering wick.** This is to be his firm policy right to the end, when he will establish God's truth victorious (by his Resurrection?). Thenceforward the whole world will find its hopes in his **name**—in his Person as revealed by his works and by those who tell of them.

Beelzebul accusation 12:22-32 (Mk 3:22-30; Lk 11:14-23; 12:10)

The miracle is similar to that of 9:32-34 with the added detail (absent from Lk 11:14) that the possessed man was not only dumb but blind. It is possible that Mt returns to the same miracle here (in the context of the condemnation of the Pharisees) to tell of the controversy merely

²⁴ the Son of David?"   But when the Pharisees heard it they said, "It is only by Beelzebul, the prince of demons, that ²⁵ this man casts out demons."   Knowing their thoughts, he said to them, "Every kingdom divided against itself is laid waste, and no city or house divided against itself will ²⁶ stand;   and if Satan casts out Satan, he is divided against ²⁷ himself; how then will his kingdom stand?   And if I cast out demons by Beelzebul, by whom do your sons cast ²⁸ them out? Therefore they shall be your judges.   But if it is by the Spirit of God that I cast out demons, then the ²⁹ kingdom of God has come upon you.   Or how can one enter a strong man's house and plunder his goods, unless he first binds the strong man? Then indeed he may ³⁰ plunder his house.   He who is not with me is against me, ³¹ and he who does not gather with me scatters.   Therefore I tell you, every sin and blasphemy will be forgiven men, but the blasphemy against the Spirit will not be forgiven. ³² And whoever says a word against the Son of man will be forgiven; but whoever speaks against the Holy Spirit will not be forgiven, either in this age or in the age to come."

hinted at in 9:34. Alternatively, 9:32-34 may be an anticipation. It is possible that we have two distinct miracles, but this hypothesis would seem to imply that our Lord did not reply to the grave calumny of 9:34. This would be surprising. Moreover, the "doublet" phenomenon (repetition of discourse or event in different contexts) is not unusual in Mt (about sixteen times). **23** – Among the crowd there are tentative murmurs: this may be the **Son of David** (the Messiah; cf 1:1 note. **24** – With the Pharisees are scribes from Jerusalem (Mk) – evidently the plot, 14, goes forward and the Jerusalem Sanhedrin is in action. **This man,** they say, scornfully echoing the crowd's phrase, "is himself possessed by the prince of devils (Mk) who, through him, casts out the minor demons." For "Beelzebul" cf 10:25 note.

Jesus, supernaturally aware of the Pharisees' mind, first demonstrates the absurdity, 25-26, and dishonesty, 27, of the charge. He then passes to the positive conclusion to be drawn from his exorcisms, 28-29, and throws down a challenge, 30. **25** – The general principle is axiomatic: a divided kingdom (as Israel knew to its cost) is devoured piecemeal by its foes; indeed civil dissension in even smaller communities (civic or domestic) is calamitous. **26** – The particular and topical application is obvious. The great adversary (**Satan** cf 4:10 note) of all goodness is himself no exception. Jesus appeals implicitly not to a single instance of exorcism (which Satan might instigate for his own subtle ends) but to repeated examples; cf e.g. 8:16. If this were a set policy it would be the policy of a fool, which Satan is not. Satan, therefore, does not cast out himself (i.e. his satellites) – the paradoxical expression underlines the contradiction in the Pharisaic argument. **27** – The argument, moreover, issues from prejudice. The Pharisees were the spiritual leaders of the nation at large. Among their disciples, therefore (**sons** – a Semitism) were some who at least claimed to enjoy a certain success in exorcism (Jos, *Ant.* 8, 2, 5; Ac 19:13-14; Mk 9:38). Why did not the Pharisees denounce them? Such exorcists are therefore living witnesses and (were the question put to them) perforce judges of their own spiritual teachers. **28** – Satan excluded, there remains the one alternative – the spiritual power of God. That Jesus freely wields this power, without effort or restriction, is clear proof that he is the founder of a new era – the the phrase "spirit of God"). **29** – How can it be otherwise, since Christ is already pillaging Satan's kingdom? Satan, therefore, must be helpless. He is helpless not because weak or careless but because Jesus, stronger than he, has overcome him just as a robber may overpower a strong and vigilant householder. This victory has already taken place (with the Incarnation?); it remains only to gather the spoils. **30** – It is a climax of history, a time for decisions. There are only two possible choices – God or Satan. Jesus speaks with a calm assurance of dignity which recalls his manner of speech in Jn. He will not accept tolerant neutrality or

Words reveal the heart 12:33-37

33 "Either make the tree good, and its fruit good; or make the tree bad, and its fruit bad; for the tree is known by 34 its fruit.   You brood of vipers! how can you speak good, when you are evil? For out of the abundance of the heart 35 the mouth speaks.   The good man out of his good trea-

benevolent suspension of judgment. The words are addressed probably to the waverers, hardly to the Pharisees who are clearly his enemies. The "gathering" and "scattering" metaphor is obscure. It is probably neither agricultural nor pastoral but general: all work is dissipation of energy when not united with the cause of Jesus.

31 – The meaning of **blasphemy against the Spirit** is to be determined from the context. This context (to which 31-32 are closely tied; cf **therefore** in 31 and even more explicitly Mk 3:30) is decisive. The sin referred to is one of which an example has just been furnished by the Pharisees. They have perversely attributed to Satan what is clearly the work of God. This is only one example of conscious, hardened rejection of God's proffered light – the root vice of the Pharisees (cf Jn 9:41; 3:19f) as of others. This is the direct affront of the Spirit of wisdom; cf. e.g. 1 Cor 2:10-13. It is the sin "that remains", Jn 9:41. Why does it "remain"? Why is it unforgivable? Of its very nature. Man cannot be saved without the gifts of God, one of which is forgiveness. If these gifts are persistently refused nothing can be done. "It is called 'unforgivable' because of its very nature it precludes those things (i.e. the dispositions) which induce forgiveness. However we cannot thus exclude the power and mercy of God which can find a way of forgiveness . . . by which, as it were miraculously, he heals such sinners", Aquinas. Even in this hypothesis of a "quasi-miraculous" grace the sinner is presumed to accept it. At that moment and to that extent he ceases to affront the Spirit; he ceases to be a blasphemer of the Spirit because he has (though tardily) accepted God's light. Christ's statement is therefore literally true: it will never be forgiven because it refuses to be forgiven. **32** – The **word against the Son of man** is, though grave, forgivable. To assail the human conduct of Jesus (e.g. 9:11 or even 16:22) is an insult to his compassionate humanity, but it proceeds from a misreading of God's ways. It may presuppose a religious, if indocile, spirit. It finds some excuse in the fact that the Word has taken flesh and is, to that degree, veiled. But an attack upon the Son of man when manifestly wielding the power of the Spirit is conscious malice – an attack upon the Spirit himself.

Words reveal the heart 12:33-37 (Lk 6:43-45)

33 – A maxim already used by our Lord, 7:17-20, is now given a different turn. It is a direct assault on the Pharisees for their blasphemous words, 24, an appeal, in the spirit of 30, for a downright attitude and for clear issues. Nature knows no deception; from good fruit one may argue a healthy tree. Not so the Pharisees. From their customary pious discourses one would not guess at their inward corruption. They are as dangerous, therefore, as a brood of vipers. Let them reform inwardly or at least show their corruption outwardly in speech. The form of 33 is awkward. It has been suggested that the Aramaic original read: A

sure brings forth good, and the evil man out of his evil
36 treasure brings forth evil. I tell you, on the day of
judgment men will render account for every careless word
37 they utter; for by your words you will be justified, and
by your words you will be condemned."

The sign of Jonah 12:38-42
38 Then some of the scribes and Pharisees said to him,
39 "Teacher, we wish to see a sign from you." But he
answered them, "An evil and adulterous generation seeks
for a sign; but no sign shall be given to it except the sign
40 of the prophet Jonah. For as Jonah was three days and
three nights in the belly of the whale, so will the Son of man
be three days and three nights in the heart of the earth.
41 The men of Nineveh will arise at the judgment with this
generation and condemn it; for they repented at the
preaching of Jonah, and behold, something greater than
42 Jonah is here. The queen of the South will arise at the
judgment with this generation and condemn it; for she
came from the ends of the earth to hear the wisdom of
Solomon, and behold, something greater than Solomon
is here."

good tree makes, i.e. produces, good fruit etc. – the participle for "makes" having been read as an imperative. **34-35** – They are an unnatural and repellent phenomenon because words are customarily the "heart's overflow" (Knox) and if the store of the heart is good, the mouth dispenses what is good. **36-37** – (Mt only). In the present context Christ's words sound a grave warning for the Pharisees. If every **careless** (*argos*, i.e. do-nothing, lazy) **word** will be accountable for (the text does not necessarily imply "condemned"), how searching will be the examination of considered pronouncements like the deliberate blasphemy of the Pharisees! **37** – This has the ring of a proverb, particularly as the "you" (plural) of v. 36 is now singular in the Greek ("thine", "thou"). The **words** are a sure criterion of acquittal (justification) or condemnation since, if we except the Pharisaic monstrosity of 34, they are the index of the heart, 34, 35.

The sign of Jonah 12:38-42 (Lk 11:29-32)

38 – After the rebuff of the Pharisees, 24-34, others continue the conversation (lit. "answered saying", cf the Aramaic idiom in which there is no suggestion of answering a question but merely of reacting to certain circumstances or words; e.g. Dan 2:26). They ask for a convincing proof of our Lord's messianic mission – a **sign** of their own choosing more startling than the miracles so far witnessed; see 16:1. **39** – Ignoring the veneer of politeness Jesus directly attacks the questioners as representatives of an **evil and adulterous** race, faithless to God, Israel's spouse; cf Ho 2; Ez 16, etc. A sign will indeed be given but, as a race, they will reject it; cf 41. **40** – The sign is the Resurrection, though the word is not spoken and the allusion remains cryptic until the event unveils it. If we remember that analogies are not designed to be urged too far, the likeness is striking between the O.T. presentation of Jonah's story and Christ's burial (though again the term is not used) and Resurrection. As the fish (*ketos*, sea-beast, Knox) swallows Jonah, so the earth will swallow the Son of man. The disappearance is for **three days and three nights** in each case. In Jon 1:17 this phrase may or may not indicate 72 hours; Heb. usage makes the expression ambiguous (cf e.g. Est 4:16 with Est 5:1 and the Jewish method of reckoning part of a day, month or year for the whole). In our Lord's case it certainly does not indicate 72 hours as the evangelist, though faithfully recording the expression, well knew, 16:21; 17:23; 20:19. In any case, the general analogy is enough and this point should be remembered also when it is objected that Jonah was body and soul in the fish and Christ's body only in the tomb, or when it is urged that **the heart of the earth** is as deep in the earth (and therefore Limbo?) as the **belly** is in the fish. **41** – The example of the Ninevites will rise accusing at the final reckoning. (It is possible, however, that the words **at the judgment** have been added by the Greek translator; the original Aramaic would then read

Return of the unclean spirit 12:43-45

⁴³ "When the unclean spirit has gone out of a man, he passes through waterless places seeking rest, but he finds ⁴⁴ none.   Then he says, 'I will return to my house from which I came.' And when he comes he finds it empty, ⁴⁵ swept, and put in order.   Then he goes and brings with him seven other spirits more evil than himself, and they enter and dwell there; and the last state of that man becomes worse than the first. So shall it be also with this evil generation."

True kindred of Jesus 12:46-50

⁴⁶ While he was still speaking to the people, behold, his mother and his brothers stood outside, asking to speak to ⁴⁸ him.   But he replied to the man who told him, "Who is ⁴⁹ my mother, and who are my brothers?"   And stretching out his hand towards his disciples, he said, "Here are my ⁵⁰ mother and my brothers!   For whoever does the will of my Father in heaven, is my brother, and sister, and mother."

simply "will arise with this generation", i.e. in the Aramaic idiom "dispute with, reproach"). It will put the incredulous Pharisees to shame – their missionary was not a mere prophet but the Son of man himself. **42** – Cf 1 Sam (Kg) 10:1ff. This fresh contrast is of another order: it suggests not the impenitence of the Pharisees but their refusal to recognize the true wisdom offered them. The queen of Sheba (in S.W. Arabia, called the Yemen, i.e. "the south") travelled far to hear one whose wisdom, though proverbial in Israel, did not compare with this.

Return of the unclean spirit 12:43-45 (Lk 11:24-26)

By means of a comparison suggested by the present exorcism incident, 22-24, Jesus warns his opponents against a false sense of security. There is peril in over-confidence – in the calm assurance of the Pharisees conscious of Israel's privileged status, unconscious of spiritual need. They cannot afford to refuse the help of Jesus who alone opposes Satan with the Spirit of God, 28-29. **43** – **The unclean spirit** ("unclean" as opposed to the "holy" Spirit) appears as a tenant not necessarily evicted but perhaps simply seeking a change of residence. **44** – He finds the waterless countryside unsuitable and decides to return to his old home. To his delight it is still untenanted, cleaned and in good order. **45** – Anxious to share his good fortune (there is no suggestion of gathering forces for a battle) he invites a whole band (**seven** – the number of completion) of like-minded spirits. Packed with this unclean horde the house is made dirtier than ever. Applied to this **evil generation** the comparison invites it to consider the possibility that the God-favoured house of Israel may, through sheer indifference, be open with vacant possession to Satan. Such indifference will make the state of Israel more desperate (though not yet hopeless) than its condition was before God's call of Abraham. The unprivileged pagans will be in better case.

True kindred of Jesus 12:46-50 (Mk 3:31-35; Lk 8:19-21)

46 – The episode has no obvious logical connexion with the rest of the section nor is it clear that it took place at this time: Mt's apparently precise indication, **while he was still speaking,** is in reality his own vague connecting formula, 9:18; 17:5; 26:47. Mt, who is primarily interested in our Lord's pronouncement, 48-49, does not say why his **brothers** sought him (see Mk 3:21 where the "friends" are probably relations, i.e. "brothers" cf Mk 3:31-32). Of this passage Lagrange pointedly remarks: "The presence of our Lord's mother on this occasion no more proves that she shares the sentiments of the others than does her presence at the foot of the Cross". She is there simply because she wants to be near him. The house (cf 13:1) is full, Mk 3:20. Mary and the "brothers" are outside. **48** – Jesus is informed. [Note: many MSS

add, probably mistakenly: Some one told him, "Your mother and your brothers are standing outside, asking to speak to you"]. Jesus takes up the words of his informant to drive home a lesson. **49-50** – With a gesture and a word he sets the example of complete detachment (enjoined on his followers in 10:37) in the interests of the Father. He acknowledges no kinship but with those who are obedient, and therefore genuine children of the one Father. His mother was dear to him for the same reason, Lk 1:38. For such he uses the nearest and dearest terms – **brother, sister, mother** – but "father" is reserved for his Father in heaven. The terms "brother" and "sister" in 50 do not necessarily define the word "brothers" of 46f. which (cf Mk 3:32; 6:3) is actually to be understood of "relations" in general. To indicate relationship of affection Jesus was restricted to the terms "brother", "sister", because the terms of more distant relationship ("cousin", "aunt", etc.) would be absurd used in a figurative sense.

The sower 13:1-9

¹ That same day Jesus went out of the house and sat beside
² the sea.   And great crowds gathered about him, so that
he got into a boat and sat there; and the whole crowd
³ stood on the beach.   And he told them many things in
⁴ parables, saying; "A sower went out to sow.   And as he
sowed, some seeds fell along the path, and the birds came
⁵ and devoured them.   Other seeds fell on rocky ground,
where they had not much soil, and immediately they

II

Discourse: The Parables 13:1-13:52

The foregoing chapter presented our Lord and the Pharisees; in ch. 13 Jesus turns to ordinary folk. In contrast with the direct teaching of the Sermon, ch. 5-7, his teaching is now in "parables". They are of various kinds, but the subject throughout this "day of parables" is one: the kingdom of God, the great subject of Christ's preaching, 4:17; 10:7; cf Lk 4:42-43; 10:9; Ac 1:3. The Greek word *parabolé* means "comparison". The Gospel parables may be defined as fictitious though likely stories designed to clarify a moral lesson or doctrinal truth by means of comparison. The parable is a comparison to be taken as a whole; its details are inserted merely to make the story live. In this it is distinguished from the allegory, which is a chain of metaphors of which each link has its own significance. It follows that the lesson of the parable inclines to simplicity and clarity; the lessons of the allegory are multiple and tend to obscurity. Yet some allegories may be clear and some parables obscure by reason of the circumstances of their utterance or of the difficulty of the subject treated. The Gospel parables, expecially those concerning the kingdom, often contain allegorical elements. This phenomenon has been used to prove that such parables have been decorated with allegory by the evangelists. Jesus, it has been claimed, would not have used allegory since it would obscure his message. In this theory the evangelists, anxious to explain to pagan and Jew the blindness of the Messiah's own people, have deliberately obscured the parable with allegorical elements. The theory is exaggerated. Allegory and parable are similar literary forms and the intrusion of allegory into parable is a natural process (C. H. Dodd, *The Parables of the Kingdom*, London 1936). Moreover, the mixture of the two is equally characteristic of the rabbinic "parables" in the first centuries of the Christian era.

The Sower 13:1-9 (Mk 4:1-9; Lk 8:4-8)
1-2 – Mt's phrase **that same day** may be as vague as his other phrase "at that time", or (if intended to be exact) may apply only to some of the parables in the chapter. Leaving the house (cf 12:46; Matthew's own with some probability) Jesus goes down to the lakeside. So that all may see and hear, he addresses the throngs from one of the boats moored there. **3-4** – In Palestine the farmer sows after the first autumn rains (usually November). His hedgeless fields are bordered, and often traversed, by stony paths. Willy-nilly some seed, scattered from his basket, must fall on the track. The greedy Palestinian sparrow is not slow to seize it. **5-6** – Even in Galilee the stony soil lies thin on outcrops of rock. The very lightness of such soil favours too rapid

⁶ sprang up, since they had no depth of soil,   but when the
sun rose they were scorched; and since they had no root
⁷ they withered away.   Other seeds fell upon thorns, and
⁸ the thorns grew up and choked them.   Other seeds fell
on good soil and brought forth grain, some a hundredfold,
⁹ some sixty, some thirty.   He who has ears, let him hear."

Purpose of parables 13:10-17

¹⁰ Then the disciples came and said to him, "Why do you
¹¹ speak to them in parables?"   And he answered them,
"To you it has been given to know the secrets of the
kingdom of heaven, but to them it has not been given.
¹² For to him who has will more be given, and he will have
abundance; but from him who has not, even what he has
¹³ will be taken away.   This is why I speak to them in
parables, because seeing they do not see, and hearing
¹⁴ do not hear, nor do they understand.   With them indeed
is fulfilled the prophecy of Isaiah which says:
'You shall indeed hear but never understand,
and you shall indeed see but never perceive.
¹⁵   For this people's heart has grown dull,
and their ears are heavy of hearing, and their eyes
they have closed,
lest they should perceive with their eyes,
and hear with their ears,
and understand with their heart, and turn for me to
heal them.'
¹⁶ But blessed are your eyes, for they see, and your ears, for
¹⁷ they hear.   Truly, I say to you, many prophets and righteous men longed to see what you see, and did not see it,
and to hear what you hear, and did not hear it."

growth (perhaps within a few hours) and the sun, still strong in November, will shrivel the delicate shoots unsustained by moisture from a deep root. **7-8** – The Palestinian farmer prefers not to cut his weeds. The result is disastrous: they stifle everything in the vicinity. As for the more fortunate seeds, it is a mistake to look for botanical precision in a parable. Our Lord's figures are selected at random to illustrate the abounding virtue of the seed. In special cases one seed may produce (even in Palestine) two or three hundred grains of cereal, but the ordinary Palestinian farmer (from whom our picture is taken) is content with an average yield of 12 to 1. **9** – Far from wishing to puzzle his audience, Jesus seriously asks them to reflect upon his words. His formula (again in 11:15; 13:43, cf Deut 29:4 where the absence of the listening "ear" suggests guilt) implies that in these matters goodwill facilitates understanding; cf Jn 3:21.

Purpose of parables 13:10-17 (Mk 4:10-12; Lk 8:9-10)
The disciples (not only the twelve; cf Mk 4:10) seem puzzled at this indirect method of teaching. Their question, however, was not put until they were alone with Jesus, Mk 4:10. **11** – The notion of the **kingdom of heaven** embodies the hidden design, **secrets** of God. The mass of the Jewish people were ill-prepared for a direct and sudden revelation of the true nature of the messianic kingdom. The indirect teaching by parable must for the time suffice; direct light would only blind. But the inner circle of disciples, willing to be taught and destined to teach, can and must be told. It should however be noticed that this inner circle was not a closed circle. It was open for all who heard the parables to show their goodwill by making further inquiries. **12** – Jesus observes that a worldly practice, common but not admirable, here finds its spiritual application. The rich are flattered with gifts, the poor suffer violence and loss. Those who accept and are rich in the gifts of God (which include docility, pliant will, generous heart) amass further treasures: cf Jn 1:16. The spiritual pauper has only himself to blame (cf "Ask and it will be given", 7:7) – and this explains how an axiom of unjust worldly practice can have its counterpart in the spiritual order. He is said, by a paradoxical hyperbole, to lose what he has – which is nothing. The application of this dictum to the present situation seems to presuppose some fault (as it does in 25:29 where it is used again) on the part of the people at large. **13** – This fault is a lack of spiritual perception. Confronted with this, Jesus did not withdraw as he did from the actively malignant Pharisees, 12:15. He mercifully remained to do what he could in the circumstances. Like stupid children the people could learn only from little stories – analogies which, though helpful, could not plumb the depths of the mysterious "kingdom". **14-15** – Cf Is 6:9-10. Isaiah had been thwarted by the same dispositions. His experience rehearsed that of the Messiah-Prophet as the O.T. history

Explanation of the sower parable 13:18-23

18 "Hear then the parable of the sower. When any one
19 hears the word of the kingdom and does not understand
it, the evil one comes and snatches away what is sown in
20 his heart; this is what was sown along the path. As for
what was sown on rocky ground, this is he who hears the
21 word and immediately receives it with joy;   yet he has
no root in himself, but endures for a while, and when
tribulation or persecution arises on account of the word,
22 immediately he falls away. As for what was sown among
thorns, this is he who hears the word, but the cares of the
world and the delight in riches choke the word, and it
23 proves unfruitful. As for what was shown on good soil,
this is he who hears the word and understands it; he
indeed bears fruit, and yields in one case a hundredfold,
in another sixty, and in another thirty."

in general was a rehearsal of the messianic era. Mt reproduces the LXX version; this softens the harsh (but heartbroken) irony of the Semitic imperatives: 'Hear and understand not! See and comprehend not! Harden the heart . . . ' (cf Is 6:9). The words expand, by more literal quotation, those of 13, and like them they explain why Jesus is forced to use parables. Whether the purpose of the parables is of chastisement or of benefit is much discussed. In effect we cannot exclude either element. The difficulties of the texts, however, (especially Mk) must be resolved in the light of three certain facts. First: Christ's own love for his people; his mission is mercy not judgment; he has come to save that which was lost, 18:11. Second: the parable is designed not to obscure but to clarify; absolutely speaking, it is not the most direct and efficient form of teaching, but relatively to the capacity of the audience's mind and heart it may be the only possible one; the only alternative would be silence. Third: graces refused become matter for condemnation. **16-17** – Jesus does not praise the docility of the disciples, but invites them to be grateful for God's free gift. Born in less happy times men as good as they and even the prophets could only peer into the great dim future, I Pet 1:10ff. In that future, now present, the disciples are privileged to live and not only to live but to be the pupils of the Master in the new era; cf "Hear, *then*" in 18.

Explanation of the sower parable 13:18-23 (Mk 4:13-20; Lk 8:11-15)
18 – The disciples have just heard the parable; it is the *meaning* of the parable that they are about to hear, but in Aramaic there is no exact expression for "significance, explanation"; (cf similar defective phrases in Mk 4:10; 9:10; Lk 8:11). **19** – The seed is the doctrine, **word,** of the kingdom, sown by Jesus and later by the apostles. For three classes of men it remained fruitless. In some it is a total lack of spiritual appreciation. The "word" lies unregarded. Satan alone benefits. "This is he who (the more exact translation) was sown along the path": the various kinds of soil represent the various kinds of hearers. But since the fate of the seed really represents the spiritual fate of the hearers, the seed and the hearers are in part identified. **20-21** – In others there is a thin layer of spiritual perception, but the superficial are given to sudden and ephemeral enthusiasms. The quick growth is not of deep root and soon disappears; the personal sacrifice entailed, and even active opposition, very quickly prove a snare in the moral path of such men. **22** – The third category is of those in whom the roots strike deepest. Yet here too the seed will not come to maturity if, side by side with it, grow preoccupation with the affairs of the world and particularly with the seductive glamour of **riches.** **23** – Not all the successful seed bears the same fruit, but in all cases it is abundant; cf 8 note.

The darnel 13:24-30

24 Another parable he put before them, saying: "The kingdom of heaven may be compared to a man who sowed
25 good seed in his field; but while men were sleeping, his
enemy came and sowed weeds among the wheat, and
26 went away. So when the plants came up and bore grain,
27 then the weeds appeared also. And the servants of the
household came and said to him, 'Sir, did you not sow
28 good seed in your field? How then has it weeds?' He
said to them, 'An enemy has done this.' The servants said
to him, 'Then do you want us to go and gather them?'
29 But he said, 'No; lest in gathering the weeds you root up
30 the wheat along with them. Let both grow together
until the harvest; and at harvest time I will tell the
reapers, Gather the weeds first and bind them in bundles
to be burned, but gather the wheat into my barn.' "

The mustard-seed 13:31-32

31 Another parable he put before them, saying, "The kingdom of heaven is like a grain of mustard seed which a
32 man took and sowed in his field; it is the smallest of all
seeds, but when it has grown it is the greatest of shrubs
and becomes a tree, so that the birds of the air come and
make nests in its branches."

The leaven 13:33

33 He told them another parable. "The kingdom of heaven
is like leaven which a woman took and hid in three
measures of meal, till it was all leavened."

The darnel 13:24-30

The parable has a setting similar to the previous one and completes it. **24** – From the outset Jesus makes it clear that he is speaking of the kingdom; contrast 3. But, in the rabbinic manner, the term of the comparison is said to be **a man who sowed** when, in reality it is the whole situation which is thus compared; cf also 13:31, 33, 45, 47; 20:1; 22:2; 25:1. **25-26** – The **weeds** (darnel) are the *lolium temulentum* (so named from its effect of dizziness on men and cattle). It is sown secretly and in spite. The weed is indistinguishable from the wheat until its more slender ear appears. **27-29** – This plant (rare in England) is common in Palestine, but the servants are astonished at its amount. The farmer himself immediately senses the hand of an enemy, but it is too late, or too early, to act: the roots of weed and wheat are interwined. **30** – He must wait until the ears are ripe and then the wheat, which grows higher than the weed, may be cut near its head while the sickle leaves the weed untouched. It is unusual to sheave weeds, but then it is unusual to sow them: this is an unusual operation to meet an unusual case. Nevertheless there may be allegory here, though the sheaving is not mentioned again in the explanation; v. 40 mentions only the gathering and burning. For explanation of parable see notes to 37-42.

The mustard-seed 13:31-32 (Mk 4:30-32; Lk 13:18-19)

Once again it is not precisely to the seed that the kingdom is compared but to the whole situation; see on 24. It would seem wiser, therefore, not to attempt to emphasize the pungency or any other property of the seed except its apparent insignificance, which is an integral part of the parable. This would be allegory without warrant. In the world of nature, as in the world of history, insignificant beginnings may be misleading. It is so with the world-event known as the kingdom of heaven. The human activity of Jesus was limited, its immediate results unspectacular. The mustard-plant is the *brassica nigra* of the botanists. The seed, proverbially tiny (cf 17:20) is not in fact the smallest known, but Jesus is not giving a lesson in botany. It is the smallest of the familiar seeds. Its bush is common on the banks of the Jordan and of the Galilean Lake, often reaching a height of 12 ft and therefore called a "tree" by the Arabs. That the **birds of the air come and make nests in its branches** recalls the prophecy of Ez 17:22-24 where the "tree" (a cedar) is the future messianic kingdom and "every bird and winged thing" the people of all the nations. This reminiscence seems to warrant for the "birds" the allegorical sense of all peoples.

The leaven 13:33 (Lk 13:20-21)

The preceding parable stressed the contrast between small beginnings and enormous end; the present one covers the intermediate process. The kingdom's development is not a matter of almost inevitable, natural

Parabolic teaching prophesied 13:34-35
³⁴ All this Jesus said to the crowds in parables; indeed he
³⁵ said nothing to them without a parable.   This was to
   fulfil what was spoken by the prophet:
      "I will open my mouth in parables,
      I will utter what has been hidden since the foundation
         of the world."

Explanation of the darnel parable 13:36-43
³⁶ Then he left the crowds and went into the house. And his
   disciples came to him, saying, "Explain to us the parable
³⁷ of the weeds of the field."   He answered, "He who sows
³⁸ the good seed is the Son of man;   the field is the world,
   and the good seed means the sons of the kingdom; the
³⁹ weeds are the sons of the evil one,   and the enemy who
   sowed them is the devil; the harvest is the close of the age,
⁴⁰ and the reapers are angels.   Just as the weeds are gathered
⁴¹ and burned with fire, so will it be at the close of the age.
   The Son of man will send his angels, and they will gather

growth from its Old Testament beginnings. It is the issue of forces intrinsic to the element (the yeast) now for the first time implanted in the world. These forces work powerfully, secretly, in every corner. The yeast is small compared with the dough, perhaps one ounce to sixteen or seventeen pounds of flour nowadays in Palestine. The amount chosen by Jesus for his parabolic purpose is a large one, slightly more than one bushel; this large amount is chosen to illustrate not the size of the kingdom (cf previous parable) but the power of the "yeast".

Parabolic teaching prophesied 13:34-35 (cf Mk 4:33-34)

Mt again seizes the opportunity of pointing out the reflection of the New Order in the Old. The psalmist in 78 (77): 2, about to expound the mystery of God's way with his people, dubs his exposition a "parable" (*mashal; LXX parabolé;* in this case a didactic poem). Struck by the word itself, so apt to the teaching he describes, Mt points to the divinely constituted precedent. He insinuates the uniformity existing between the teaching method in the word of God of old and that of the Son of God now. But he insinuates, too, as elsewhere when he quotes the O.T. that the psalmist's words would be more profoundly true on Christ's lips. This last point appears to be emphasized by the form in which Mt puts the second half of the quotation. Unlike the first half it is not identical with LXX but seems to be a more impressive translation of the Heb. "Enigmatic things of old" (Heb., LXX, referring in the psalm to the early days of Israel's history) becomes: **what has been hidden from since the foundation of the world**; cf 25:34. The psalmist ("Asaph" is named in Ps 78 (77):1 and called "prophet" in 2 Chr (Par) 29:30) had a much more restricted purpose. Christ's doctrine is not contained within the temporal or spatial bounds of Israel.

Explanation of the darnel parable 13:36-43

Not all the elements of the parable are allegorical. The "men sleeping" of 25, for example, are not careless pastors; nor does the "binding" of 30 indicate that not one of the wicked shall escape. Such applications may tentatively be made, and often were made by the Fathers, but they were not made by Jesus. He explains the allegory of the main elements only. The conditions described in the parable are said to be those of the early Church. This is not impossible (cf Introduction, pp.23-4), but it should be noted that "the most important expansions and recastings of the parables occur where it is a question of the meaning and application of the stories" (Jeremias, *The Parables of Jesus*, London, 1954). The expansion of the parable story itself is a rare practice. In our present example it is worth observing that in the early Church the "weed" was not always allowed to go unmolested until the "harvest" (cf 1 Cor 5:2), a fact which shows that the early Christians did not consider our Lord as laying down exhaustive legislation for a fully

out of his kingdom all causes of sin and all evildoers,
42 and throw them into the furnace of fire; there men will
43 weep and gnash their teeth. Then the righteous will
shine like the sun in the kingdom of their Father. He who
has ears, let him hear."

The treasure and the pearl 13:44-46
44 "The kingdom of heaven is like treasure hidden in a field,
which a man found and covered up; then in his joy he
45 goes and sells all that he has and buys that field. Again,
the kingdom of heaven is like a merchant in search of
46 fine pearls, who, on finding one pearl of great value, went
and sold all that he had and bought it."

constituted society. On the other hand, vv. 36-43 are full of Matthean linguistic characteristics (Jeremias, *l.c.*, p. 65f), suggesting that this interpretation of the darnel parable is the work of Matthew himself. (Note: both parable and interpretation are absent from Mk and Lk.)

36 – Dismissing the crowds, Jesus returns to the house; 13:1 note. The disciples, emboldened by his words, 11, ask a more detailed explanation of the parable of which, doubtless, they already have the general meaning. **37-38 – the field** is the world; **the good seed** is every loyal subject of the kingdom, **sons of the kingdom** in Semitic phrase, **the weed** is the offspring of the **evil one, 39,** who himself is the spiteful enemy of the Son of man, attacking him indirectly and by stealth. The explanation takes a leap to the end of the world; the intermediate period of growth is not mentioned, presumably because here it is not significant. It appears, therefore, that the object of the parable is not to define the duties of the leaders in the early Church but simply to explain God's tolerance of evil. The **angels** of the Son of man (16:27; 24:31), who execute his judgments, gather the crop, wheat and weed. **40** – The emphasis on the fact of the **weeds** (40-42; the "wheat" goes unmentioned) is in accord with the purpose of the parable: the exercise of retribution is only delayed. **41** – The **Son of man** must present a perfect kingdom to his Father (1 Cor 15:24), hence it is he who executes judgment (cf Jn 5:27) through his ministers. These will cleanse the kingdom of **causes of sin** (acts constituting a moral snare for the faithful) and of those responsible for them (cf the same distinction in 18:7; cf also in Heb., Zp 1:3 of which the sentence phrase is probably a reminiscence: "I will destroy . . . scandals together with the wicked"). **42** – The weeds will be thrown into the **furnace of fire,** a contemporary synonym for the place of the damned. The "weeping and gnashing (or 'grinding') of teeth" sorts ill with the suggestion of burning, but the phrase is stereotyped in Mt (8:12; 22:13; 25:30; in which places it is more naturally associated with the "exterior darkness"). **43** – Finally a word of comfort for the disciples. Their future glory is expressed in terms familiar to Jewish thought (Dan 12:3; Wis 3:7 and the uncanonical 4 Ezr 7:97). The kingdom thus purified now passes from the hand of the Son and becomes the kingdom of the Father; cf 1 Cor 15:24. For the concluding formula cf 13:19 note.

The treasure and the pearl 13:44-46

Mt records this and the following parable without either preamble or explanation. Doubtless the two were proposed to all, like the previous parables. Explanation was scarcely necessary; they are already sufficiently clear. A man finds buried treasure, struck perhaps by his random spade, in another's field – a not unlikely experience in a country familiar with invasion and sudden flight. He buries it again for security and **in his joy** goes off and sells his possessions (the significant trait of

The drag-net 13:47-50

⁴⁷ "Again, the kingdom of heaven is like a net which was
⁴⁸ thrown into the sea and gathered fish of every kind; when
it was full, men drew it ashore and sat down and sorted
⁴⁹ the good into vessels but threw away the bad. So it will
be at the close of the age. The angels will come out and
⁵⁰ separate the evil from the righteous, and throw them
into the furnace of fire; there men will weep and gnash
their teeth."

Conclusion 13:51-52

⁵¹ "Have you understood all this?" They said to him,
⁵² "Yes." And he said to them, "Therefore every scribe
who has been trained for the kingdom of heaven is like a
householder who brings out of his treasure what is new
and what is old."

this parable as of the next). He buys the field, clearly without acquainting the owner (landlord or employer, presumably) of his discovery. The morality of his action need not be discussed: it lies outside the purpose of the parable which is to teach that the kingdom is worth the sacrifice of all worldly possessions (cf 10:37-39).

45-46 – The pearl parable is a pendant of the former with the same moral. The parable naturally finishes with the acquisition (again, at all costs) of the single and valuable pearl. The merchant may have turned connoisseur but, in any case, he is parabolically pictured as retaining the pearl; suggestion of resale would have injured the parable.

The drag-net 13:47-50

From pictures of farm and kitchen and market-place Jesus turns to that of lake fishing, equally familiar to the Galileans. The net (often about one-quarter of a mile in length and about 6 to 10 feet in depth) is sustained by cork floats and weighted with lead. The men on shore pay out the net as the boatmen, holding the other end, describe a wide arc in the lake until they disembark further along the bank. The net, now semicircular, is evenly drawn towards the shore by both parties. Of the thirty or so species of fish in the Lake of Galilee none is worthless, (*sapros*, here rendered **bad**) though the cat-fish (*clarias macracanthus*) being scaleless was not eaten by practising Jews, Lev 11:9; Deut 14:9. It is unnecessary, however, to seek ichthyological exactitudes: the moral of the parable demands a mixture of bad and good (as in the darnel parable) and the picture becomes subservient. **49-50** – The application of the parable (probably Matthew's own, cf p. 167) is similar to that of the darnel (without the epilogue concerning the "just") of which it is a twin. Both parables make it clear that the kingdom exists in earthly conditions before it reaches its final stage of perfection.

Conclusion 13:51-52

The disciples assert that they have grasped the implications of the foregoing parables of the kingdom. Jesus in reply defines the advantage of such understanding. It is only when he possesses this comprehension of the kingdom that the **scribe,** thus instructed, becomes comparable to the careful householder. Old garments have not been destroyed but put away in his store-cupboard ready for emergencies. The new must not be used to patch the old, 9:16, but the old has its subservient uses. The "scribe" (or law-learned) of the new order (cf. 23:34), unlike his counterpart of the old, has the essentials of the Old Law at his fingertips precisely because he possesses the knowledge of the kingdom which is the perfection of the Law, 5:17. He is in a position to expound the working-out of God's design not only in its preliminary expression (the Mosaic dispensation) but in its present activity (the kingdom in being) and even in its consummation, 39-43; 49-50.

Visit to Nazareth 13:53-58
⁵³ And when Jesus had finished these parables, he went
⁵⁴ away from there, and coming to his own country he
taught them in their synagogue, so that they were
astonished, and said, "Where did this man get this wisdom
⁵⁵ and these mighty works? Is not this the carpenter's son?
Is not his mother called Mary? And are not his brothers
⁵⁶ James and Joseph and Simon and Judas? And are not
all his sisters with us? Where then did this man get all this?"
⁵⁷ And they took offence at him. But Jesus said to them,
"A prophet is not without honour except in his own
⁵⁸ country and in his own house." And he did not do many
mighty works there, because of their unbelief.

Jesus and Herod 14:1-2
¹ At that time Herod the tetrarch heard about the fame of
² Jesus; and he said to his servants, "This is John the
Baptist, he has been raised from the dead; that is why
these powers are at work in him."

The Nucleus of the Kingdom:
The Twelve 13:53—18:35

I

Narrative: Formation of the Twelve
13:53 – 17:27

Visit to Nazareth 13:53-58 (Mk 6:1-6)

53-54 – From the account of the parables, Mt (having already, in ch. 8—9, narrated the miracles of Mk 4:35-41; 5:1-20, 21-43) takes us straight to Nazareth, our Lord's home town; cf 21:11, Mk 1:9. It is Jesus' second visit; cf 4:13 and Lk 4:16-30. His teaching in their synagogue astounds them, 7:29 note. They know that he has not been trained in the rabbinic schools at Jerusalem. Moreover, they have heard of miracles worked, though not at Nazareth (another source of complaint; cf Lk 4:23-29). **55-56** – With the public Jesus passed for the son of Joseph the carpenter (*tekton:* joiner and housebuilder, etc.). His **brothers** are known to the people of Nazareth: James, Joseph (or Joses; Mk 6:3) Simon, Judas. James is called "brother of the Lord" in Gal 1:19;, nevertheless he is certainly not a son of our Lady but of another Mary ("of Cleophas" cf Mt 27:56; Mk 15:40; Jn 19:25) who is also the mother of Joseph (Joses). If the first two named are only cousins (the Greek term *adelphoi*, "brothers", represents the more general Aramaic *aha*) it is scarcely likely that Simon and Judas, named last, are closer relations. **57-58** – Contemptuous familiarity was a psychological obstacle. Jesus sadly notes this irrational but common attitude. He works only a few unspectacular cures (Mk), evidently for some of the few who accepted him. He could give nothing to those who refused his gifts.

Jesus and Herod 14:1-2 (Mk 6:14-16; Lk 9:7-9)

1-2 – **Herod**, son of Herod the Great by Malthace the Samaritan, was **tetrarch** ("ruler in that quarter", Knox) of Galilee and Perea (4 B.C. to 39 A.D.). He was probably living in his new town of Tiberias on the S.W. bank of the lake when reports of our Lord's activity became

The Baptist beheaded 14:3-12

³ For Herod had seized John and bound him and put him
in prison, for the sake of Herodias, his brother Philip's
⁴ wife;   because John said to him, "It is not lawful for you
⁵ to have her."   And though he wanted to put him to
death, he feared the people, because they held him to be
⁶ a prophet.   But when Herod's birthday came, the
daughter of Herodias danced before the company, and
⁷ pleased Herod,   so that he promised with an oath to give
⁸ her whatever she might ask.   Prompted by her mother,
she said "Give me the head of John the Baptist here on a
⁹ platter."   And the king was sorry; but because of his
¹⁰ oaths and his guests he commanded it to be given;   he sent
¹¹ and had John beheaded in the prison,   and his head was
brought on a platter and given to the girl, and she
¹² brought it to her mother.   And his disciples came and
took the body and buried it; and they went and told Jesus.

First miracle of loaves 14:13-21

¹³ Now when Jesus heard this, he withdrew from there in a
boat to a lonely place apart. But when the crowds heard it,
¹⁴ they followed him on foot from the towns.   As he went
ashore he saw a great throng; and he had compassion on

too persistent to ignore. Only guilty superstition could have prompted his absurd conjecture, if, indeed, it is to be taken seriously; cf Lk 9:9. His courtiers had other ideas, Mk 6:15.

The Baptist beheaded 14:3-12 (Mk 6:17-29)

The imprisonment of John had taken place before Jesus began his Galilean ministry, 4:12. Its cause was John's denunciation of Herod's adulterous marriage, Lev 18:16; 20:21. Herodias was the wife of his half-brother Philip – not Philip tetrarch of Trachonitis and Iturea, Lk 3:1, but a son of Herod the Great by Mariamne II. To make the case worse, Herod, though the Baptist does not mention it, was the uncle of Herodias. **5** – Mt, unlike Mk, content with general statements of events, does not mention the murderous intent of Herodias, though cf. 8. Nor does he represent as adequately as Mk 6:20 Herod's vacillating character, fascinated by John, half-persuaded by Herodias, held back by fear of John's many supporters. This perplexity seems to have lasted for nearly a year. **6** – The scene was the banquet-hall of the fortress-palace of Machaerus (*Mkawer;* cf Jos., *Ant.* 18, 5, 2). The castle, rebuilt by Herod the Great, lay between Callirhoe and the Arnon. It stood in the mountains of Moab on the southern border of Herod's Perean dominion. The occasion was the birthday of Herod. In place of the usual courtesans danced Salome, daughter of Herodias by her first husband. This condescension of a young princess of the blood (perhaps about fifteen years old at the time, certainly not more than twenty) was doubtless instigated by the far-sighted Herodias. **7-8** – Herod fell into the trap. The girl's mother then instructed her to ask for the head of the Baptist who lay in the dungeons. The girl herself pertly added **here, on a platter**; cf Mk 1:24-25. **9** – The unexpected and cold-blooded request sobered Herod. He was being rushed into an act which did not suit his policy, 5, nor entirely answer his feelings, Mk. 6:20. He was a king (tetrarch in fact, "king" in popular speech), and a royal, if drunken, oath could not be recalled, if uttered in public! **10-11** – The courageous Baptist died a martyr's death for the sanctity of marriage. His head went fitly back to the woman who had schemed so carefully for it. **12** – Herod possibly silenced his strange conscience by allowing the disciples of John to bury the body. For the subsequent history of Herod, Herodias, Salome, cf Jos, *Ant.* 18, 5, 1-4.

First miracle of loaves 14:13-21 (Mk 6:30-44; Lk 9:10-17; Jn 6:1-15)

13 – **Now when Jesus heard this:** If Mt's formula is not a transitional cliché, it implies that Christ's suggestion of repose for his disciples (Mk) was reinforced by the fate of the Baptist, 12, and Herod's sinister reflexion, 2. The people were evidently excited; Herod might act; Jesus used his human prudence and retired to a place **apart**, i.e. not so much secluded as removed from the crowds. He and his disciples were

¹⁵ them, and healed their sick. When it was evening, the disciples came to him and said, "This is a lonely place, and the day is now over; send the crowds away to go into ¹⁶ the villages and buy food for themselves." Jesus said, "They need not go away; you give them something to ¹⁷ eat." They said to him, "We have only five loaves here ¹⁸ and two fish." And he said, "Bring them here to me." ¹⁹ Then he ordered the crowds to sit down on the grass; and taking the five loaves and the two fish he looked up to heaven, and blessed, and broke and gave the loaves to the disciples, and the disciples gave them to the crowds. ²⁰ And they all ate and were satisfied. And they took up ²¹ twelve baskets full of the broken pieces left over. And those who ate were about five thousand men, besides women and children.

Jesus walks on the water 14:22-33
²² Then he made the disciples get into the boat and go before him to the other side, while he dismissed the crowds.

on the west side of the lake (cf 23, 34), presumably near Capernaum, Mk 6:32. They quietly withdrew from Herod's territory and sailed to that of Philip the tetrarch, to the neighbourhood, perhaps, of Bethsaida Julias in Gaulanitis on the N.E. shore of the lake. The crowds, not to be thwarted, followed on foot; doubtless they had observed whither the boat was heading. If we accept this itinerary, the distance (c. 6 m.) was almost twice that by sea, but the disciples, in need of rest, were in no hurry and the crowd arrived first, Mk 6:33. Its numbers had increased as it went. **14** – Our Lord's heart could never resist suffering. In the broad, uncultivated plain that lies to the S.E. of Bethsaida Julias between hills and sea, he healed the sick. He taught the simple folk, too, Mk 6:34. **15** – The work went on until evening (*opsias*, late afternoon, cf v. 23). Jesus took no heed, but the hungry disciples called his attention to the fact that the time (for refreshment?) had slipped by. **16-17** – The master's command must have left them dumbfounded. It was Peter's brother, Jn 6:8, who told of the boy with the five cheap (barley) loaves and the two dried fish. The remark of Andrew was not meant to be helpful – Philip had already calculated that two hundred days' labour would not buy the necessary provender. **18-19** – The plain of Bethsaida is green in spring at the time of the Pasch, Jn 6:4, and all sat down on the grass in companies, Mk 6:40, at Christ's bidding. He evidently wished to give the impression of a formal meal and, in the same spirit, he invoked a blessing, like the father of a family. The breaking of the bread also, being mentioned by all four evangelists, is evidently significant: Jesus repeated this action just one year later, at the Last Supper, 26:26. It would appear that the ceremony was deliberately symbolic of the Holy Eucharist but the symbolism is Jesus's: the very sober account of the evangelists suggests historical intention on their part and not mere symbolism. Moreover, the presence of the fish and the absence of wine does not suggest that we have here a mere symbol of the Eucharist. Whether the bread increased in Christ's hands or in the apostles' does not appear. **20-21** – The prodigality of God's gifts does not excuse human waste, and the remnants are gathered up. They fill **twelve baskets** (the property, perhaps, of the twelve apostles) whereas the original amount had been carried in one – the boy's. The baskets here are "hampers" in 15:37 (second multiplication) and the distinction is preserved when Jesus recalls the two miracles, 16:9-10. It would seem that the distinction is not merely literary: the *kophinos* of 14:20 appears to have been a strong wicker 'basket' (as used for farmwork) the *spuris* of 15:37 a larger 'hamper' used chiefly for food cf Ac 9:25).

Jesus walks on the water 14:22-33 (Mk 6:45-52)
23 – The miracle of the loaves had dangerously excited the people, Jn 6:14f. It was important that the apostles should not share their

23 And after he had dismissed the crowds, he went up into
the hills by himself to pray. When evening came, he was
24 alone, but the boat by this time was many furlongs
distant from the land, beaten by the waves; for the wind
25 was against them.   And in the fourth watch of the night
26 he came to them, walking on the sea. But when the
disciples saw him walking on the sea, they were terrified,
27 saying, "It is a ghost!" And they cried out for fear.   But
immediately he spoke to them, saying, "Take heart, it is
28 I; have no fear."   And Peter answered him, "Lord, if it
29 is you, bid me come to you on the water."   He said,
"Come." So Peter got out of the boat and walked on the
30 water and came to Jesus; but when he saw the wind,
he was afraid, and beginning to sink he cried out, "Lord,
31 save me."   Jesus immediately reached out his hand and
caught him, saying to him, "O man of little faith, why
32 did you doubt?"   And when they got into the boat, the
33 wind ceased. And those in the boat worshipped him,
saying, "Truly you are the Son of God."

Cures at Gennesaret 14:34-36
34 And when they had crossed over, they came to land at
35 Gennesaret.   And when the men of that place recognized
him, they sent round to all that region and brought to
36 him all that were sick,   and besought him that they might
only touch the fringe of his garment; and as many as
touched it were made well.

The traditions of the Pharisees 15:1-20
1 Then Pharisees and scribes came to Jesus from Jerusalem
2 and said,   "Why do your disciples transgress the tradition
of the elders? For they do not wash their hands when they
3 eat."   He answered them, "And why do you transgress

political frenzies; Jesus therefore ordered them into the boat while he sent the people home. He did not rejoin the apostles who seem to have waited at the lakeside until night fell (Jn 6:17. In Mt and Mk *opsia* as in 15, but here, apparently, bearing the meaning " night".) Instead, he slipped away from the crowd to pray in the hills surrounding the plain. **24-25** – The apostles left without him but made poor progress against the high (Jn) and contrary wind. Driven, no doubt, off their course they were in mid-lake (over 3 m. out: Jn) making little headway. There was only one way to rejoin the dispirited apostles and Jesus took it. The time was between 3 and 6 in the morning – the **fourth watch** of the night according to the Roman reckoning used by the Jews at this time. The cry of the apostles: **It is a ghost** proceeded from the apparent impossibility of any other explanation. The familiar voice calmed and convinced. **28-31** – (Mt only) Peter now appears for the first time with his high qualities and their endearing human defects. He is devoted to his master and sublimely confident in him but, conscious suddenly of self, he cries out in fright. The hand of Jesus is ready and his reproach gentle: **Of little faith!** **32-33** – To Peter on the water and now to the apostles in the boat it is clear that they are safe with their master; the wind drops as he joins them. The apostles, **those in the boat,** cf 22, are carried away. They acknowledge their master as **Son of God** (without the definite article in Greek). The title indicates at least a "sonship" of loving adoption (cf 2:14), and here the outburst seems to suggest something more (God himself walks the waters in Job 9:8), however undefined. Nevertheless, the evangelist evidently regarded Peter's profession of faith as more significant (cf 16:17).

Cures at Gennesaret 14:34-36 (Mk 6:53-56)

Stretching for about 4 miles along the west side of the lake between 'Ain Tabgha and Magdala, and less than 2 m. S. of Capernaum is a rich plain about 2 m. broad at its widest part. It is not improbable that the name of this plain was Gennesar and that the name Gennesaret, with the feminine suffix, is that of a village in the vicinity of Capernaum. The inhabitants immediately recognized Jesus, who was well known in neighbouring Capernaum. As usual, they ran (Mk) to fetch their sick. Many were healed by the touch of the tassel (cf 9:20 note) of his cloak.

The traditions of the Pharisees 15:1-20 (Mk 7:1-23)

1-2 – The quiet atmosphere of the last two chapters is now broken into by the renewed attack of the Pharisees who meanwhile have not been idle. This time, reinforcements for the local Pharisees have come from Jerusalem itself in the person of scribes. (The distinction is Mk's; Mt is not concerned with this detail.) These complain that the disciples do not observe the prescribed ceremonial handwashings before,

the commandment of God for the sake of your tradition?
⁴ For God commanded, 'Honour your father and your
mother,' and, 'He who speaks evil of father or mother, let
⁵ him surely die.'   But you say, 'If any one tells his father
or his mother, What you would have gained from me is
⁶ given to God, he need not honour his father.'   So, for
the sake of your tradition, you have made void the words
⁷ of God.   You hypocrites! Well did Isaiah prophesy of
you, when he said:

⁸   'This people honours me with their lips,
but their heart is far from me;
⁹   in vain do they worship me,
teaching as doctrines the precepts of men.' "

¹⁰ And he called the people to him and said to them. "Hear
¹¹ and understand: not what goes into the mouth defiles a
man, but what comes out of the mouth, this defiles a man."
¹² Then the disciples came and said to him, "Do you know
that the Pharisees were offended when they heard this
¹³ saying?"   He answered, "Every plant which my heavenly
¹⁴ Father has not planted will be rooted up.   Let them
alone; they are blind guides. And if a blind man leads a
¹⁵ blind man, both will fall into a pit."   But Peter said to
¹⁶ him, "Explain the parable to us."   And he said, "Are
¹⁷ you also still without understanding?   Do you not see that
whatever goes into the mouth passes into the stomach,
¹⁸ and so passes on?   But what comes out of the mouth
¹⁹ proceeds from the heart, and this defiles a man.   For out
of the heart come evil thoughts, murder, adultery, fornica-
²⁰ tion, theft, false witness, slander.   These are what defile
a man; but to eat with unwashed hands does not defile
a man."

during, and after the meal (lit. "When they eat bread" – a Semitism). These prescriptions were carefully laid down not in the Law but in the oral tradition of the **elders** (i.e. of the early rabbis). Towards the end of the 2nd. cent. A.D. they were codified in written form in the Mishnah (tract: *Yadayim* or "Hands"). Such traditions were held in even higher esteem than the Law itself; for the minutiae of the hand-washing ordinances, Edersheim 2, 9-12. **3** – Jesus declines an aimless discussion of sophistries, and sharply attacks the spirit that prompted the objection. As once before (12:7 note) he might have denounced explicitly the legal zeal that had suffocated charity. Instead, he fights his opponents on their own ground and shows how this blind devotion to the **tradition** of the elders had driven them to **transgress** (he uses their own word, v. 2) the law of God himself. He supports the accusation with an example. **4** – The law of God on duties to parents was unequivocal (the citations are from Ex 20:12, or Deut 5:16, and Ex 21:17). **5** – This, most certainly, God said; "whereas *you* say that if anyone should utter this sentence to father or mother: 'Any property of mine from which you might draw is Qorban', then he will not (need to) honour his father". Mt obscures the already involved sentence by translating the technical term "Qorban" (offering, gift consecrated, i.e. to God); Mk keeps the Aramaic term and explains it. The use of this word, "Qorban", though not implying that the property in question would be actually given to the temple, had the effect of a sacred oath isolating that property from any claims. That these claims included those even of filial duty was the opinion of at least some of the rabbis in the time of Christ (cf Babylonian Talmud, *Nedarim*, 3, 2; cf also Edersheim 2, 21). Later reforms may have been due to criticism such as that of Jesus in the present passage. To sustain the validity of such a vow, therefore, was in effect (though the Pharisees would not deduce this conclusion in so many words) to relax the divine command always to honour father and mother, 4a; indeed such an oath is equivalent to a curse, 4b. It declares null, **makes void** the divine law. **7-9** – Again sacred history repeats itself (13:14f note). Isaiah, 29:13, had also been confronted with hypocrites, and his denunciation applied equally to this messianic age. The quotation, practically identical with Mk 7:6f, is from LXX, slightly adjusted though not abbreviated. It is given a slightly different turn. The prophet (cf Heb.) had complained of the Law observed from human motives; the evangelists complain of the Law unobserved through human "traditions". On the lips the word "Qorban" had a pious sound but, as Christ's instance shows, it may hide the heart's contempt for the express will of God.

In the verses that follow, 10-20, Jesus proceeds to put the laws of legal purity in their true perspective. We observe three grades of teaching adapted to three classes of listeners. The malevolent have their charge rebutted, and no more, 3-9; the ordinary folk, now gathered

together by Jesus, receive positive, though prudently veiled, instruction with an invitation to reflect on it, 10-11. To the disciples, interested enough to ask, Jesus explains himself more fully, 15-20. **10-11** – It seems odd that Jesus should summon the crowd to hear this one sentence. It is possible, therefore, that Mt and Mk have selected it from a longer discourse. The dictum of 11 would remain obscure for the multitude who, it seems, were unaware of the circumstances, 1-2, that prompted it. Moreover, for those imbued with the food distinctions of the Law (Lev 11 etc.) the implications of 11b would be unthinkable. The startling implications are there nevertheless, as Mk 7:19 observes. But the immediate application of our Lord's saying is determined by the context. The unwashed hand, thought the Pharisees, communicates its uncleanness to the food and so to the eater. There is no suggestion, 2, that the food itself was illegal, and consequently our Lord's retort to the crowds does not explicitly touch the Mosaic distinction of foods but only the superstitious precautions of the "tradition of the elders". He affirms that to eat with clean or unclean hands can have no moral significance because the very food handled has none. He will explain later, 18-19, what he means by **what comes out of the mouth. 12-14** – (Mt only, but cf Lk 6:39). The disciples are perturbed, the recognized religious leaders, evidently present in the crowd, have taken serious offence at **this saying** of 11. Perhaps they saw more clearly than the simple folk that Christ's words touched not only the "tradition" but – in their logical conclusion – the Law itself. What they could not see was the possibility that certain elements of the Law might be transient and ill-suited to the fullness of time. Such incomprehension was excusable and the apostles long shared it; cf Ac 10:9-15. Not blindness only but refusal to see was the sin of the Pharisees, Jn 9:41. They would not lower themselves by humbly asking explanations. But their whole regime being not of God would pass, and Jesus warns the disciples against setting any store by hostility even on the part of those who were the accepted guides. Only the blind would mistake those for guides who are blind themselves. Jesus, therefore, opens his disciples' eyes to the blindness of the Pharisees and urges them to have nothing to do with them. **15-16** – It is Peter who speaks up and asks an explanation of the **parable** (here, as sometimes in O.T., enigmatic saying) of 11. He speaks for the disciples. Jesus reproaches them: Are even you (the Greek is emphatic) still without understanding? **17** – With unusual energy and realism Jesus declares that food, of itself, is an object indifferent to the spiritual life; it is matter only for the digestive process. **18** – Of no spiritual import, therefore, what goes into the mouth, but what proceeds from it. For the mouth is the overflow of the inmost heart, 12:34, and the heart, in Semitic idiom, is the factory of evil or good intent. **19** – Having reached this point in the reasoning there is no further need for the opposition (into the mouth; out of the

The daughter of the Canaanite 15:21-28

²¹ And Jesus went away from there and withdrew to the
²² district of Tyre and Sidon. And behold, a Canaanite
woman from .that region came out and cried, "Have
mercy on me, O Lord, Son of David; my daughter is
²³ severely possessed by a demon." But he did not answer
her a word. And his disciples came and begged him,
²⁴ saying, "Send her away, for she is crying after us." He
answered, "I was sent only to the lost sheep of the house
²⁵ of Israel." But she came and knelt before him, saying,
²⁶ "Lord, help me." And he answered, "It is not fair to
²⁷ take the children's bread and throw it to the dogs." She
said, "Yes, Lord, yet even the dogs eat the crumbs that
²⁸ fall from their master's table." Then Jesus answered her,
"O woman, great is your faith! Be it done for you as you
desire." And her daughter was healed instantly.

mouth) of 17-18. The sins mentioned in 19 are therefore not confined to sins of the tongue. They are embraced by the term "wicked purposes" (rather than **evil thoughts**) and include four sins of act and two (false witness; blasphemies) of the tongue. **20** – Jesus (in Mt, not Mk) rounds off the whole controversy with a concluding reference to its starting-point, 2 (the Semitic literary phenomenon known as "inclusion").

The daughter of the Canaanite 15:21-28 (Mk 7:24-30)

This incident, one of the most touching in the Gospel and treated with a delicate realism unusual in Mt, takes place in the pagan district of Tyre and Sidon; cf 11:21 note. This Phoenician territory borders Galilee on the north. It is possible that Jesus leaves Israelite ground to give his disciples the respite which they had been recently denied, 14:13 note. **22** – Mt uses the term **Canaanite** (Mk "Syrophoenician") to underline the significance of a miracle worked for one who belonged to the hereditary enemies of Israel. The term is not inaccurate: this district, colonized by Canaanites, Gen 10:15, was still basically Canaanite. The woman salutes Jesus with the messianic title **Son of David:** see note on 1:1; 9:27. The phrase must have spread with his reputation beyond the confines of Israel, 4:42 note. **23** – (Mt only). The realistic reference to the disciples' intervention is strangely absent from Mk. The Greek Matthew (cf pp. 30f) is evidently independent of Mk here. Since it is not the habit of Gk Mt to enter into detail of this kind, it is clear that the detail is not invented to heighten the effect but rather that the translator has under his eye a second and longer account (than Mk's). Yet even here the lifelike quality of the incident is due as much to what is implied as to what is expressed. Our Lord's silence (we gather) naturally drives the poor mother to the disciples. These are more concerned to rid themselves of the annoyance but, as Christ's reply in 24 hints, they suggest that the only way to do so is to dismiss her with the request granted. **24** – The personal concern of Jesus (like that of the apostles on their first mission; 10:6 note) is with Israel. His remark recalls the one made to his mother at Cana, Jn 2:4, where, evidently, the tone was sufficiently kindly to encourage. **25** – In any case, the woman's quick eyes have seen him at last open his mouth. She seizes the slight advantage and falls at his feet with a cry for pity. **26** – The words of Jesus are not as harsh as they read and they seem deliberately to invite a riposte. That they are a little parable turned into allegory only by the situation lessens the shock of the words. (On parable and allegory cf notes to ch. 13). Moreover, the Greek word used in Mt and Mk would be better rendered "little dogs", "pet dogs"; it serves to bring out the importance of priority for the children, yet eliminates the absolute idea of contempt. **27** – Nevertheless the remark would have checked one with a vestige of pride (contrast Naaman, 2 (4) Kg 5:11-12) as Jesus

Cures near the lake 15:29-31

²⁹ And Jesus went on from there and passed along the Sea of Galilee. And he went up into the hills, and sat down
³⁰ there.   And great crowds came to him, bringing with them the lame, the maimed, the blind, the dumb, and many others, and they put them at his feet, and he healed
³¹ them,   so that the throng wondered, when they saw the dumb speaking, the maimed whole, the lame walking, and the blind seeing; and they glorified the God of Israel.

Second miracle of loaves 15:32-39

³² Then Jesus called his disciples to him and said, "I have compassion on the crowd, because they have been with me now three days, and have nothing to eat; and I am unwilling to send them away hungry, lest they faint on
³³ the way."   And the disciples said to him, "Where are we to get bread enough in the desert to feed so great a
³⁴ crowd?"   And Jesus said to them, "How many loaves have you?" They said, "Seven, and a few small fish."
³⁵ And commanding the crowd to sit down on the ground,
³⁶ he took the seven loaves and the fish, and having given thanks he broke them and gave them to the disciples,
³⁷ and the disciples gave them to the crowds.   And they all ate and were satisfied; and they took up seven baskets
³⁸ full of the broken pieces left over.   Those who ate were
³⁹ four thousand men, besides women and children.   And sending away the crowds, he got into the boat and went to the region of Magadan.

well knows. But the woman's simple humility rises to the occasion and there is wit in her reply: "How true, Lord", or "Please, Lord" cf Phil 4:3; Phm 20, (rather than **yes, Lord**) "for the little dogs also get their meal – from the crumbs that fall". The woman quaintly turns the parable to her own advantage: what you say is true, she implies, as far as it goes, but it has not been taken far enough. As a mother she knows that she would not thus rob her children of bread, but she also knows their table manners and how the floor is kept clean. **28** – Jesus is won by a faith that has stood so sharp a test. When the woman gets home she finds her child well again (Mk).

Cures near the lake 15:29-31 (cf Mk 7:31-37)
Jesus with his disciples leaves the district of Tyre and Sidon for the Lake of Galilee; for this journey cf Mk 7:31. The scene of the miracles appears to be the N.E. side of the lake where the hills fall to the plain. From the fact that the crowds praise **the God of Israel** it would be bold to argue that they were pagans; cf Lk 1:68; Ac 13:7.

Second miracle of loaves 15:32-39 (Mk 8:1-10)
The evangelists plainly record the multiplications as two separate miracles. Each narrates them in close succession (Mt ch. 14—15; ch. 6 and 8) and subsequently refers to them as two separate events, Mt 16:9-10; Mk 8:19-20. If the unexpected attitude of the disciples on this second occasion seems surprising, we should remember the months that had elapsed since the former miracle, the occasions on which the disciples must since have gone hungry without a miracle being worked, their very proper diffidence in asking for a miracle, 23. **32** – The disciples therefore leave it to Jesus to comment on the hunger of the crowds. He does so. Their provisions are exhausted after three days with him, far from their homes (Mk). Jesus proposes a dilemma: they have no food here yet he will not send them elsewhere. He is clearly inviting the disciples to ask for a solution like the previous one, 14:19. So far, the text does not exclude (rather it suggests) a previous multiplication of loaves. **33-34** – The disciples' remark is cautious, perhaps even a sly suggestion: **where are we** – (emphatic) . . . ? They express their own helplessness, not necessarily his. Moreover, their answer to the question: **How many loaves?** is not the helpless one of 14:17 ("only five") but simply **Seven,** as if in this case the information was not regarded as useless. **35-37** – The multitude (4,000 here, 5,000 in ch. 14) sat on the ground — there was no "green grass" as on the previous occasion, Mk 6:39; it was summer. The number of baskets (see 14:20 note) corresponds, not to the number of the apostles (unlike 14:20) but to the original number of loaves, this more directly signalizing the abundance of the miracle. **39** – It appears that Jesus sets sail for the western bank of the lake, since it is on this bank that he would be most

The Pharisees ask for a sign 16:1-4

¹ And the Pharisees and Sadducees came, and to test him
² they asked him to show them a sign from heaven. He
answered, "When it is evening, you say, 'It will be fair
³ weather; for the sky is red.' And in the morning, 'It
will be stormy today, for the sky is red and threatening.'
You know how to interpret the appearance of the sky,
⁴ but you cannot interpret the signs of the times. An evil
and adulterous generation seeks for a sign, but no sign
shall be given to it except the sign of Jonah." So he left
them and departed.

The leaven of the Pharisees 16:5-12

⁵ When the disciples reached the other side, they had for-
⁶ gotten to bring any bread. Jesus said to them, "Take
heed and beware of the leaven of the Pharisees and
⁷ Sadducees." And they discussed it among themselves,
⁸ saying, "We brought no bread." But Jesus, aware of
this, said "O men of little faith, why do you discuss
among yourselves the fact that you have no bread?
⁹ Do you not yet perceive? Do you not remember the five
loaves of the five thousand, and how many baskets you
¹⁰ gathered? Or the seven loaves of the four thousand, and
¹¹ how many baskets you gathered? How is it that you fail
to perceive that I did not speak about bread? Beware of
¹² the leaven of the Pharisees and Sadducees." Then they
understood that he did not tell them to beware of the
leaven of bread, but of the teaching of the Pharisees and
Sadducees.

likely to meet the Pharisees, 16:1, and since it is to the eastern side that he later sails, 16:5, to go to Caesarea Philippi, 16:13, via Bethsaida Julias, Mk 8:22. But the point of arrival, **Magadan,** ("Dalmanutha" in Mk) is unknown. It is probable however (Abel 2,373) that the form, certainly authentic, represents "Magdala" (cf 27:55 note) just as the "Migdal" of Jos 15:37 is transcribed "Magada" in the Vatican Codex.

The Pharisees ask for a sign 16:1-4 (Mk 8:11-13; Lk 11:16; 12:54-56; 11:29)

The incident serves as introduction to the lesson of 5-12. **1 – Pharisees and Sadducees** forget their differences and make common cause against the new teacher. The situation is similar to that of 12:38ff (see note) but the Sadducees here take the place of the scribes, and our Lord's answer is notably different. They issue a cynical challenge – **to test him.** They demand a messianic **sign** descending **from** the physical heavens. The sign asked for is possibly of the "manna" miracle of Mosaic times (cf Jn 6:30ff) which times were in Jewish tradition (Edersheim, 1, 176) a rehearsal of the messianic age; in particular the Messiah was to bring down manna from heaven for his people. Their ill-will had contrived to explain away Christ's miracles (e.g. 9:34; cf Jn 9:18-29) and he refuses to work wonders at their dictation; cf his similar attitude in Lk 23:8-9. **2-3 –** He ironically concedes their ability to notice natural portents in the heavens but adroitly invites them to discern supernatural portents on earth among the blind, the lame, the deaf (cf 11:4f), announcing the new messianic day. **4 –** This verse, with the exception of the ominous, valedictory phrase, has possibly been imported hither by translator or copyist from 12:39.

The leaven of the Pharisees 16:5-12 (Mk 8:14-21; Lk 12:1)

5 – Jesus and his disciples sail for the eastern shore of the lake. Distracted by dispute or by the unexpected departure, the disciples had not made their usual provision; only one old loaf lay in the boat, Mk 8:14. **6-7 –** Jesus bids his disciples beware of the corrupting element (**leaven,** cf 1 Cor 5:6) which is the outlook (**teaching,** 12) of his recent questioners, but the disciples, as so often the interlocutors in the fourth Gospel (e.g. Jn 4:11; 6:34), are reminded only of material bread. **8-12 –** After witnessing the two miracles of the loaves (14:17-21; 15:34-38 with notes) the disciples needed no great faith to exclude worry about material things; still less should they have implicitly attributed this worry to their master. Jesus has only to repeat his original remark (doubtless with an emphasis on its second half) to make its metaphorical meaning clear. Doctrinally the Pharisees and Sadducees had little in common, the **teaching** therefore is their common cynicism, so recently displayed, with regard to the "signs of the times". Christ's warning is not unnecessary: unlike the Pharisees and Sadducees the disciples did

Peter's profession of faith 16:13-20

13 Now when Jesus came into the district of Caesarea
Philippi, he asked his disciples, "Who do men say that
14 the Son of man is?"   And they said, "Some say John the
Baptist, others say Elijah, and others Jeremiah or one of
15 the prophets."   He said to them, "But who do you say
16 I am?"   Simon Peter replied, "You are the Christ, the
17 Son of the living God."   And Jesus answered him,
"Blessed are you Simon Bar-Jona! For flesh and blood
has not revealed this to you, but my Father who is in
18 heaven.   And I tell you, you are Peter, and on this rock
I will build my church, and the powers of death shall not
19 prevail against it.   I will give you the keys of the kingdom of heaven, and whatever you bind on earth shall be
bound in heaven, and whatever you loose on earth shall
20 be loosed in heaven."   Then he strictly charged the
disciples to tell no one that he was the Christ.

not ignore his Galilean miracles but they were in danger of missing their full significance, 8-10.

Peter's profession of faith 16:13-20 (Mk 8:27-30; Lk 9:18-21)

13 – After reaching the east bank of the lake and after the cure of the blind man at Bethsaida Julias, Mk 8:22-26, (Mt omits), Jesus takes his disciples to the district of Caesarea Philippi on the extreme northern frontier of Palestine, 2 or 3 m. E. of Dan. Here in fertile country rises one of the largest sources of the Jordan. It is a natural site for the sanctuary of Pan (hence Paneas; Arab. Baniyas) built there by the predominantly Greek population in the 3rd cent. B.C. In Christ's time the town itself was new-built by Philip the tetrarch in 3-2 B.C. and named Caesarea in honour of Caesar Augustus. It boasted a temple to Augustus built by Herod the Great c. 20 B.C. Here Jesus invites his disciples to compare their own reflections on his own personality with those of popular rumour. In Mt (**Son of man**; Mk and Lk: "I") we are already prepared for **Son of God** which is to follow, 16. **14** – In Galilee at Herod's court there was a superstitious rumour of the Baptist's resurrection. Other circles felt the messianic atmosphere and thought of Elijah the precursor (but cf 17: note) or of Jeremiah, Israel's champion at a time of national crisis (cf 2 Mac 15:13-16); the messianic age was associated, too, with the return of other prophets; cf 4 Ezr 2:18. It is strange that none of them mention rumours of the Messiah himself which must have been recently circulating; (cf Jn 6:15). **15-16** – Jesus expects more from his companions and pupils, but it is only Peter who makes the decisive and immediate reply acknowledging his messiahship. In Mt (only) he goes on to profess, with much more emphasis than the less considered exclamation of 14:33, that Jesus is **the Son of the living God.** The formula is found with slight variation, on the lips of Caiaphas, Mk 14:61, and for its acceptance Jesus is declared guilty of blasphemy. He accepts it here, and in terms which make it clear that Peter's conception of his dignity is not merely a deduction of messiahship from adequate human premises cf 11:4-6. The confession of sonship is absent from Mk and is probably Gk Mt's insertion. **17-19** – Human considerations (**flesh and blood**) such as reasoning from miracle and prophecy could have led Peter to a confession of messiahship – no great marvel there. That the **Father,** not the Son, had revealed shows how profound was the significance of Peter's words, even if Peter himself had not yet fully sounded their depth. By this revelation the Father had singled out Peter as the natural foundation for his Son's society and Jesus, as ever, follows his Father's lead. Faith in the divinity of Christ must henceforth be a criterion of the true society of Christ. The Son of God now echoes and outdoes the generosity of the son of Jonah. At last he explains the name (apparently of his own invention) promised to Simon at the first encounter, Jn 1:42, and con-

firmed on the occasion of Simon's call, Mt 4:18; cf 10:2. The name
in Aramaic is *Kepha*, i.e. **rock** or stone. The Greek translator judged
petros "stone" more suitable, being masculine in form, for Simon's name
and kept *petra* "rock" for the foundation-material demanded by the
metaphor. The original language, however, leaves no room for distinction: You are *Kepha* and on this *Kepha* . . . The **church** (*ekklesia*, the
customary LXX rendering of the Hebrew *qahal*, i.e. religious assembly,
congregation) is the new society of Christ's faithful, answering to and
supplanting the O.T. *qahal*. Simon is to be the ultimate authority on
earth of this society which is itself the hierarchical body described
in 18:15-18. By reason of this rock-foundation the malignant powers
will not prove stronger than the citadel-society. The phrase **powers of
death,** lit. "gates of Hell", needs some explanation. The term "gates" in
Hebrew is often used of the fortified city itself (Gen 22:17; 24:60; Is 14:
31, etc.). "Hell" (Hades), dwelling-place of demons (four times in this
sense in the Apocalypse, and cf Lk 16:23) seems to imply more than
death (an idea which would confuse the warlike image): it indicates
every activity of the forces hostile to the cause of Good. In 19 the metaphor
changes, the besieged citadel founded on a rock now becomes the
kingdom with its Chancellor, to whom Christ will in due time commit
his own keys, Jn 21:15-17. The gift of the keys implies responsible
stewardship as the keys of Eliakim, Is 22:22, implied stewardship of the
Davidic household. This idea serves as a bridge from the rock-metaphor
to the more direct definition of Peter's powers. These powers are of
effective "binding" and "loosing" in the spiritual order on earth. The
"binding and loosing" (rabbinical terms for excluding from – "binding"
– or granting readmission to the community, or for declaring forbidden
or permitted according to the Law) must be understood as containing
all that is implicit in the gift of the keys, i.e. all powers necessary to the
well-being of the kingdom including any positive legislative power
which may prove necessary in the future. **20** – Mt, having inserted a
second title (absent from Mk and Lk) in v. 16, has to say **tell no one
that he was the Christ** (Mk: "tell no one about him"). The word
"Messiah" was politically inflammatory.

Note on the genuineness and implications of Mt 16:17-19: These verses are
absent from Mk and Lk, and it is probable that their insertion here is
due to Mt's habit of synthesis. There is no doubt (a) that they have
always belonged to the text of Greek Matthew – the textual tradition is
firm; or (b) that they derive from a very ancient oral Palestinian tradition. This last point, on which almost all modern scholars are agreed,
seems undeniable: the passage has a strong Semitic flavour (Simon is
surnamed *bar-yonah;* human reasoning is *flesh and blood;* the familiar
rabbinic expression *bind and loose* is used; the play on the nickname is
more exact in Aramaic; in rabbinical literature Abraham is called the
rock of the world; the word *church – ekklesia,* equivalent to *sunagogé* or

First prophecy of the passion 16:21-23

21 From that time Jesus began to show his disciples that he must go to Jerusalem and suffer many things from the elders and chief priests and scribes, and be killed, and on 22 the third day be raised.   And Peter took him and began to rebuke him, saying, "God forbid, Lord! This shall 23 never happen to you."   But he turned and said to Peter, "Get behind me, Satan! You are a hindrance to me; for you are not on the side of God, but of men."

"gathering" – occurs about one hundred times in the Greek translation of the Old Testament for Israel, the congregation of God; the metaphor of *building* such a community flows naturally from the O.T. phrase "the house of Israel" – and cf Jn 2:19). There is no adequate reason, therefore, for denying that these words were spoken by Christ, especially as it would be strange if he never explained the nickname given at the outset (Mk 3:16; Jn 1:42). When were they spoken? Possibly after the Resurrection (cf Jn 21:15ff), possibly at the Last Supper (cf Lk 22:31ff).

It is much more difficult to decide *from the text itself* how much is implied for the post-Resurrection Church, but it is certain from all four Gospels and the Acts that among the disciples Peter was chosen for the leading role, and subsequently played this part in the Jerusalem church (cf O. Cullmann, *Peter*, London, 1953, pp. 23-55). Now, it seems legitimate to put the question not why Christ chose *Peter* (an answer would be purely conjectural), but why he chose an individual apostle at all. Christ himself is the one foundation, and there is no other (1 Cor 3:11). But just as he is the one shepherd and yet appoints Peter to shepherd his flock (Jn 21:15ff), so he communicates his own rock-strength to the same apostle. This, presumably, because he intends the post-Resurrection community to have a *visible* authority, an individual. We may even ask a further question: did Christ intend that there should be no such visible authority after Peter's death (prophesied in Jn 21:18f)? And since Jesus did not explicitly speak of this, is it not possible – and likely – that the Spirit of Jesus spoke through history?

First prophecy of the passion 16:21-23 (Mk 8:31-33; Lk 9:22)

21 – Caesarea Philippi marks a turning-point of the apostles' faith. Jesus now ventures to break the strange news of his approaching passion. The titles "Messiah", "Son of God", were to the apostles far removed from the idea of Israel's official rejection (through the Sanhedrin) and from the prospect of death. All three passion predictions, 16:21f; 17:21f; 20:18f are accompanied by a prophecy of resurrection which, however, seems to be overwhelmed in the apostles' mind by the shocking prediction preceding it. Moreover, the nature of this resurrection is relatively vague and its prospect remote; compare their mentality perhaps with Martha's, Jn 11:23-24. **22-23** – Peter **took him** (i.e. to one side; or possibly translate "tried to be helpful") and remonstrated with him: (lit.) "may (God) be merciful to you!" But Peter is a stumbling block, **hindrance,** in the path traced by the Father and willingly taken by the Son; Jesus orders him out of the way. Peter cannot yet appreciate God's ways. He is unwittingly playing the part of their great adversary (**Satan**). Through him Satan, who had left Jesus only "for a time", Lk 4:12, renews the original temptation, 4:1-11. The faithful report of this rebuke is a tribute to the candour of the evangelist who has just reported the promise of the primacy.

Conditions for following Christ 16:24-28

²⁴ Then Jesus told his disciples, "If any man would come after me, let him deny himself and take up his cross and ²⁵ follow me.   For whoever would save his life will lose it, ²⁶ and whoever loses his life for my sake will find it.   For what will it profit a man, if he gains the whole world and forfeits his life? Or what shall a man give in return for ²⁷ his life?   For the Son of man is to come with his angels in the glory of his Father, and then he will repay every ²⁸ man for what he has done   Truly, I say to you, there are some standing here who will not taste death before they see the Son of man coming in his kingdom."

Transfiguration 17:1-8

¹ And after six days Jesus took with him Peter and James ² and John his brother, and led them up a high mountain apart.   And he was transfigured before them, and his face shone like the sun, and his garments became white ³ as light.   And behold, there appeared to them Moses and ⁴ Elijah, talking with him.   And Peter said to Jesus, "Lord, it is well that we are here; if you wish, I will make three booths here, one for you and one for Moses and one for ⁵ Elijah."   He was still speaking, when lo, a bright cloud overshadowed them, and a voice from the cloud said, "This is my beloved Son, with whom I am well pleased;

Conditions for following Christ 16:24-28 (Mk 8:34 – 9:1; (Lk 9:23-27)
Like master, like man: the disciple must himself be prepared to
shoulder a cross in imitation of Christ. The saying is even more natural
in this passage than it is in 10:38 (see note) because it here follows a
prediction of the passion. **25** – The exhortation is reinforced by a
prospect of the great issues involved (cf 10:39) – no less than the loss
or gain of eternal life. **26** – How great is this gain appears from a
literary balance of the world's riches against the worth of man's whole
person (**life** here, *psuché*, like the corresponding Hebrew word *nephesh*,
is a complex notion embracing not physical life only but supernatural
also). **27** – Man cannot buy this life: it will be awarded according to
his works i.e. according to his loyalty to Christ's cause. The fitting
judge of this loyalty is Christ himself. Of him, with his cross, one might
be tempted to be ashamed (Mk, Lk), but the true dignity and reward
of his following will appear from his glory and his sentence in the
final judgment. **28** – This sentence, though juxtaposed to 27, was perhaps originally a separate dictum, as Mk 9:1 seems to hint. If this is so,
we should not interpret v. 28 from v. 27: v. 28 appears to imply that the
dignity of Christ's discipleship will be manifested *before* the final judgment, even in the lifetime of some of the bystanders. The kingdom of
the Son (not "of the Father", cf 13:43 note) will establish itself shortly
"in power" (Mk; cf Cor 4:20). This power, following the "weakness"
of the cross, 1 Cor 1:23-25, manifests itself progressively from the
Resurrection onwards, Rom 1:4ff. To those who could see it the glory
of this spiritual kingdom on earth was already plain in St Paul's time,
e.g. 1 Thess 2:12, Eph 2:6f. The destruction of Jerusalem in 70 A.D.
served only to show that the kingdom stood alone. (For further notes
cf pp. 261-2).

Transfiguration 17:1-8 (Mk 9:2-8; Lk 9:28-36)
1 – The Father had already revealed the dignity of his Son to Peter
16:17; he now, about one week later, reveals it more publicly. As his
companions, Jesus takes the three favoured witnesses of one of his
greatest miracles, Mk 5:37, and of his deepest distress, Mk 14:33. The
high mountain apart is not known, but a fourth century tradition
names Tabor, a few miles S.E. of Nazareth and two or three days'
direct journey from Caesarea Philippi; it rises, symmetrical and isolated,
about 1,000 ft above the plain. **2** – Before the eyes of the disciples the
aspect of Jesus was profoundly changed, the result of an inner brilliance
affecting even his garments. **3** – Moses the legislator and Elijah the
prophet-champion of Yahwism (cf Ecclus 48:1-10) show by their
presence that the old order is not destroyed but fulfilled in the person and
work of Jesus – fulfilled even in the "scandal" of the cross, the subject
of their converse with him, Lk 9:31. Wearied with the climb, the three
apostles are asleep; they waken to see the vision (Lk). **4** – Peter's

⁶ listen to him." When the disciples heard this, they fell
⁷ on their faces, and were filled with awe. But Jesus came
and touched them, saying, "Rise, and have no fear."
⁸ And when they lifted up their eyes, they saw no one but
Jesus only.

Question about Elijah 17:9-13

⁹ And as they were coming down the mountain, Jesus commanded them, "Tell no one the vision, until the Son of
¹⁰ man is raised from the dead." And the disciples asked
him, "Then why do the scribes say that first Elijah must
¹¹ come?" He replied, "Elijah does come, and he is to
¹² restore all things; but I tell you that Elijah has already
come, and they did not know him, but did to him whatever they pleased. So also the Son of man will suffer at
¹³ their hands." Then the disciples understood that he was
speaking to them of John the Baptist.

The epileptic demoniac 17:14-20

¹⁴ And when they came to the crowd, a man came up to him
¹⁵ and kneeling before him said, "Lord, have mercy on my
son, for he is an epileptic and he suffers terribly; for often
¹⁶ he falls into the fire, and often into the water. And I
brought him to your disciples, and they could not heal
¹⁷ him." And Jesus answered, "O faithless and perverse
generation, how long am I to be with you? How long
¹⁸ am I to bear with you? Bring him here to me." And

suggestion is a wild one (Mk, Lk), based apparently on the assumption that Moses and Elijah have come to stay and to herald Jesus in his glory. "It is fortunate we are here", he says. He means that, being there, he and his companions will be able to improvise **booths** (huts of branches). He forgets that such guests need no shelter. **5** - As in the O.T. (cf Ex 24:15; 33:9-11 etc.) the cloud is the visible manifestation of the divine presence. It envelops them all. The Voice repeats the words spoken at the Baptism, 3:17, and approves Peter's profession, 16:17, but the added command **listen to him** warns the apostles against questioning the words of the Son; cf 16:22. **6-9** - The glory passes and Jesus is once more the familiar friend. He enjoins silence: the vision is not to be spoken of until after the Resurrection, presumably to avoid premature and mistaken messianic enthusiasm. Few, knowing of the transfiguration, would learn to appreciate the necessity of the cross.

Question about Elijah 17:9-13 (Mk 9:9-13)

The appearance and disappearance of Elijah had been troubling the apostles. He has appeared after our Lord and disappeared without furthering Christ's mission in any way. This was not the Elijah, herald of the Messiah, depicted by the scribes (cf Edersheim 2, 706-9) from their reading of the prophet Malachi (Mal 4:5-6). Jesus grants the expression of the scribal teaching; Elijah is to come and restore (i.e. bring back to perfection) . . ., but he corrects its perspective. This herald-Elijah has already come in the person of the Baptist. The "great day of the Lord" before which Elijah was to come, Mal 4:5, is therefore the day of messianic visitation. Jesus declares the profound sense of the prophecy (missed by the scribes): not the person but the spirit of Elijah returns - in the person of the Baptist; cf Lk 1:17. Jesus then turns this discussion to advantage: if the great Elijah is the martyred Baptist, it is not surprising that the glorious Messiah should prove to be the crucified Son of man. The fate of the Baptist was a hint of God's messianic plan. John was a precursor in more ways than one.

The epileptic demoniac 17:14-20 (Mk 9:14-29; Lk 9:37-43)

14 - It seems that the night was spent on the hill, Lk 9:37. On the following day Jesus and the three descend to find a crowd gathered round three groups: the nine apostles, certain scribes, and a father with a son. The boy has all the symptoms of epilepsy, Mk 9:17-25, called "lunacy" by the ancients by reason of its periodicity. **15-16** - In the absence of Jesus the father has approached the disciples without success; he now eagerly approaches the master. **17** - Our Lord's tone is one of lament rather than of rebuke. His words "are not merely those of a man among men; it is a divine being speaking - one whose own home is heaven" (Lagrange). The lament embraces the whole faithless and misguided (**perverse**) human race among whom Jesus

Jesus rebuked him, and the demon came out of him,
19 and the boy was cured instantly. Then the disciples
came to Jesus privately and said, "Why could we not
20 cast it out?" He said to them, "Because of your little
faith. For truly, I say to you, if you have faith as a
grain of mustard seed, you will say to this mountain, 'Move
hence to yonder place,' and it will move; and nothing will
be impossible to you."

Second prophecy of the passion 17:22-23
22 As they were gathering in Galilee, Jesus said to them,
"The Son of man is to be delivered into the hands of men,
23 and they will kill him, and he will be raised on the third
day." And they were greatly distressed.

The temple tax 17:24-27
24 When they came to Capernaum, the collectors of the half-
shekel tax went up to Peter and said, "Does not your
25 teacher pay the tax?" He said, "Yes." And when he
came home, Jesus spoke to him first, saying, "What do
you think, Simon? From whom do kings of the earth
26 take toll or tribute? From their sons or from others?" And
when he said, "From others," Jesus said to him, "Then

came to work. It is immediately evoked, however, by the impotence of his own apostles (their own fault, cf 19-20) and perhaps by the malevolence of the carping scribes, Mk 9:13. **18** – The child was not only epileptic but possessed, since Jesus not only cures but exorcizes, Mk 9:14; Lk 19:34. The father, however, does not distinguish the two states nor does Jesus instruct him: he did not come to teach the natural sciences. **19-20** – The apostles, puzzled at their inability to exorcize (their first failure?), ask the reason. Jesus underlines his earlier hint ("unbelieving" generation; 16) – lack of confidence in God. The tiniest grain of such **faith** (cf 13:32) can work the impossible. He uses the current rabbinic hyperbole of "moving mountains", suitable to their situation at the foot of Tabor. After v. 20 some Mss. read: "But this kind never comes out except by prayer and fasting." This is a harmonization with Mk 9:29.

Second prophecy of the passion 17:22-23 (Mk 9:30-32; Lk 9:43-45)
22 – **As they were gathering** (or "one day when they were all together") **in Galilee,** and about to leave for Jerusalem, Jesus again warns the disciples of his death. **Delivered into the hands of men** takes the place of the suffering from "the elders, scribes, high-priests" of the prediction (16:21, see note). The phrase suggests a terrible fate, 2 Sam (Kg) 24:14, and there is pathetic irony in the juxtaposition of **Son of man** and **the hands of men.**

The temple tax 17:24-27
24 – From Tabor it is a full day's walk direct to Capernaum. On their arrival, Peter is approached by the tax-collectors for the tribute which, in the absence of Jesus and the apostles, has evidently become overdue. The **half-shekel,** or two-drachma silver-piece (Westminster Version: "florin") is the annual subscription towards the upkeep of the temple. (1 Greek drachma$=\frac{1}{4}$ stater$=\frac{1}{4}$ Jewish shekel$=$1 Roman denarius. The denarius was the recognized daily wage of a labourer; cf Mt 20:2). This tribute affected all male Jews at home and abroad, aged twenty and over. The subscription was traditional (cf Ex 30:11-16; Neh 10:32-34), the amount fluctuating. The diffident approach of the collectors (who were usually local men) may be due to respect for the dignity of their great townsman; they were aware that priests at least were not forced to pay the temple-tax. **25-26** – Peter, knowing his master's custom, unhesitatingly answers **Yes,** and goes into the house (his own? cf 9:10, 28; 13:1, 36) where Jesus is staying. Our Lord forestalls Peter's words. He already knows Peter's difficulty – either supernaturally or because he has overheard the conversation. He frames a small parable in the form of a question, the answer to which is obvious. **Toll** (customs dues) and **tribute** (direct, capitation, tax) would certainly not be exacted of members of an oriental royal family – the royal

²⁷ the sons are free.   However, not to give offence to them, go to the sea and cast a hook, and take the first fish that comes up, and when you open its mouth you will find a shekel; take that and give it to them for me and for yourself."

children are exempt. Now the temple dues are a tribute "which each offers to God", Jos., *Ant.* 18, 9 1. It is therefore clear (especially to Peter who, in Mt, has recently confessed the divine sonship) that Jesus is exempt. **27** – Nevertheless, refusal to pay would savour of impiety for those ignorant of Christ's dignity and rights. Doubtless the necessary money could have been obtained by ordinary means but the miraculous means chosen has the advantage of avoiding the "scandal" while yielding nothing to the principle (**the sons are free**) because the money does not come from the apostolic purse after all. The miracle is certainly one of supernatural knowledge, probably more, though the *hemichromis sacra* of Lake Galilee has been found with e.g. pebbles in its mouth. Simon here (as the disciples elsewhere; 12:1-8) is associated with the immunity of one who is greater than the temple. The incident of the miracle is discountenanced in many circles as a pious story later (c. 97 A.D.?) elaborated, partly to clear up early difficulties on the relationship of early Church and State, partly to enhance the dignity of Peter and of the Roman church. This accusation is subject to the general remarks regarding "Form Criticism" (cf pp. 38-9) but in particular it should be observed that late invention is improbable for this passage. After the destruction of the temple in 70 A.D. the tax remained but was diverted to the temple of Jupiter in Rome. Against this background the argument of Jesus – resting on the fact that the collection was for the Father's temple – would be meaningless.)

Who is the greatest? 18:1-4

¹ At that time the disciples came to Jesus, saying, "Who is
² the greatest in the kingdom of heaven?"   And calling to
³ him a child, he put him in the midst of them,   and said,
"Truly, I say to you, unless you turn and become like
children, you will never enter the kingdom of heaven.
⁴ Whoever humbles himself like this child, he is the greatest
in the kingdom of heaven.

Scandal 18:5-10

⁵ "Whoever receives one such child in my name receives
⁶ me;   but whoever causes one of these little ones who believe in me to sin, it would be better for him to have a
great millstone fastened round his neck and to be drowned
⁷ in the depth of the sea.   Woe to the world for temptations to sin! For it is necessary that temptation come, but
⁸ woe to the man by whom the temptation comes!   And if
your hand or your foot causes you to sin, cut it off and

II

Discourse: Relationships within the New Community 18:1-35

Our Lord addresses himself principally to those who were to carry on his work. His discourse is far from being a systematic and exhaustive charter for the Church's leaders, but it inculcates fundamental dispositions: childlike spirit, 1-4; care for the simplest of the faithful, 5-8; zeal for the wayward, 10-14, but salutary firmness and exercise of full authority, 15-20; and all this without personal rancour, 21-35.

Who is the greatest? 18:1-4 (Mk 9:33-37; 10:15; Lk 9:46-48; 18:17)

Despite, or even because of (?), the promise of primacy to Peter, 16:19, the apostles debate, not without personal interest, the question of precedence. The dispute takes place on the way to Capernaum (Mk) and the apostles are ashamed to tell our Lord (Mk, Lk) who, however, knows their thoughts. Mt characteristically ignores these details and summarily presents the incident in the form of Jesus' own question and answer. **1** – The question concerns present dignity, not degrees of reward in heaven (cf Mk 9:33 "which of them was greatest"). The **kingdom of heaven** is, therefore, the kingdom in its earthly stage. This is shown also by the theme of the whole chapter which deals with mutual relations of the disciples on earth. **2** – The child is a flesh-and-blood parable. Ambition is not a common trait of childhood. **3** – Our Lord's words are particularly stern in Mt "Unless you become like little children *again*" (**turn and** appears to be a Hebraism), far from achieving eminence in the kingdom you cannot even qualify for entrance. Ambition in this matter defeats itself; cf. 20:20ff. with note. **4** – The greatest stature in the kingdom (i.e. true dignity before God) is paradoxically that of the man who makes himself small. High function in the kingdom absolves no one from personal humility.

Scandal 18:5-10 (Mk 9:37; 42-48; Lk 9:48; 17:1-2)

5 – The **child** suggests all, young or old, who have simple faith in Jesus. He therefore passes to the duties of the twelve towards the least sophisticated of the faithful. Care devoted to such, if it be given because they belong to Christ (**in my name**) as his chosen ones, becomes an act of devotion to Jesus himself. **6** – The care for the **little ones** demanded in 5 is explained by its opposite vice – the providing of a snare ("scandal") in the moral order by one's own conduct – bad example or direct seduction. This is a danger for those destined to occupy high places in the community. Better that those who so seduce

throw it from you; it is better for you to enter life maimed or lame than with two hands or two feet to be thrown into ⁹ the eternal fire. And if your eye causes you to sin, pluck it out and throw it from you; it is better for you to enter life with one eye than with two eyes to be thrown into the ¹⁰ hell of fire. See that you do not despise one of these little ones; for I tell you that in heaven their angels always behold the face of my Father who is in heaven."

The lost sheep 18:12-14

¹² "What do you think? If a man has a hundred sheep, and one of them has gone astray, does he not leave the ninety-nine on the hills and go in search of the one that went ¹³ astray? And if he finds it, truly, I say to you, he rejoices over it more than over the ninety-nine that never went ¹⁴ astray. So it is not the will of my Father who is in heaven that one of these little ones should perish."

should be securely out of the way of doing harm – weighed down in the depth of the sea. The **millstone** (lit. "ass-mill") in question is the lower of two stones which is like a hollow inverted cone with a wide hole at the narrower end allowing the flour to fall through when the grain has been crushed against its sides by the upper millstone. The mill is set in motion by an ass harnessed to a beam. This hollow cone could be put on a man collar-fashion. **7** – Human nature being what it is, scandal, here translated **temptations to sin**, is inevitable, but woe to the one who provides it, because he takes the evil initiative.

8-9 – The transition to this new idea is made, in Semitic fashion, by means rather of a word (**cause to sin**) than by a direct logical connexion with vv. 5-7, which deal not with obstacles in oneself but with obstacles put in the way of others. A similar thought has been expressed in 5:29-30, but here the context (dealing with mutual relations in a society) suggests that the "hand, foot, etc" further represent those dear to us who may prove occasions of sin. Our Lord's words are severe because so much is at stake: **life or eternal fire.** The "life" is the unending life of the world to come (cf Wis 5:15f; 2 Mac 7:9, 36) where sacrifice of mortal life and limb will be repaired. Eternal fire or the hell (gehenna) of fire (5:22 note) is proposed as the one alternative without prospect of end, and this was the prevailing Jewish belief. **10** – After the short digression on the removal of obstacles within oneself, Jesus returns to the care for the "little ones", 5-7, with a parable to which Luke (Lk 15:3-7, note) gives a different emphasis. These **little ones** (5, note) are not contemptible; they have their **angels,** their representatives at the court of God to plead vindication of their wrongs or neglect. That these angel-representatives are also companions of the just on earth (cf Ps 90:11) is a doctrine found in rabbinic writings (Edersheim 2, 752): the just man on his journey is accompanied by two good angels, the wicked by two evil spirits. Later rabbis speak of angels assigned to the permanent care of each individual. Here Jesus clearly speaks of angelic advocates in heaven and, if we take into account the background of Jewish angelology, implies that they accompany their charges on earth. This doctrine of "guardian angels", based on our text (and cf Ac 12:15), is not defined by the Church, but is consecrated in her practice. On the manuscript evidence editors rightly omit 11, ("for the Son of man came to save the lost") as an importation from Lk 19:10.

The lost sheep 18:12-14 (Lk 15:3-7)

The parable speaks for itself. The lesson is implicit: if the Father thinks so much of these **little ones,** how far should the disciple be from despising them! The shepherd is, of course, not a perfect image of God; his impetuosity in leaving the ninety-nine, his disproportionate joy in finding the one, are very human qualities. Yet, by their very excess they serve admirably to illustrate the Father's concern for his little ones.

Fraternal correction 18:15-18

15 "If your brother sins against you, go and tell him his fault, between you and him alone. If he listens to you, 16 you have gained your brother. But if he does not listen, take one or two others along with you, that every word may be confirmed by the evidence of two or three wit- 17 nesses. If he refuses to listen to them, tell it to the church; and if he refuses to listen even to the church, let him be 18 to you as a Gentile and a tax collector. Truly, I say to you, whatever you bind on earth shall be bound in heaven, and whatever you loose on earth shall be loosed in heaven.

Prayer in common 18:19-20

19 "Again I say to you, if two of you agree on earth about anything they ask, it will be done for them by my Father 20 in heaven. For where two or three are gathered in my name, there am I in the midst of them."

The disciples' duty is clear: not only the negative obligation of averting scandal, but the positive one of leading the little ones back to the fold when they stray.

Fraternal correction 18:15-18 (Lk 17:3)

This duty of seeking the straying Christian (**brother**) is to be exercised with discretion. **15** – The sinner (**against you** should probably be omitted) must be won back to God (**gained**) as sweetly as may be. If there is no need for public reprimand, charity forbids it: one must show him his fault privately. **16** – in juridical matters the old Law required at least two witnesses: "it is by the deposition of two or three witnesses that the case is to be established", Deut 19:15. The principle is transferred to this affair which is not yet juridical. The persons called are therefore not witnesses of the fault but are called in as independent opinions helping not to convict but to convince the sinner of his fault. **17** – Only in the last resort must the matter be brought to official notice – this for the sake of the individual and of the community. Jesus prudently and naturally provides for the future (as in 16:17-19, notes) when he will be no longer at hand to settle difficulties. His **church** (*ekklesia*, gathering) appears as a compact, defined body with powers to exclude the recalcitrant from its society. After such a sentence the sinners stand outside the society as the pagans and the Jewish tax collectors (cf 9:10 of note) are beyond the pale of the synagogue. **18** – Vv. 15-17 have been addressed, in the singular (lit. "*thy* brother" etc.), to any Christian; now Jesus addresses the apostles ("you"; cf 18:1), not the members of the Church at large. He associates their powers with Peter's without prejudice to Peter's exclusive custodianship of the keys or to his function as the one foundation, 16:17-19. The apostolic body, with Peter, is given wide powers which include that of formal excommunication or reconciliation.

Prayer in common 18:19-20

Though the connexion with the preceding may be loose (cf **Again I say to you**) it seems probable that the words, in Mt's context, still have reference to the apostles. They appear to guarantee efficacious help for any agreed course of action concerning which the apostles ask divine assistance. Most commentators, however, refer Christ's promise to the prayer of the faithful in general and refuse any close connexion with 18. **20** – In any case, the reason why the Father's help is certain is based on a general principle: the beloved Son himself whom the Father always hears, Jn 11:42, is mystically present in the smaller gathering convoked to do him honour (**in,** but literally "to", **my name** suggests the idea of appurtenance, consecration, devotion to). We may compare the words with the rabbinic saying (c. 135 A.D.): "When two are together and discussing the Law, the Glory (i.e. God himself) is

Forgiveness 18:21-22

²¹ Then Peter came up and said to him, "Lord, how often shall my brother sin against me, and I forgive him? As ²² many as seven times?" Jesus said to him, "I do not say to you seven times, but seventy times seven.

Parable of the unforgiving debtor 18:23-35

²³ "Therefore the kingdom of heaven may be compared to a king who wished to settle accounts with his servants. ²⁴ When he began the reckoning, one was brought to him ²⁵ who owed him ten thousand talents;   and as he could not pay, his lord ordered him to be sold, with his wife and children and all that he had, and payment to be made. ²⁶ So the servant fell on his knees, imploring him, 'Lord, have patience with me, and I will pay you everything.' ²⁷ And out of pity for him the lord of that servant released ²⁸ him and forgave him the debt.   But that same servant, as he went out, came upon one of his fellow servants who owned him a hundred denarii; and seizing him by the ²⁹ throat he said, 'Pay what you owe.'   So his fellow servant fell down and besought him, 'Have patience with me, and ³⁰ I will pay you.'   He refused and went and put him in ³¹ prison till he should pay the debt. When his fellow servants saw what had taken place, they were greatly distressed, and they went and reported to their lord all ³² that had taken place.   Then his lord summoned him and said to him, 'You wicked servant! I forgave you all that ³³ debt because you besought me;   and should not you have

in the midst of them". Jesus takes the place of the Law as the purpose of the gathering and assumes the role of the Glory itself.

Forgiveness 18:21-22 (Lk 17:4)

The instruction on reconciliation of erring brethren, 15-18, has said nothing of repeated faults. It is Peter (naturally enough, in view of his position, 16:17ff) who seeks precision on this matter, though he introduces a personal note (**against me**) hitherto absent; cf 15, note. **Seven** is a round (Semitic) number and therefore, Peter thinks, generous. Jesus multiplies and multiplies the sacred number to leave the impression of limitless pardon. Repeat them as he will, our neighbour's offences against us can never compare with ours against God – and still God forgives. Nevertheless, our forgiveness of neighbour is the condition of God's pardon of us. This is the lesson of the parable which follows.

Parable of the unforgiving debtor 18:23-35

The parable is a drama in three scenes: Mercy, 22-27, Cruelty, 28-30, Justice, 31-34, with an epilogue, 35. **23** – Because this notion of pardon is so indispensable it is possible to represent the kingdom in terms of mercy and justice. The time has come for the king's officials (provincial governors or financial administrators) to settle their account with the Treasury. **24** – At the very outset one is brought to the king's presence who owes nearly three million pounds (**10,000 talents:** one talent is a weight of silver equivalent to 6,000 Greek drachmas – more than a labourer could earn in fifteen years; cf 17:23, note). The sum is fantastic even for a highly-placed official; its choice has in view the application of the parable to our debt towards God. **25-27** – The king, using his royal prerogative, orders the man and his family to be sold into slavery and a small percentage of the debt to be paid for the sale of his person and possessions. The king, though he knows the absurdity of the man's wild promises, relents; he remits the whole debt – a kingly gesture. **28-30** – The contrast that follows is emphatic and detailed. The forgiven debtor meets his equal, not his subject; he is owed a paltry sum – one six-hundred-thousandth of his own forgiven debt; he assails his fellow debtor with violence, not giving time to speak; he spurns him when his attitude and words (ironically the image and echo of his own) must have recalled the recent interview with the merciful king. Finally he throws his debtor into prison to force him to raise the money by some means (selling-up, borrowing etc.). **31-34** – The shocking contrast between the king's conduct and his servant's is made explicit in this third tableau. The matter is reported to the king who exacts the rigorous justice which the merciless servant has just demanded. The unhappy man is handed over to the torturers who will force him perhaps to disclose some hidden reserves. He is handed over **till he should pay.** There is no likelihood that he will be able. **35** – The epilogue is on a

had mercy on your fellow servant, as I had mercy on you?'
34 And in anger his lord delivered him to the jailers, till he
35 should pay all his debt.   So also my heavenly Father will
do to every one of you, if you do not forgive your brother
from your heart."

threatening note, but it plainly identifies the Father with the king whose first characteristic is limitless mercy, 23-27. The enormity of our debt to the Father is immeasurable: it is represented arithmetically only because a parable in human terms demands it, and because the figure serves to dwarf our neighbour's "debt" to us. But the Father lays down two firm conditions, and only two: that we ask for forgiveness; that we exercise it ourselves. The first condition is implicit in the parable, the second explicit. The parable is the graphic development of the pregnant and sobering prayer "Forgive us as we forgive", 6:12. And the forgiveness must be "from our hearts", profound and absolute. "I forgive but cannot forget" is not a Christian saying.

Question about Divorce 19:1-9

1 Now when Jesus had finished these sayings, he went away from Galilee and entered the region of Judea beyond the 2 Jordan; and large crowds followed him, and he healed 3 them there. And Pharisees came up to him and tested him by asking, "Is it lawful to divorce one's wife for any 4 cause?" He answered, "Have you not read that he who made them from the beginning made them male and 5 female, and said, 'For this reason a man shall leave his father and mother and be joined to his wife, and the two 6 shall become one'? So they are no longer two but one. What therefore God has joined together, let no man put 7 asunder." They said to him, "Why then did Moses command one to give a certificate of divorce, and to put 8 her away?" He said to them, "For your hardness of heart Moses allowed you to divorce your wives, but from 9 the beginning it was not so. And I say to you: whoever divorces his wife, except for unchastity, and marries another, commits adultery."

The Approaching Advent
of the Kingdom 19:1–25:46

I

Narrative: Mounting Opposition of Judaism 19:1 – 23:39

Question about divorce 19:1-9 (Mk 10:1-12)

The common plan of the Synoptic Gospels gives preference to the Galilean ministry, omitting the various visits of our Lord to Jerusalem, Jn 2:13; 5:1; 7:2; 10:22. After the visit of Jn 10:22 (for the feast of Dedication in December) John says, 10:40, like Mt and Mk, that Jesus went "beyond Jordan". It is probable that the journey described by Mt and Mk took place in September and that it included Jn's two visits to Jerusalem – for Tabernacles (Sept-Oct; Jn 7:2) and for Dedication (Jn 10:22). In 19:1 Mt rounds off his fourth group of discourses with his familiar formula, 7:28 note. Jesus seems (Mk) to go first into Judea and from there to the plain just across Jordan, Jn 10:40, which, though strictly part of mountainous Perea and under Herod's jurisdiction, was commonly regarded as the **region** of Judea. **3** – The Pharisees put him to the test. Their question must be seen against its background. In Christ's time there were two schools of thought, divided on the question of sufficient motive for divorce in the full sense. The followers of the Rabbi Shammai allowed it on grounds of adultery only. Those of Hillel (Shammai's pre-Christian contemporary) for less grave, even trivial, reasons: see Edersheim 2, 331-5. The controversy turned on the interpretation of Deut 24:1. There the Mosaic Law prescribed that a husband give his wife a "bill of divorce" (lit. "document of cutting-off") if he discover in her "some uncleanness" ("indecency of (in) something"; apparently some sexual irregularity). This last phrase was the subject of bitter argument. It appears that in the 1st cent. A.D. the school of Shammai was gaining ground at least among the ordinary folk in Palestine, but that divorce was more common in the upper classes. The Pharisees' question is therefore equivalent to: "Is Hillel right? Can divorce for any cause whatever be tolerated?", or:

"Is a man permitted to send away his wife however the case stands?".
4-6 – To their chagrin Jesus pronounces for neither school but, as
in 15:3f, goes straight to the act and words of God, Gen 1:27; 2:24.
Having created a woman for Adam, God (through the inspired author)
had insisted that the union was even closer than that of blood. It produced, as it were, one single and indivisible person (one flesh). Jesus
emphasizes his conclusion, claiming that no man, not Shammai nor
Hillel, dare interfere with the express will of God. **7** – The answer was
disconcerting. It struck at the practice of divorce itself. Whether the
questioners be of the Hillel or of the Shammai school they are forced
now to defend common ground. They in their turn appeal to scripture,
Deut 24:1. Their implication is that our Lord's conclusion from Gen is
in plain opposition to the enactment of Moses himself. **8** – Jesus removes
the contradiction by correcting their terms. Divorce was not a Mosaic
"command" but a toleration of existing custom. This custom itself
was due to Israel's **hardness of heart**, i.e. (cf Deut 10:16; Jer 4:4;
Ecclus 16:10) to a moral immaturity insensitive to God's will – a will
made plain, as Jesus says, in Gen 1:27. The Mosaic "bill of divorce"
made the best of an existing situation by demanding a formality which
restrained hasty action and which safeguarded the divorced wife from
recall at her divorcing husband's whim. **9** – Jesus restores the stability
of the primal institution on his own authority, **I say to you**; cf 5:21-44.
His attitude is so uncompromising, indeed, that the disciples are
shocked, 10, as they would never have been had he merely declared
for the severe view of Shammai. Moreover, his words as reported by
Mk 10:11f, and by Lk 16:18, and used by Paul, I Cor 7:10f, contain no
hint of an exception made for unchastity. It is in the light of these
certain facts that the obscure "exceptive" clause of Mt, here and 5:32,
must be explained. In view of the marked Jewish tone of Mt's words
it seems probable that he is near to the actual words of our Lord. In any
case, an evangelist would not have been so bold as to intrude an exception of his own making, nor so stupid as to contradict his own context.
It is still less likely that Jesus is reversing his uncompromising attitude
by means of a parenthesis thrown out casually. It follows that the so-
called "exceptive" clause cannot permit re-marriage on the grounds
even of unchastity. Its positive explanation is, however, a matter of
dispute. The "classical" Catholic explanation takes **unchastity**
(*porneia*) as being here "adultery", as it is a question of married persons.
The disputed clause is not strictly an "exception" but reserves the case
of adultery. That it is a "reservation" appears more clearly from
5:32 where "except" is *parektos*, "setting aside", than it does from 19:9
where "except" is the awkward Greek *me* (*epi*). It does not positively
provide for the case of adultery. This provision, however, must have
been made at some time, explicitly or implicitly, by Jesus. It consists in
separation *a mensa et toro* and is found explicitly in Paul, 1 Cor 7:10.

Continence 19:10-12

¹⁰ The disciples said to him, "If such is the case of a man
¹¹ with his wife, it is not expedient to marry."   But he said
to them, "Not all men can receive this precept, but only
¹² those to whom it is given.   For there are eunuchs who
have been so from birth, and there are eunuchs who
have been made eunuchs by men, and there are eunuchs
who have made themselves eunuchs for the sake of the
kingdom of heaven. He who is able to receive this, let him
receive it."

Jesus and the children 19:13-15

¹³ Then children were brought to him that he might lay
his hands on them and pray. The disciples rebuked the
¹⁴ people;   but Jesus said, "Let the children come to me,
and do not hinder them; for to such belongs the kingdom
¹⁵ of heaven."   And he laid his hands on them and went
away.

The reservation was made to avoid the impression that Jesus was imposing the hardship of living with a faithless partner. An alternative Catholic explanation objects that the usual O.T. and N.T. word for "adultery" is *moicheia*, and that *porneia* here means concubinage (cf 1 Cor 5:1) – incestuous marriage within the degree forbidden by the Mosaic Law, Lev 18:1-17. In such a case a man in dismissing (divorcing) the woman is not only guiltless but is actually doing his duty. Jesus inserts the clause in order to hint that the Mosaic injunctions remain.

Continence 19:10-12

10 – The disciples express their concern. Such severity is unheard of. If such be the position of the married state, marriage is too dangerous, because irrevocable. **11** – Jesus does not withdraw his severe pronouncement but, doubtless to the disciples' surprise, passes from their own phrase, **not expedient to marry** to an even higher teaching. All this doctrine of the due perspective on marriage and its expediency or non-expediency can be fully appreciated ("received") not by the carnal man but by those alone whose understanding is of God (**given**); cf 13:11. **12** – **For,** says Jesus, explaining that such an understanding and perspective is so given, not accident of birth alone, nor malice of men, (the case of the first two classes of eunuch) but the high motive of the kingdom (cf 1 Cor 7:32) has succeeded in inducing virginity – and, in this last case, of free choice. To these last the divine sense of due proportion has been "given" and put into practical effect, not by self-mutilation but by self-denial. Jesus thinks, perhaps, of the Baptist and of others who like Jeremiah, Jer 16:2, had thus sacrificed themselves in the interests of the kingdom. He is proposing an ideal foreign to Judaism which held marriage as a sacred duty for all men. "Let him who is capable of appreciating ('receiving' cf v. 11) the true order of values apply his faculty to this case." It is fairly evident that Jesus is not appealing only for speculative appreciations: a gentle invitation underlies his words.

Jesus and the children 19:13-15 (Mk 10:13-16; Lk 18:15-17)

13 – Jesus has just shown himself the champion of family life; it is perhaps not without significance that the mothers bring their children for a blessing. The disciples were used to the throngs of sick, but they rebuke the parents for this waste of their master's time and strength. **14** – One of the rare occasions when Jesus shows himself really displeased with his disciples ("he was indignant" Mk): "Leave the little children alone!" This adult contempt is misplaced; their elders should not interfere but rather watch how he loves their simplicity and themselves learn to imitate it, 18:1-4 notes. He takes the children into his arms (Mk) and touches their heads with a murmured blessing.

The rich young man 19:16-22

16 And behold, one came up to him, saying, "Teacher, what
17 good deed must I do, to have eternal life?"   And he
said to him, "Why do you ask me about what is good?
One there is who is good. If you would enter life, keep
18 the commandments." He said to him, "Which?" And
Jesus said, "You shall not kill, You shall not commit
adultery, You shall not steal, You shall not bear false
19 witness, Honour your father and mother, and, You
20 shall love your neighbour as yourself." The young man
said to him, "All these I have observed; what do I still
21 lack?" Jesus said to him, "If you would be perfect, go,
sell what you possess and give to the poor, and you will
22 have treasure in heaven; and come, follow me." When
the young man heard this he went away sorrowful; for he
had great possessions.

Danger of riches 19:23-26

23 And Jesus said to his disciples, "Truly, I say to you, it
will be hard for a rich man to enter the kingdom of
24 heaven.   Again I tell you, it is easier for a camel to go
through the eye of a needle than for a rich man to enter

The rich young man 19:16-22 (Mk 10:17-22; Lk 18:18-23)

16 – A young man of wealth and (Lk) position who, no doubt, had been watching and listening, hurried (Mk) after our Lord. Jesus had spoken, 14, of a necessary disposition for the kingdom – a disposition less acceptable than the observance of the Decalogue; this has perhaps brought uneasiness to the youth's mind. The form of the question in Mk is different: "Good Teacher, what must I do . . . " (the adjective "good" being transposed). **17** – The answer, correspondingly, is different in Mk: "Why do you call me good? No one is good but God alone." It is commonly held that Mt has softened Christ's rejection of the title "good". This is not improbable but, on the other hand, emendations are usually made from obscure to clear, whereas Mt's text is more obscure than Mk's. In Mt the implication seems to be that the youth leans too heavily upon one who, as he thinks, is a rabbi and no more. Jesus declines the compliment, cf e.g. 20:23; 23:9. He seeks to put the inquiring soul into immediate contact with God who is personified Good. God himself, the one absolute Good, is the model of sanctity; cf 5:48. Nevertheless, Jesus goes on, in magisterial tone, to exercise the sovereign authority of his human office by confidently pointing the way to eternal life. **18-19** – He doubtless surprises the youth when he lays down as necessary conditions the elementary prohibitions of the Decalogue, Ex 20:13-16; cf Deut 5:17-20. But he passes then to positive commands that admit of degrees of perfection in their observance. First, the young man's duty to his parents (Ex 20:12a; cf Deut 5:16a); secondly, the great precept of charity towards one's fellows, Lev 18:19, not found in the Decalogue. **20-21** – In view of the last, and difficult, command the youth's confident reply appears hasty but evidently has little trace of self-sufficiency since (Mk) our Lord's affection is aroused. The young man has a generous heart and Jesus invites it to a perfection exceeding what is, absolutely speaking, necessary to eternal life. If the youth is content to have his **treasure** (and so, all his heart; cf 6:21) only in heaven, then he is fit for Christ's inner circle, 27. **22** – The young man, who might have become an apostle, was taken aback ("his face fell" Mk) and went away dismayed.

Danger of riches 19:23-26 (Mk 10:23-31; Lk 18:24-30; 13:30)

23 – The departure of the youth is the occasion of a sad warning to the disciples. It is with difficulty that the rich shall enter the kingdom of heaven. The saying surprises after our Lord's distinction of moral precept, 17ff, and counsel of poverty, 21. He speaks, however, not of impossibility, 26, but of difficulty. Nor does he condemn the rich young man but illustrates from his case how riches may grip and even suffocate the heart. **24** – Indeed, for merely human reasons it is inconceivable that those whose heart is possessed by riches should enter the kingdom. Jesus expresses this with a slight adaptation of the Jewish proverb that

²⁵ the kingdom of God." When the disciples heard this
they were greatly astonished, saying, "Who then can be
²⁶ saved?" But Jesus looked at them and said to them,
"With men this is impossible, but with God all things are
possible."

Reward of renunciation 19:27-30
²⁷ Then Peter said in reply, "Lo, we have left everything
²⁸ and followed you. What then shall we have?" Jesus said
to them, "Truly, I say to you, in the new world, when the
Son of man shall sit on his glorious throne, you who have
followed me will also sit on twelve thrones, judging the
²⁹ twelve tribes of Israel. And every one who has left
houses or brothers or sisters or father or mother or children
or lands, for my name's sake, will receive a hundredfold,
³⁰ and inherit eternal life. But many that are first will be
last, and the last first.

"a man even in his dreams does not see an elephant pass through a needle's eye'. **25-26** – He has deliberately provoked the astonishment of the disciples in order to impress on them the spiritual menace of riches. If possessions are such an obstacle – and there are few who have no possessions – **who can be saved**? In words reminiscent of Gen 18:14; Job 42:2; Zec 8:6, Jesus explains that divine grace accomplishes the humanly impossible. Grace may leave the riches but loosen their grip on the heart.

Reward of renunciation 19:27-30 (Mk 10:28-31; Lk 18:28-30)

27 – During this discussion Peter's mind has turned to the situation of himself and of his companions. They have accepted the invitation, 4:22, refused by the rich young man. What reward? A natural and honest question, if somewhat brusque. **28** – The solemn promise surpasses expectation. Its meaning turns on the sense of the word *paliggenesia* (here translated **new world**) used in N.T. only here and in Tit 3:5 (of the "new birth" by baptism in the Christian era). A similar idea, though not the term, is found in the O.T. ("the new heavens and new earth" of Is 65:17; 66:22) referring, in apocalyptic style, to the messianic age. The reference is pointed by Paul, 2 Cor 5:17, for whom the Christian era here on earth is already a "new creation". It appears probable, therefore, that Jesus refers to the kingdom established on earth rather than to the world to come and the Last Judgment. This opinion is supported by the similar text of Lk 22:28-30 which also refers to the kingdom of the Son on earth – not "of the Father" in heaven; cf 13:43, note. The **Son of man** seated **on his glorious throne** recalls Dan 7:9 and (as in 26:64; see note) refers to our Lord's presiding from heaven (cf Ps 110 (109):1 quoted in 22:43f) over his kingdom on earth. Associated with him in this royal function of judgment (i.e. of government, cf Ps 72 (71):2 etc. – the Last Judgment is reserved exclusively to the Son in Jn 5:27) are the Twelve. This office they are to exercise on earth (and, doubtless, when they pass from earth and the Church remains); they will be thus associated with their master in heaven. Since the horizon has not yet widened for the apostles, 10:5; 15:24, Jesus speaks in terms of Israel. It will be clear to them later, 28:19, that the sphere of their authority is to be the whole world – the Israel "of God", Gal 6:16. Our Lord addresses the Twelve as a body. He has already hinted at the defection of Judas, Jn 6:71, but this is not the place to mention it; moreover, their number was later supplied by the election of Matthias, Ac 1:26. **29** – In the new era the apostles occupy a privileged position, but those who have imitated their detachment, leaving family or estates for Christ, will have their abounding reward too. The reward, though on earth (Mk), is clearly of the spiritual order since it is compatible with persecution, Mk 10:30. And finally (closing the whole section as it opened; cf 16) in the world to come, **eternal life. 30** – Introduces

Parable of the vineyard labourers 20:1-16

¹ "For the kingdom of heaven is like a householder who went out early in the morning to hire labourers for his ² vineyard. After agreeing with the labourers for a ³ denarius a day, he sent them into his vineyard. And going out about the third hour he saw others standing ⁴ idle in the market place; and to them he said, 'You go into the vineyard too, and whatever is right I will give ⁵ you.' So they went. Going out again about the sixth ⁶ hour and the ninth hour, he did the same. And about the eleventh hour he went out and found others standing; and he said to them, 'Why do you stand here idle all day?' ⁷ They said to him, 'Because no one has hired us,' He said ⁸ to them, 'You go into the vineyard too.' And when evening came, the owner of the vineyard said to his steward, 'Call the labourers and pay them their wages, ⁹ beginning with the last, up to the first.' And when those hired about the eleventh hour came, each of them received ¹⁰ a denarius. Now when the first came, they thought they would receive more; but each of them also received a ¹¹ denarius. And on receiving it they grumbled at the ¹² householder, saying, 'These last worked only one hour, and you have made them equal to us who have borne the ¹³ burden of the day and the scorching heat.' But he replied to one of them, 'Friend, I am doing you no wrong; ¹⁴ did you not agree with me for a denarius? Take what belongs to you, and go; I choose to give to this last as I ¹⁵ give to you. Am I not allowed to do what I choose with what belongs to me? Or do you begrudge my generosity? ¹⁶ Or is your eye evil because I am good?' So the last will be first, and the first last."

the following parable which it serves also to conclude, 20:16, note.

Parable of the vineyard labourers 20:1-16

1 – Not the householder but the whole situation in which he figures is comparable to the **kingdom,** 13:24, note. He goes to the bazaar at daybreak to find men standing waiting for hired work. Since we are in parable and not in allegory (see note to ch. 13) it is unnecessary to seek an individual significance for the "vineyard", though in the allegory of Is 5:1-7 it represents Israel. **2** – After the usual bargaining, no doubt, the day's wage is formally agreed upon (a circumstance to be remembered in view of what transpires)—**a denarius,** 17:24, note. **3-5** – At nine, noon and three p.m. (the hours are reckoned from 6 a.m.) the man returns to the bazaar. His first visit was presumably at 6 a.m. The times, however, are merely schematic and should not be scrutinized for hidden meanings. No sum is yet mentioned other than a fair wage. In human affairs one would expect three-quarters, one half, one quarter of a denarius respectively. **6-7** – One hour before sunset (the time-scheme is violently broken into to emphasize the lesson) the man hires the last of the unemployed – more, it would appear, from pity than from need. **8** – The foreman is evidently given two unusual instructions. The first, though this is mentioned later to suspend the interest, is to give the same wage to all – and in this the point of the parable lies. The second is to begin with **the last,** with the latecomers. The purpose of this odd procedure is to hold back the firstcomers as witnesses, hostile and critical, who will make objection and thus pave the way to the master's reply. This reply, 13-15, holds the lesson of the parable. **9-12** – The disgruntled bystanders complain only of the most extreme case of "injustice", though they might have complained of the other later groups. **These last** have worked for one hour, and that in the cool of the evening! **13-15** – The master addresses the chief grumbler. His gentle tone (**friend**) recalls that of the Prodigal's father addressing the elder son, Lk 15:31. He calmly reminds him of the agreement, duly observed by both parties. When justice has been done, should anyone complain if kindness plays its part? The eye (of the mind) should not see evil where there is only good. If it does, it must be a diseased eye. **16** – Jesus has explained by parable his initial epigram: "Many that are first will be last, and the last, first", 19:30, and concludes: "*It is in this way* (**so**) that the last will be first and the first last".

It may be that we have in this parable only a striking picture of the divine generosity which gives without regard to the measures of strict justice. In this case the parable insinuates a mistrust of works for their own sake (perhaps as a corrective to the reward promised in 19:27-29) to the advantage of the divine liberality. The concluding sentence, stripped of the violent contrast imposed by paradoxical form, implies simply that "first" and "last" (long or short service) merge into one

Third prophecy of the passion 20:17-19

17 And as Jesus was going up to Jerusalem, he took the twelve
18 disciples aside, and on the way he said to them, "Behold,
we are going up to Jerusalem; and the Son of man will be
delivered to the chief priests and scribes, and they will
19 condemn him to death,   and deliver him to the Gentiles to
be mocked and scourged and crucified, and he will be
raised on the third day."

Ambition of the sons of Zebedee 20:20-23

20 Then the mother of the sons of Zebedee came up to him,
with her sons, and kneeling before him she asked him for
21 something.   And he said to her, "What do you want?"
She said to him, "Command that these two sons of mine
may sit, one at your right hand and one at your left, in
22 your kingdom."   But Jesus answered, "You do not know
what you are asking. Are you able to drink the cup that
23 I am to drink?" They said to him, "We are able."   He
said to them, "You will drink my cup, but to sit at my
right hand and at my left is not mine to grant, but it is
for those for whom it has been prepared by my Father."

another before God – not that he is indifferent to the distinction but that his mercy refuses to be restrained. (The ominous: Many are called but few are chosen, is perhaps not authentic here – Mark omits – but drawn from 22:14, where see note.) The grumblers of 11 do not necessarily figure the Pharisees; they may appear only with a parabolic purpose (8 note) similar to that of the Elder Brother in Lk 15:25ff. This general lesson may not exhaust the parable. In Lk 13:30 the dictum of Mt 20:16a is connected with the personnel of the kingdom to which there may also be reference here. If so, the latecomers are the Gentiles (cf Lk 13:29) who will flock to the kingdom ahead of the mass of Israel; cf Rom 11:25f. And this because, although the whole Jewish race has been "called" to the kingdom, only a few – the "remnant" spoken of by the prophets, e.g. Is 1:9 – have deserved to be "chosen" to belong to it.

Third prophecy of the passion 20:17-19 (Mk 10:32-34; Lk 18:31-34)
17 – Passing from the plain across Jordan (19:1-2, note) our Lord hurries ahead of his apprehensive disciples and of others who follow (Mk) towards Jerusalem which lies on the western mountains before him. He turns to them as they follow and, for the third time (cf 16:21; 17:22-23), speaks to the disciples alone of his coming passion and resurrection. **18-19** – The prophecy is more detailed than before. The death-sentence is to be engineered by the Sanhedrin and executed by the Romans. Mocking, scourging and (Mt only) crucifixion appear now for the first time. For the apostles Jesus evidently wishes to soften the harsh notion of such an inglorious Messiah by showing that he goes to his death consciously and freely. There is no remonstrance this time; cf 16:23. It is clearly useless.

Ambition of the sons of Zebedee 20:20-23 (Mk. 10:35-40)
20 – Zebedee's wife, probably the Salome of Mk 15:40 (cf Mt 27:56), on her knees before Jesus has evidently some great favour to ask. Her presence suggests that of the other holy women whom we find later at the Cross and at the tomb. **21** – Mother-like she is interested in her sons' career, but it appears that she profoundly misreads its true character. Christ's **kingdom**, though doubtless spiritual, is for her, as for the expectant Jews in general, a place also for honours as the world knows them – a religion-state. For James and John (cf 4:21) she asks the first and second rank in the king's hierarchy. **22** – The mother has asked (in Mt, not Mk: indication that Mt is nearer the facts here?) but the sons are answered: presumably they had confided their hopes to her, possibly even prompted her to ask. Though there is ambition here to be corrected, Jesus does not display the indignation he reserves for the Pharisees, 23:6. It must, therefore, have something of simplicity in it. Moreover, it is accompanied by docility, since the brothers profess them-

Leadership with service 20:24-28

²⁴ And when the ten heard it, they were indignant at the
²⁵ two brothers.   But Jesus called them to him and said,
"You know that the rulers of the Gentiles lord it over
them, and their great men exercise authority over them.
²⁶ It shall not be so among you; but whoever would be
²⁷ great among you must be your servant, and whoever
²⁸ would be first among you must be your slave;   even as
the Son of man came not to be served but to serve, and
to give his life as a ransom for many."

Blind men of Jericho 20:29-34

²⁹ And as they went out of Jericho, a great crowd followed
³⁰ him.   And behold, two blind men sitting by the roadside,
when they heard that Jesus was passing by, cried out,
³¹ "Have mercy on us, Son of David?"   The crowd rebuked

selves ready to drink our Lord's own bitter cup; cf 26:42. The **cup** is a Hebrew metaphor for destiny – happy, as in Ps 16 (15):5, or unhappy, as in Ps 75 (74):9. **23** – Like all our Lord's worthy followers, 10:38f, the brothers are to share his cross – an imitation of Christ which does not always suppose a martyr's death. James was in fact beheaded in 44 A.D.; John suffered torture and exile. Nevertheless Jesus, speaking as the envoy of his Father, reserves to the Father's eternal decree the honours of the kingdom. He himself has already designated the primate of the kingdom on earth, 16:18f, but here he answers the question as it has been put, Mk 10:37, and speaks of the kingdom in its final, glorious stage.

Leadership with service 20:24-28 (Mk 10:41-45; Lk 22:24-27)

24-27 – Nor will Jesus tolerate the spirit of ambition in his kingdom on earth. This spirit shows itself in the indignation of the ten even more than in the request of the two. It is a commonplace of political kingdoms that rulers are heavy-handed and their ministers officious. There will be rank in Christ's kingdom, 16:18f; 19:28, but it must not be used for selfish ends. Let all know who would seek that rank that it is the rank of **servant,** 26, even of **slave,** 27. **28** – In this too (cf 22) Jesus is the model – Lord by nature, servant by deliberate choice, Jn 13:13ff. He has already hinted, 18, 19, 22, the lengths to which he is prepared to go in this service; now he states it clearly, and his phrase contains, in germ, the whole dogma of redemption later developed by Paul. The Servant is to give his life in **ransom** – one life for the many. The Greek word used (*lutron*) is found twenty times in LXX where its meaning is variously the sum offered either in compensation for injury, or for the purchase of an object, or as the price of a slave's manumission. It is the term used (in Num 3:12: LXX) even of human beings – the Levites, substituted for the firstborn in the temple-service. The evidence of contemporary profane Greek literature shows that the most natural sense of the word in the time of Christ was certainly that of a slave's ransom. The idea of a *human life* offered as ransom (*lutron*) is found in the 1st cent. A.D. Moreover, our Lord's phrase must be read in the light of contemporary Jewish thought not unfamiliar with the idea of an expiatory death, 2 Mac 7:37f. The same idea of expiation is found in Is 53:10 where, as here, the expiation is the function of a Servant – the "Servant of Yahweh".

Blind men of Jericho 20:29-34 (Mk 10: 46-52; Lk 18:35-43)

29 – Our Lord, making his way from Perea, 19:1, towards Jerusalem, 20:17, passes through **Jericho**, the beautiful garden-town adorned architecturally by Herod the Great and by Archelaus. It lies little more than 5 m. to the W. of Jordan and 15 m. to the E. of Jerusalem but in the plain 3,300 ft below the capital. The approach of the Passover season brought crowds to the neighbourhood. **30-31** – On the way out

them telling them to be silent; but they cried out the more,
32 "Lord, have mercy on us, Son of David?" And Jesus
stopped and called them, saying, "What do you want me
33 to do for you?" They said to him, "Lord, let our eyes
34 be opened." And Jesus in pity touched their eyes, and
immediately they received their sight and followed him.

The Messiah enters Jerusalem 21:1-11

1 And when they drew near to Jerusalem and came to
Bethphage, to the Mount of Olives, then Jesus sent two
2 disciples, saying to them, "Go into the village opposite
you, and immediately you will find an ass tied, and a
3 colt with her; untie them and bring them to me. If any
one says anything to you, you shall say, 'The Lord has
4 need of them,' and he will send them immediately." This
took place to fulfil what was spoken by the prophet, saying,
5   "Tell the daughter of Zion,
      Behold, your king is coming to you, humble, and
         mounted on an ass,
      and on a colt, the foal of an ass."

of the town two blind men sit begging. Hearing that the passer-by is Jesus, the wonder-worker from Nazareth, they cry loudly for pity, and refuse to be silenced. They address him as **Son of David,** an indubitably messianic title, and Jesus this time does not enjoin silence (contrast 9:30; see note). Open proclamation of Messiahship is no longer untimely: Jesus is himself about to enter Jerusalem as Messiah, 21:1-9; he is himself to raise the question of the Messiah in public, 22:42ff, to speak openly as Israel's saviour, 23:37-39, and solemnly to declare himself, 26:64. **32-34** – The faith of the blind men is encouraged by our Lord's call and by his gentle question, and they dare to give definite shape to their vague hopes. As at Capernaum, 9:29, the fingers of the Light (cf Jn 9:5-6) touch the blind eyes. *Note on the Synoptic accounts:* There is no doubt that Mt, Mk, Lk all speak of the same incident, though only one blind man is mentioned in Mk, Lk. It is probable that Mk, consciously or unconsciously, omits the second because he is interested in the first whom he evidently knows ("Bar Timaios" Mk 10:46). Lk, though here somewhat independent of Mk, follows him in this detail. The exact place of the miracle is uncertain: going out of Jericho (Mt, Mk), approaching Jericho (Lk). It may be that one was healed on the way in, the other on the way out. Or Lk may refer to the Herodian Jericho, Mt, Mk to the old, deserted site a mile or two N.N.W. and through which Jesus would pass to the inhabited Jericho. Such harmonizations, however, smack of artificiality, and it is more likely that the inspired authors are content with a vague indication ("near Jericho") – an attitude which they so often adopt towards the chronological order of events.

The Messiah enters Jerusalem 21:1-11 (Mk 11:1-11; Lk 19:28-38; Jn 12:12-16)

1 – From Jericho Jesus had gone to **Bethany,** on the eastern slope of Olivet nearly 2 m. from Jerusalem. There, on the Saturday, he had been anointed by Mary; cf Jn 12:1-8; Mt 26:6-13. It is now Sunday, Jn 12:1, 12. **Bethphage** lay higher up the eastern flank of Olivet nearer Jerusalem and between Bethany and the summit, a summit which from its 2,500 ft looks downwards and westwards, across the Kedron valley, upon the temple 200 ft. below. The old steep road from Jericho to Jerusalem passed to the right of Bethany and through Bethphage. **2** – Bethphage is the village that the disciples have almost reached (v. 1: **came to,** perhaps better "came near to", *eis*) it lies straight ahead of (**opposite**) them. Just inside the village, Jesus assures them, they will find an ass and her foal tethered. **3** – If any watchful bystander objects they are to say that **the Lord** (*kurios;* perhaps "the master", i.e. the owner of the ass, who, in this hypothesis, would be with Jesus at the time). **4-5** – Mt (and Jn 12:15) is struck by the literal fulfilment of the prophecy of Zechariah 9:9. In view of the sombre prospect of

⁶ The disciples went and did as Jesus had directed them;
⁷ they brought the ass and the colt, and put their garments
⁸ on them, and he sat thereon.　Most of the crowd spread
their garments on the road, and others cut branches from
⁹ the trees and spread them on the road.　And the crowds
that went before him and that followed him shouted,
"Hosanna to the Son of David! Blessed is he who comes
¹⁰ in the name of the Lord! Hosanna in the highest!"　And
when he entered Jerusalem, all the city was stirred,
¹¹ saying, "Who is this?"　And the crowds said, "This is
the prophet Jesus from Nazareth of Galilee."

the Passion, Mt introduces the citation not with the "shout for joy" of Zec 9:9, but with the sober words in which Isaiah announces the Saviour in 62:11. The promise to "the daughter of Zion" (Jerusalem) is fulfilled. The substance of the prophecy is the humble advent of the triumphant king, but Jesus chooses to fulfil it to the letter and so to declare his messianic character. The Hebrew prophecy (here translated from the Heb., not incorporated from LXX) displays the parallelism (synonymous here) inherent to Heb. poetic form. We should therefore read: "on an ass, yes [not "and"] on a colt, the foal of a beast of burden" (here rendered "ass"). That this is the meaning of Mt is evident: a translator of the Hebrew would not so misread the poetic device nor would an intelligent writer intend the absurdity of a rider using two mounts apparently at the same time. The "ass" of 5 is therefore equivalent to the "colt" of v. 2, as the prophetic context demands, and not to the she-ass of 2. This last is the "beast of burden" of v. 5. **6-7** – The colt was not yet broken in, Mk 11:2, note; its dam is brought only to steady it. Nevertheless it seems from the text as it stands that the two disciples, 1, made their cloaks into saddles for both beasts (7: **on them**). This is odd, but possibly it was done to leave Jesus the choice of mount. On the other hand, many competent commentators prefer to read the singular "on *it*" (the colt) with some not unimportant MSS and versions. **8** – The news of our Lord's approach has spread to the capital where he was expected, Jn 11:55f, for the Passover feast. The excited **crowd** collecting at Bethphage is thus reinforced by another from Jerusalem, Jn 12:12, which escorts Jesus down the western slope of Olivet, across the Kedron and up the opposite slope to the temple. Some paved his path with their cloaks in sign of reverence, 2 (4) Kg 9:13, others with branches broken from the olives in the fields. Those who came from Jerusalem waved palm-branches, Jn 12:13, which, as they set out, they had torn from the trees in the warm Kedron valley. **9** – At the feast of Tabernacles it was customary for the people to carry **branches** in procession and to wave them as they sang "Hosanna Yahweh!" (cf Edersheim 2, 159) and the branch itself was called "the hosanna". The crowd now, waving branches, associates the action with the word **Hosanna!** an abbreviated form (*hosha-na*) of the biblical *hoshiah-nna*, Ps 118 (117): 25, lit.: "Oh save!" or "Oh be propitious to . . . !" Their cry is: "God save the Messiah!" and (26 of the same psalm with a slight change): **Blessed is he who comes in the name of the Lord!** – i.e. with the Lord's glory in view. In the final cry **Hosanna in the highest** the "hosanna" is a mere shout of joy, the phrase being equivalent to "Glory (to God) on high!"; cf Lk 19:38. **10-11** – (Mt only). The capital is in a turmoil: the triumphal approach has been seen and heard. There are visitors from abroad who know nothing of the new prophet. Probably they have heard his messianic rank acclaimed and they ask only his identity.

Expulsion of the buyers and sellers 21:12-17

¹² And Jesus entered the temple of God and drove out all
who sold and bought in the temple, and he overturned
the tables of the money-changers and the seats of those
¹³ who sold pigeons.   He said to them, "It is written, 'My
house shall be called a house of prayer'; but you make it
¹⁴ a den of robbers."   And the blind and the lame came to
¹⁵ him in the temple, and he healed them.   But when the
chief priests and the scribes saw the wonderful things that
he did, and the children crying out in the temple, "Ho-
¹⁶ sanna to the Son of David!" they were indignant;   and
they said to him, "Do you hear what these are saying?"
And Jesus said to them, "Yes; have you never read,
   'Out of the mouth of babes and sucklings
    thou hast brought perfect praise'?"
¹⁷ And leaving them, he went out of the city to Bethany and
lodged there.

Expulsion of the buyers and sellers 21:12-17 (Mk 11:15-19; Lk 19:45-46; Jn 2: 13-22)

If the episode is the same as that described by Jn, as seems highly probable, it is likely that Jn gives it its actual chronological setting, viz. at the beginning of Christ's public life. Mt who (like Mk, Lk) mentions only this one journey to Jerusalem would be bound to insert the incident here if he was to narrate it at all. And indeed the priests, though custodians of the temple, do not here (15; though see 21:23) refer to the incident, which perhaps suggests that it did not take place at this time. On the other hand, in view of the notable differences between Jn's account and that of the Synoptics, it is possible that our Lord took this action twice – the need for it would certainly recur. **12** – At festal times temporary booths were erected in the great outer court of the temple where tradesmen turned pilgrim piety to profit. The materials for sacrifice, both animal and bloodless, were sold in noisy markets with the usual oriental haggling. Some sold oxen and sheep, Jn 2:14, others doves, the sacrifice of the poor; cf Lev 12:8. Since Tyrian coinage only was accepted for temple-offerings, Roman and Greek coins were exchanged at a fee by the money-changers who set up their tables in the court. Jesus drove out the animals and their anxious owners. He was content to upturn the tables of the money-changers and the chairs of the dove-sellers. It is to these, it seems, he speaks. **13** – All three Synoptics remember the striking words: the joyful prophecy of Isaiah, 56:7, joined to the subsequent lament of Jeremiah, 7:11. The Jews themselves had profaned the temple by making it an unseemly and dishonest market, and prayer impossible

The importance of the incident lies, not in its detail, or even in the authority that Christ implicitly claims, but in its messianic significance. In two ways Mt (not Mk, Lk) emphasizes this. First, he makes the cleansing of the temple the immediate sequel of the messianic entry into the city. Second, he notes that **the blind and lame** came to Jesus in the temple. This observation is almost certainly a reference to 2 Sam (Kg) 5:6ff: whereas David would not allow "the blind and lame" into the house of God, the Son of David does: there is no exclusiveness in Christ's outlook. Further to this last, the scene is the Court of the Gentiles: the Cleansing is therefore in defence of devout men of all creeds who wish to pray in Jerusalem (the lesson of the incident in all the Gospels, Mk 11:17 being most explicit). Here in the Synoptics is already latent the theology of Jn 2:19-21: that the worship of God is not confined to a stone building (cf Jn 4:23): Christ spoke of the Temple of his Body.

15 – The chief priests and the scribes, though of different schools of thought (Sadducee and Pharisee respectively; cf 2:7-10 note), are at one. They are irritated by the miracles but particularly by the shouts of the children. Echoing the cry of their elders, 9, doubtless without

The barren fig-tree; faith and prayer 21:18-22

¹⁸ In the morning, as he was returning to the city, he was ¹⁹ hungry.   And seeing a fig tree by the wayside he went to it, and found nothing on it but leaves only. And he said to it, "May no fruit ever come from you again!" And ²⁰the fig tree withered at once.   When the disciples saw it they marvelled, saying, "How did the fig tree wither at ²¹ once?"   And Jesus answered them, "Truly, I say to you, if you have faith and never doubt, you will not only do what has been done to the fig tree, but even if you say to this mountain, 'Be taken up and cast into the sea,' it will ²² be done.   And whatever you ask in prayer, you will receive, if you have faith."

understanding, they hail Jesus as the Messiah, and he allows it. **16** – In answer to the objectors he clearly approves it. He sends the scribes back to their Bible, Ps 8:3, leaving them to complete the quotation in their minds ("to reduce the enemy to silence"). The Heb. text of the psalm declares that the smallest children acknowledge the Creator's glory; those who do not are the Creator's enemies. The implication is sharply pointed by the present circumstances and recalls Christ's appeal for simplicity, 18:3, 14. LXX (quoted by Mt) renders substantially the same sense as Heb. text, but more clearly underlines his approval of the children's cry: **"Out of the mouths of babes . . . thou has brought perfect praise".** **17** – On this note Jesus leaves them. He spends the night at Bethany (1, note) where his friends Martha and Mary and Lazarus lived.

The barren fig-tree; faith and prayer 21:18-22 (Mk 11:12-14; 20-24)

It is characteristic of Mt that he presents the miracle and the lesson to be derived from it without breaking up the episode as Mk does in 11:15-18. In view of this telescoping process there is no need to stress the "at once" of 19, though the words may in fact be intended literally. **18-19** – On the Monday morning Jesus left Bethany for the city. The fig-tree stood, perhaps, on the slopes of Olivet; it was in leaf, as it would be at the Paschal season (beginning of April). Jesus had evidently not broken his fast and he approached the tree. He knew, as well as the evangelist knew, that "it was not the season for figs" (Mk 11:13) – figs are not ripe till June. He laid a curse on the tree. There is no impatience in the words since he expected no fruit and it would be a curious sentimentality that could read cruelty there – especially as the insentient tree becomes a signpost for men. The tree withers. The unusual severity of Christ's tone, the strange rebuke addressed to a mere tree – a tree, moreover, obedient to the Creator's law – betray the fact that his action is entirely symbolic. It resembles the extraordinary symbolic actions of the prophets, e.g. Is 20:1-6, Jer 13:1-11. But Jesus did not explain it. The action, so far as we know, stood isolated. It was only on the following day (Tuesday; Mk 11:19f) that our Lord chose to draw from the incident a further, personal lesson for the disciples, 21f. The meaning of the symbol, therefore, can be decided only from its foregoing and subsequent historical context. Israel had welcomed its Messiah, on the previous day, with wild enthusiasm. In a day or two it will reject him. Judaism is condemned by Jesus for its deceptive, fruitless show (cf 21:43) – a show that should normally have proclaimed its spiritual summer, Cant 2:12f. When, in the course of the week, the apostles heard the Lord's rejection of Israel and his condemnation of the vine-dressers who refused the Master his own fruit, they would come to understand. **20-22** – Meanwhile the present lesson for the disciples, struck by the display of power rather than by the symbolism, is strong

The Jews question the authority of Jesus 21:23-27

23 And when he entered the temple, the chief priests and the elders of the people came up to him as he was teaching, and said, "By what authority are you doing these things, 24 and who gave you this authority?" Jesus answered them, "I also will ask you a question; and if you tell me the answer, then I also will tell you by what authority I do 25 these things. The baptism of John, whence was it? From heaven or from men?" And they argued with one another, "If we say, 'From heaven,' he will say to us, 'Why 26 then did you not believe him?' But if we say, 'From men,' we are afraid of the multitude; for all hold that 27 John was a prophet." So they answered Jesus, "We do not know." And he said to them, "Neither will I tell you by what authority I do these things.

Parable of the two sons 21:28-32

28 "What do you think? A man had two sons; and he went to the first and said, 'Son, go and work in the vineyard

faith to carry them through this difficult week and beyond. Nor is this lesson entirely independent of the symbolism, since Jesus has implicitly demonstrated his power over his enemies (cf 26:53) by causing this figure of hostile Israel to wither. Underlying the exhortation to faith is this invitation to believe in the power of their master when, in the passion, he is to appear most powerless. Nevertheless, the explicit invitation is to faith in their own power through prayer, or rather an invitation to pray with lively faith. This will move all obstacles – and what obstacles lie ahead for the disciples! With his eyes on Olivet (**this mountain**) Jesus uses the common rabbinic hyperbole for accomplishing the impossible: "rooting-up mountains"; cf Edersheim 2, 376, note.

The Jews question the authority of Jesus 21:23-27 (Mk 11:27-33; Lk 20:1-8)

23 – The priests particularly are concerned at our Lord's unauthorized temple teaching, possibly also (if his cleaning of the temple was recent) at his assumption of authority over the sacred precincts by expelling the buyers and sellers. With representatives of the other sections of the Sanhedrin (including scribes; cf Mk) they ask if he acts on his own initiative or at least (and they think this impossible) to name his accreditor. **24-25** – After the manner of rabbinic discussion Jesus answers question with question, not disrespectful to the established authority but pointed enough for those who wield authority dishonestly. The question concerns the mission of the Baptist. He sums up this mission in the word **baptism** – significantly, because this baptism was a rite preparatory for Jesus' own work, 3:11f. Whence did the "authority" of the Baptist derive? They had once asked that question themselves, Jn 1:25, but since that day to the day of John's martyrdom it had become increasingly plain to those of good faith that John was a man of God and his work "of heaven", heavenly. **26** – The objectors, over-anxious to save their face, miss the implication of the question – namely, that if John's mission was supernaturally accredited so also was that of the one he announced (Jn 1:29-37; 3:25-30; 5:33ff). They assume instead that Jesus will attack them for never having countenanced John, 3:7-10. On the other hand, the public esteem in which the Baptist was held (e.g. Ac 19:3; Jos, *Ant.* 18, 5, 2) kept them from denying to John the status of prophet. **27** – The weak reply, surely damaging in the ears of those present, reveals that they are guided only by motives of policy. To such dishonest witnesses Jesus need make no answer; let honest bystanders judge between them! Nevertheless, he pursues the theme of the Baptist in the parable that follows.

Parable of the two sons 21:28-32

28-30 – The significant point of the parable is the contrast between a farmer's two sons: one, beginning with flat refusal, ends with obedience:

²⁹ today.'   And he answered, 'I will not'; but afterward he
³⁰ repented and went.   And he went to the second and
said the same; and he answered, 'I go, sir,' but did not go.
³¹ Which of the two did the will of his father?" They said,
"The first." Jesus said to them, "Truly, I say to you,
the tax collectors and the harlots go into the kingdom
³² of God before you.   For John came to you in the way of
righteousness, and you did not believe him, but the tax
collectors and the harlots believed him; and even when
you saw it, you did not afterward repent and believe him.

Parable of the wicked husbandmen 21:33-46
³³ "Hear another parable. There was a householder who
planted a vineyard, and set a hedge around it, and dug a
wine press in it, and built a tower, and let it out to
³⁴ tenants, and went into another country.   When the
season of fruit drew near, he sent his servants to the
tenants, to get his fruit; and the tenants took his servants
³⁶ and beat one, killed another, and stoned another.   Again
he sent other servants, more than the first; and they did
³⁷ the same to them.   Afterward he sent his son to them,
³⁸ saying, 'They will respect my son.'   But when the tenants
saw the son, they said to themselves, 'This is the heir;
³⁹ come, let us kill him and have his inheritance.'   And they
took him and cast him out of the vineyard, and killed him.
⁴⁰ When therefore the owner of the vineyard comes, what
⁴¹ will he do to those tenants?"   They said to him, "He will
put those wretches to a miserable death, and let out the
vineyard to other tenants who will give him the fruits in

the other, in appearance at least readily submissive, is in effect recalcitrant. **31** – There can be no doubt which did the will of the father (or possibly "the Father", the application of the parable beginning to show through at this place). Swiftly upon the inevitable answer comes the devastating application. The publicans (9:9, note) who had listened to the Baptist, Lk 3:12, and the women of evil life who had come to the Saviour, Lk 7:36ff; Jn 4:4ff; 8:2ff, are going into the kingdom even now. There is as yet no sign (and this is a warning) that Christ's interlocutors are on their way. **32** – It was John's preaching that tested the "I will not" of the sinners and the "I go" of professional righteous men. John had come **in the way of righteousness,** i.e. respecting the traditional Law. He spoke, too, the old prophetic language of penance. Despite this, the learned in the Law did not listen. The repentance of public sinners should have shamed them.

Parable of the wicked husbandmen 21:33-46 (Mk 12:1-12; Lk 20:9-19)
From the lighter warning of 31 to a prophecy of ruin, 43, which concludes a parable that contains many allegorical details. **33** – To those familiar with Is 5:7 the image inevitably suggests Israel, vineyard of God. The stone well, the hollowed rock whence the juice of the pressed grapes passed through stone channels to a deeper rock-basin, the stone watchtower, all are present in Is 5:1-2. These details appear in the parable, not with any allegorical significance but with the purpose of establishing the identity of the vineyard by literary reminiscence of Isaiah. The listeners are now in a position to see the meaning of what follows. In his absence the owner, clearly God, commits the vineyard to farmers accountable to himself. These farmers are the centre of the story. **34-36** – It would appear from 43 that the vineyard, through the negligence of the husbandmen, had yielded nothing. In any case, to thwart the Master they maltreat or murder his servants who ask for the produce – the fate of the prophets, 23:30-31. But the Master has superhuman patience. He sends even more servants but to no better effect. **37** – The climax of gentleness is to send **his son** to persuade them. They will surely respect him. The event is to turn this hope to irony. **38** – The sight of the son only stimulates their hate. If he is removed, their possession will be for ever undisturbed. His existence threatened their possession just as our Lord's threatened the position of the Jewish leaders, Jn 11:47-53 **39** – In Mk (probably nearer the original words here) the son is first murdered and then cast out. In Mt and Lk the subsequent detail, Heb 13:12ff, has perhaps influenced the order of words. In either case, the Son is cast out of the vineyard that was his own; cf Jn 1:11. **40-41** – It is already obvious what the Master will do when the time of reckoning comes, but in Mt our Lord invites his hearers to pronounce, implicitly, their own sentence. God will choose other, more honest, workmen who will render the produce

⁴² their seasons." Jesus said to them, "Have you never read in the scriptures:

'The very stone which the builders rejected
has become the head of the corner;
this was the Lord's doing,
and it is marvellous in our eyes'?

⁴³ Therefore I tell you, the kingdom of God will be taken away from you and given to a nation producing the fruits ⁴⁵ of it." When the chief priests and the Pharisees heard his parables, they perceived that he was speaking about ⁴⁶ them. But when they tried to arrest him, they feared the multitudes, because they held him to be a prophet.

Parable of the wedding feast 22:1-14

¹ And again Jesus spoke to them in parables, saying, ² "The kingdom of heaven may be compared to a king ³ who gave a marriage feast for his son, and sent his servants to call those who were invited to the marriage ⁴ feast; but they would not come. Again he sent other servants, saying, 'Tell those who are invited, Behold, I have made ready my dinner, my oxen and my fat calves are killed, and everything is ready; come to the marriage ⁵ feast.' But they made light of it and went off one to his

promptly. As for the wicked husbandmen, they are to meet an end proportioned to their wickedness.

42 – The quotation is taken, like the "Hosanna" cry of 9, from Ps 118 (117): 22f. In the psalm the saying, probably a proverb, seems originally to refer to Israel, rejected like a useless stone by the nations as they founded their pagan polities. But in God's surprising plan and in God's building, Israel is the conspicuous angle-stone crowning and uniting the two high walls. The unexpected issue of 41 is, therefore, not without precedent in God's providence. That is why, **43** – Jesus has no hesitation in pronouncing his startling prophecy. The kingdom is to pass from the Jewish leaders and apparently from the Jewish people as a race. It will go to others who, as God's new planting, will produce the fruit for which their leaders will faithfully render timely account; cf 41.

Some MSS add a v. 44 (harmonizing with Lk 20:18): "And he who falls on this stone will be broken to pieces; but when it falls on any one it will crush him." The setting of the allegory has invited the hearers to see the cast-out Son, 39, in the rejected stone, Ac 4:11. But the "stone" is no longer considered as part of a building, it is considered in two prophetic connexions differing from this and differing from each other. In the first, Is 8:14, the "stone" is a disastrous obstacle, it is God himself becoming a severe judge for those disloyal to him. In the second, Dan 2:34-45, the "stone" is God's future, lasting kingdom, symbolized and summed-up in "one like a Son of man" – a boulder rolling down to the destruction of earthly kingdoms. Jesus, therefore, in Lk, warns the opponents of God and his kingdom with three intimidating texts, (only one in Mt, v. 42, and Mk) which he applies to himself and to his work.

45-46 – The words were too pointed to be mistaken. The enemies of Jesus knew that it was at them that the last parable was directed. The preceding one had been explicitly applied to them by Jesus himself, 31f.

Parable of the wedding feast 22:1-14 (Lk 14:16-24)

This parable-allegory, unlike 21:33-44, is not directed against the Jewish leaders as such, though there is an ominous echo of 21:38-41 in 22:6-7. It is addressed to all, and relates to the personnel of the kingdom. The distinguished ones favoured with the invitation refuse, those of no distinction take their place. But even among these (Mt only) some are unworthy and so excluded. **1-2** – Once more Jesus began to speak to them in parables, in parabolic form. The situation about to be described (cf 13:24 note) presents one aspect of the kingdom. Jewish literature (cf Edersheim 2, 425f) likened the messianic era to a feast (cf Is 25:6) and the Messiah himself to a bridegroom wedded to Israel; cf the Aramaic paraphrase or "Targum" on Ps 45 (44); Edersheim 2, 718. It is clear at the outset, therefore, that the **king** is God and the **son** the Messiah. **3-5** – It was

⁶ farm, another to his business, while the rest seized his
⁷ servants, treated them shamefully, and killed them. The
king was angry, and he sent his troops and destroyed those
⁸ murderers and burned their city. Then he said to his
servants, 'The wedding is ready, but those invited were
⁹ not worthy. Go therefore to the thoroughfares, and invite
¹⁰ to the marriage feast as many as you find.' And those
servants went out into the streets and gathered all whom
they found, both bad and good; so the wedding hall was
¹¹ filled with guests. But when the king came in to look
at the guests, he saw there a man who had no wedding
¹² garment; and he said to him, 'Friend, how did you get
in here without a wedding garment?' And he was speech-
¹³ less. Then the king said to the attendants, 'Bind him
hand and foot, and cast him into the outer darkness;
¹⁴ there men will weep and gnash their teeth.' For many
are called, but few are chosen."

usual in the East to remind invited guests when the time drew near. The servants, presumably the prophets, warn the chosen people that the marriage feast is imminent. With great forbearance the king overlooks the refusal and sends a second group of servants to say that the feast stands waiting. This circumstance indicates that the second group of servants is representative of God's envoys in the new order; cf the invitation of 3:2; 10:7. The oxen and fatted animals suggest a feast of royal proportions, but the invited are more interested in their worldly cares. **6** – Others (and the strange violence of the action suggests allegory) not content with insulting the servants (and through them their king) actually murder them. This treatment the Baptist had experienced and the apostles been taught to expect, 10:28. **7** – The king's patience is at last exhausted and his revenge terrible: death for the murderers and ruin for their city. The **city** is plainly not the king's capital which is elsewhere – perhaps (if the allegory has influenced the picture) in heaven itself. But it is as unnecessary to localize the "city" as it is to localize the "vineyard" of 21:33. The subsequent destruction of Jerusalem in 70 A.D. by the armies of Vespasian (God's instrument) would give the words a significance perhaps missed by their first hearers. **8-10** – The scene shifts to the palace. The king orders his servants (those of 3 or others) to bring in those who have not shown themselves unworthy of the royal honour. They are gathered indiscriminately from the streets, not chosen as Israel was chosen – we think automatically of the "publicans and sinners" and the Gentiles; cf Lk 13:29. No distinction is made between bad and good individuals: it is a question of God's global choice: Israel as a whole has refused the invitation to the messianic banquet, Israel as a whole is rejected (but on all this, cf Rom ch. 9 and 11). The sense of the parable is complete, and in fact Lk ends it here.

11-13 (Mt only) – The perspective changes: the morality of individuals within the newly elected group is now in question; moreover the king passes sentence on individuals and the banquet is resumed under new conditions; it is now a banquet where all are perfect. We are reminded of the parables of the drag-net and of the darnel (13:39-40, 48, 49) where the discrimination between good and wicked is postponed until the Last Judgment. The banquet which in vv. 1-10 is the messianic kingdom on earth now becomes the perfect kingdom in heaven. It seems that Mt has fused the parable preserved in Lk 14:16-24 (the man who gave a banquet) with another about a king who gave a marriage feast; the first a warning to the Jews, the second a warning to their successors in the kingdom. This hypothesis also solves the problem of v. 11: the king's expectation of a wedding garment is not unreasonable, since the culprit ceases to be one of the unexpectedly invited of v. 10.

The concluding verse, **14,** seems hardly apt to either of Matthew's two conflated parables: in the first part many are called but all refuse, in

Tribute to Caesar 22:15-22

15 Then the Pharisees went and took counsel how to entangle
16 him in his talk.   And they sent their disciples to him,
along with the Herodians, saying, "Teacher, we know
that you are true, and teach the way of God truthfully,
and care for no man; for you do not regard the position
17 of men.   Tell us, then, what you think. Is it lawful to pay
18 taxes to Caesar, or not?"   But Jesus, aware of their malice,
19 said, "Why put me to the test, you hypocrites?   Show me
the money for the tax." And they brought him a coin.

the second we are left with the impression that many are called and most are "chosen". It seems most likely that this v. is a generalizing moral dictum disjointedly inserted here. It is possible, however, that it applies to the two parts *taken together*: the invitation to the kingdom has gone out to many – to the whole nation of Israel – and the nation as a whole has refused. Add to this the thought that even in the "nation" next invited, 21:43, there are some unworthy, 22:11ff, and the "many called, few chosen" appears in its due proportions. It is to be remembered also that the term "few" is relative; they are "many" in 8:11. Moreover, the dictum refers not directly to the number of the saved (a question Jesus refuses to answer; Lk 13:23) but primarily to the members, and worthy members, of the messianic kingdom on earth. The rest is the secret of the Father.

Note: The early Church and the parables.

The story element in the parables remains very close to the actual words of Jesus, but the lesson drawn often shows signs of interpretation by the primitive community, a community living on the word of Christ, a word itself living and adaptable to the changing situation. These lessons, however reinterpreted, are still authoritative, since they are the word of Christ living in his society. Nevertheless, there has frequently been a notable shift of emphasis, the most important being that from the urgent challenge of Jesus demanding a decision on his person and mission before the last crisis of history which his death will introduce, to the conduct of a community living after his death and awaiting his return. A fairly clear example may be found in the short parable of the debtor (compare Mt 5:21-26 with Lk 12:54-59) which Matthew places in a homiletic context, a sermon on Christian conduct, but which Luke leaves in its eschatological setting, a challenge to decision before the coming crisis. (A stimulating, even indispensable book on this subject is J. Jeremias, *The Parables of Jesus*, London, 1954).

Tribute to Caesar 22:15-22 (Mk 12:13-17; Lk 20:20-26)

15-16 – The Pharisees seek to trap Jesus with a question. To hide the trap they do not approach him themselves but send their students (not yet rabbis). With these are the **Herodians,** a political and not a religious sect, supporters of the Herodian princes; in this respect they did not share the Pharisees' outlook, which was anti-Herodian. Both parties were at one, however, in their interim policy of subservience to Rome. It was to their common interest to scotch a movement which threatened or seemed to threaten the *status quo*. They open the debate with a compliment calculated to disarm. They insist, tendentiously, upon the master's well-known independence of thought (e.g. 7:29) and outspoken expression even against the person of the ruling power, Lk 13:31f. It seems from this emphasis that they hope for an anti-Roman

²⁰ And Jesus said to them, "Whose likeness and inscription
²¹ is this?"   They said, "Caesar's." Then he said to them,
"Render therefore to Caesar the things that are Caesar's,
²² and to God the things that are God's"   When they heard
it, they marvelled; and they left him and went away.

The resurrection of the dead 22:23-33
²³ The same day Sadducees came to him, who say that there
²⁴ is no resurrection; and they asked him a question,   saying,
"Teacher, Moses said, 'If a man dies, having no children,
his brother must marry the widow, and raise up children
²⁵ for his brother.' Now there were seven brothers among
us; the first married, and died, and having no children
²⁶ left his wife to his brother. So too the second and third,
²⁷ down to the seventh. After them all, the woman died.

decision which later they were forced to fabricate, Lk 23:2. **17 – taxes** (*kensos*) are apparently the poll-tax paid direct to Rome. The question is dishonest: Pharisees and Herodians had long since adjusted their conscience to the payment. But it presents Jesus with a dilemma. Should he advise non-payment, as they hope and expect, he becomes indictable to Rome. The pseudo-Messiah, Judas the Galilean, had perished for this very cause, twenty years before in 7 A.D. Should he advise payment he loses his messianic credit with the people for whom messianism spelt independence of foreign yoke. **18** – Jesus, knowing the insincerity of the question, could refuse to answer but does not. **19** – As usual (e.g. 21:31-40) he asks the objectors to contribute to their own downfall, and they show him a silver denarius (cf 17:23-26, note), the Roman coin with which the taxes were so often paid. **20** – The coin was probably of Tiberius (14-37 A.D.) with, on the obverse, the laureate head of this emperor and the inscription: "Ti(berius) Caesar Divi Aug(usti) F(ilius) Augustus". **21** – Plainly the coin came from Caesar, it is right that it should be *returned* (**rendered**) to him. These civil transactions are on one plane, God's rights on another. There is no inevitable clash, provided (as was the case in the relationship of Rome and Jewry) that the civil demands did not encroach upon the duties of man to God. **22** – The answer is a simple one. But it amazes the adversaries because they have no suspicion of the simple principle from which it emerges. Messianism is for them inevitably a political movement and their dilemma, 17, consequently exhaustive and fatal. It is the spiritual nature of our Lord's messianism that provides the third alternative which is not compromise, but due delimitation of spheres; cf Jn 18:36f.

The resurrection of the dead 22:23-33 (Mk 12:18-27; Lk 20:27-40)
The Sadducees, 3:7-10, note, now appear on the scene not, as the Pharisees had attempted, to involve Jesus with the political authorities but with a question of Jewish doctrine and practice. They seek either to score a point off the Pharisees by winning his support or else, if Jesus defends the Pharisees' doctrine, to make game of him. The **Sadducees,** despite the fact that from their ranks the priests were chosen, believed the one God to be uninterested in his creation. They therefore denied divine providence, the immortality of the soul and the resurrection of the body. The Pharisees' doctrine of bodily resurrection was firmly held but, to judge by certain texts, crass. In the question put to Jesus, therefore, another dilemma is implied: either a very material conception of resurrection or no resurrection at all. As before, Christ has a third alternative to propose, 30, which proceeds from the high spirituality of his mind. **23-27** – The Sadducees quote Deut 25:5 enunciating the "levirate" law. They propose a case in which each of seven brothers, all being childless, had successively equal rights over the one wife. What

28 In the resurrection, therefore, to which of the seven will
29 she be wife? For they all had her." But Jesus answered
them, "You are wrong, because you know neither the
30 scriptures nor the power of God. For in the resurrection
they neither marry nor are given in marriage, but are
31 like angels in heaven. And as for the resurrection of the
dead, have you not read what was said to you by God,
32 'I am the God of Abraham, and the God of Isaac, and the
God of Jacob'? He is not God of the dead, but of the
33 living." And when the crowd heard it, they were astonished at his teaching.

The greatest commandment 22:34-40
34 But when the Pharisees heard that he had silenced the
35 Sadducees, they came together. And one of them, a
36 lawyer, asked him a question, to test him. "Teacher,
37 which is the great commandment in the law?" And he
said to him, "You shall love the Lord your God with all
your heart, and with all your soul, and with all your mind.
38 This is the great and first commandment. And a second
39 is like it, You shall love your neighbour as yourself. On
40 these two commandments depend all the law and the
prophets."

when these rights become simultaneous after death? It reduces the idea of bodily resurrection to absurdity! **28-30** – The objection shows ignorance of God's power to raise man and woman bodily to the condition of the angels who, being immortal, do not need to reproduce their kind. **31-32** – It shows ignorance, too, of the very Scriptures they have ventured to quote. Jesus chooses a text from Ex 3:6 (not, e.g., from the clear text of Dan 12:1-2) perhaps because, as is highly probable, the Sadducees accepted only the Pentateuch as having full canonical authority. In its original setting in Exodus, the text strictly implies that the God now speaking with Moses was the same God as his ancestors adored. Here Jesus draws out its fuller sense after a fashion no rabbi could resent. The living God could not be named after a dead thing; yet God himself uses the title "God of Abraham". Abraham, therefore, still lives. Nor is it only of the "soul's" continuing life that Jesus speaks. In the first place, this is not the difficulty, 25, 28; in the second place, Jewish theology did not distinguish immortality and bodily resurrection, 2 Mac 12:43f. Thus the Pharisees, believing in immortality, accepted resurrection; the Sadducees denied the first and therefore the second. There was no third school. It is against this theological background that our Lord's argument must be read. If Abraham lives at all (and the Exodus text proves that he does) he lives with a view to bodily resurrection. And indeed even outside this background but within the total O.T. context the words of Exodus are significant. Setting aside explicit texts (e.g. Pss 16(15):10-11; 49(48):16; 73(72):24) the whole O.T. protests that God could never desert his servants – he is their God as he is the God of Abraham. Neither Abraham, therefore, nor any other faithful servant can perish utterly. **33** – Again the admiration (cf 22) and again, it seems, because the objectors have not grasped the simple principle, *viz.* the spiritual nature even of bodily resurrection. Evidently the Sadducees had never heard their difficulty answered like this by the Pharisees.

The greatest commandment 22:34-40 (Mk 12:28-34; Lk 10:25-28)

34 – The new approach to Jesus has in Mt the air of a conspiracy unless we read against the weight of MS evidence: the Pharisees "came round him" instead of **came together.** In this latter reading the Pharisees are presented as pursuing the attack (though, cf *infra*, they have chosen an unsuitable representative). The former reading shows them somewhat conciliated by the repulse of the Sadducees. **35-36** – One versed in the Law puts a question probably debated in the schools. The 613 **commandments** of the Law were subdivided into "light" and "grave", infringements of the latter being expiated only by death. These again were subdivided into small and great. Our Lord's question is concerned only with the greatest of all. In Mk 12:28 he seems sincere; in Mt the word **test** suggests the opposite. The solution lies perhaps

Christ, the son and lord of David 22:41-46

41 Now while the Pharisees were gathered together, Jesus
42 asked them a question,   saying, "What do you think of
the Christ? Whose son is he?" They said to him, "The
43 son of David."   He said to them, "How is it then that
David inspired by the Spirit, calls him Lord, saying,

44   'The Lord said to my Lord,
    Sit at my right hand,
    till I put thy enemies under thy feet'?
45 If David thus calls him Lord, how is he his son?"   And
46 no one was able to answer him a word, nor from that day
did any one dare to ask him any more questions.

Against the scribes and Pharisees 23:1-12

1 Then said Jesus to the crowds and to his disciples,   "The
2 scribes and the Pharisees sit on Moses' seat;   so practise
3 and observe whatever they tell you, but not what they

in the wide sense of this word, perhaps "probing", "sounding"; or possibly the lawyer's initial hostility softened as the conversation advanced. **37-38** – The words of the commandment, Deut 6:5, were familiar: they opened the twice-daily prayer – the *Shema*, cf Mk 12:29. They urged the submission of the heart (in Hebrew idiom, the centre of understanding) and the soul (principle of action) to God; and this "with all your strength" (Mt's **mind** is probably due to the Greek translator). **39** – It is more surprising that Jesus joins to this the love of **neighbour**, Lev 19:18. The fact that he speaks of the **second** commandment without being asked shows his unwillingness to separate the two. The two commandments are **like** because true love of neighbour is but an overflow of true love of God. As Jesus is the first to present these two precepts as one, so he is the first to give the widest meaning to the word "neighbour"; cf his explanation of the term on a similar, but apparently not the same, occasion in Lk 10:25-37. **40** – From this double support hang **law and prophets.** The last phrase significantly repeats 5:17 so that we now understand what this divine system was that Jesus had come not to destroy but to bring to perfection. It was essentially the law of charity.

Christ, the son and lord of David 22:41-46 (Mk 12:35-37; Lk 20:41-44) **41-42** – The recent question, 17, has betrayed a political conception of the Messiah, 22, note; our Lord now invites reflexion. That the Messiah was to be of the Davidic dynasty was the constant teaching of the prophets, Is 11:1; Jer 23:5; Ez 34:23 etc., and there is no hesitation in the Pharisees' reply. **43-46** – Yet in the Davidic psalm 110 (109) were written the inspired words: "Oracle of Yahweh to my lord: Sit at my right hand." The Pharisees evidently admitted that the Davidic "my lord" referred to the Messiah. The rabbis of the next two centuries, perhaps influenced by our Lord's argument repeated and developed by the early Christians, did not. The psalm verse, especially with its suggestion of the messianic throne of Dan 7:29, emphasized the transcendental nature of the Messiah. **Son of David** is therefore not an adequate description of him. Jesus leaves them with this thought. If honestly pursued it could take the Pharisees and others (cf Mk 12:35) from ideas of a political Messiah to the notion of one whose work was to be as spiritual as his origin.

Against the scribes and Pharisees 23:1-12 (Mk 12:37-40; Lk 20:45-47; cf 11:37-54)
The whole chapter is a warning to those who are or may be deceived by the worst elements in Pharisaism. It is with this in view that our Lord mercilessly exposes them. Note, however, that the recurrent "Woe!" is not a curse but a portentous expression of grief ("Alas!") cf 24:19.

4 do; for they preach, but do not practise. They bind heavy burdens, hard to bear, and lay them on men's shoulders; but they themselves will not move them with 5 their finger.   They do all their deeds to be seen by men; for they make their phylacteries broad and their fringes 6 long, and they love the place of honour at feasts and 7 the best seats in the synagogues, and salutations in 8 the market places, and being called rabbi by men.   But you are not to be called rabbi, for you have one teacher, 9 and you are all brethren.   And call no man your father on earth, for you have one Father, who is in heaven. 10 Neither be called masters, for you have one master, the 11 Christ.   He who is greatest among you shall be your 12 servant; whoever exalts himself will be humbled, and whoever humbles himself will be exalted.

1-4 – When the scribes and Pharisees faithfully expound the Law it is on the teaching chair of Moses that they sit (not "have sat"; the aorist is equivalent to the Semitic stative "imperfect"). Accordingly they must be obeyed. But this obedience should not lead to imitation, because they are hypocrites at heart. The letter of the law they observe, not without ingenuity, but not its spirit cf Jn 7:19-23. On the contrary, the casuistic interpretations of the Law that over-burdened the conscience of others, Ac 15:40, serve to extricate the Pharisees themselves from many an obligation; cf Edersheim 2, 777. They take pains to make neat and heavy parcels and to lift them on to the shoulders of others. **5-7** – (Mk 12:38-39; Lk 20:48). Their show is hollow though it is the basis of their prestige. They seek to impress others with their zeal for the Law by making their phylacteries more noticeable. The **phylacteries** (i.e. safeguards, amulets; Aram. *tephillin*, literally "prayers") were tiny, oblong, leather-covered cases containing four strips of parchment on which were written the texts, Ex 13:1-10, 11-16; Deut 6:4-9; 11:13-21, the monotheistic profession of faith. Here the word is evidently used to include the ribbons or thongs by which the cases were fastened, one to the forearm, another to the forehead, at the time of morning-prayer. The practice derived from an unduly literal interpretation of Ex 13:9, 16. Jesus condemns neither phylacteries nor fringes, 9:20-22, but only the ostentatious piety that makes them conspicuous. The low respectful bow in sight of all, the title **rabbi** ("master", "teacher") delighted the scribes and Pharisees. **8-12** – Jesus turns to his disciples (Mt only). As he had not condemned phylacteries, so in 7 he does not forbid the title rabbi but the vain complacency taken in it. It is in this sense that the injunction of 8 is to be understood. Jesus is not out to reform current nomenclature; he is concerned with the spirit, not with the letter. But the use, 9, or acceptance, 8, 10, of any adulation that threatens to intrude between man and God is sternly forbidden. All human titles are only shadows of God's authority from which they derive, Eph 3:15. Unless this is clearly understood, **call no man on earth Abi, father,** a term sometimes used of the great rabbis; cf Edersheim 2, 408-10. Note that Christ is not a grammarian regulating the use of terms: he is a doctor of the spirit. He forbids any acknowledgment of fatherhood that obscures the fatherhood of God, nothing more. If we make no allowance for the concreteness and brevity of his phrases we reduce either them to absurdity (e.g. 6:3) or him to inconsistency (comp. Mt 5:39 with Jn 18:23). He would not forbid a human son to use the word "father" nor would he forbid the term if addressed to one who is God's representative; in this second case, indeed, it serves to remind its user of the fatherhood of God. Nor must the Christian disciple pose as an independent spiritual guide (v. 10); he himself is subject to one teacher and one guide, Christ (the words **the Christ,** possibly a copyist's insertion, render the sense rightly). They have one Father who is in heaven. The principle of

Sevenfold denunciation of scribes and Pharisees 23:13-32

13 "But woe to you, scribes and Pharisees, hypocrites! because you shut the kingdom of heaven against men; for you neither enter yourselves, nor allow those who would 15 enter to go in. Woe to you, scribes and Pharisees, hypocrites! for you traverse sea and land to make a single proselyte, and when he becomes a proselyte, you make him 16 twice as much a child of hell as yourselves. "Woe to you, blind guides, who say, 'If any one swears by the temple, it is nothing; but if any one swears by the gold 17 of the temple, he is bound by his oath.' You blind fools! For which is greater, the gold or the temple that has made 18 the gold sacred? And you say, 'If any one swears by the altar, it is nothing; but if any one swears by the gift that 19 is on the altar, he is bound by his oath.' You blind men! For which is greater, the gift or the altar that makes the 20 gift sacred? So he who swears by the altar, swears by it 21 and by everything on it; and he who swears by the temple, 22 swears by it and by him who dwells in it; and he who swears by heaven, swears by the throne of God and by 23 him who sits upon it. Woe to you, scribes and Pharisees, hypocrites! for you tithe mint and dill and cummin, and have neglected the weightier matters of the law, justice and mercy and faith; these you ought to have done, 24 without neglecting the others. You blind guides, strain-25 ing out a gnat and swallowing a camel! Woe to you, scribes and Pharisees, hypocrites! for you cleanse the outside of the cup and of the plate, but inside they are full of 26 extortion and rapacity. You blind Pharisee! first cleanse the inside of the cup and of the plate, that the outside also

graded authority remains (11; cf 20:26, note) but the spirit in which that authority is wielded must be one of humility. For 12, cf 18:4, note.

Sevenfold denunciation of scribes and Pharisees 23:13-32 (Lk *passim*)
First: They are an obstacle to the kingdom. **13** – A general denunciation. Our Lord's anger is explained by the harm he sees done to simple folk. The formalism of scribes and Pharisees has blocked the entrance even to Christ's own kingdom. It has darkened the public mind and made it incapable of appreciating the need for inward religion or even of recognizing its presence. (Note: a verse 14 is found in many MSS; it is an insertion from Mk 12:40). *Second: They proselytize to bad purpose,* **15** – (Lk 11:52). Not content with obstructing entrance to the kingdom, the Pharisees seek, with immense zeal, to draw ignorant pagans down to their own level and to make them too consciously sin against the proffered light of Christ. (Jewish proselytism at the period was intense and successful.) Often twice as fanatical as the born Jew, the newcomer is twice as surely established in the infernal dominion (**child of** in this Semitic sense = "belonging to"). *Third: They are casuists,* **16-22** – The scribes and Pharisees, blind themselves, have absurdly assumed the role of guide. To illustrate the blindness, Jesus chooses an example (or contrives a characteristic, if non-existent, case) of their attitude to **vows.** On the annulment of these they were an ingenious court of appeal. The terms of the vow were closely scrutinized without regard to the original intention of the one who had made it. Their verdict would be either **it is nothing** (it is no vow) or **he is bound.** Two individual illustrations of this attitude are given, 16, 18. Vows naming the **gold** (apparently the votive-offerings) in the temple and vows naming the sacrifice (**gift**) on the altar. These are declared valid, vows on the temple or altar itself are declared void. But Jesus turns the casuistry against them, 17, 19. If they are determined to make these distinctions (though distinctions in this matter are out of place, cf 20-22), surely the house of God and his chosen altar are more sacred than man's possessions. These last are sacred only when, and because, they become offerings. Even casuistry should have reached a conclusion contradictory to that of the scribes. **20-22** – But, in truth, there is no room for it. A sacred vow, whatever its terms, is made in the presence of God. And (22 – a final thrust), contrary to the explicit decision of the Jewish doctors, the invocation of **heaven** in place of the divine name makes not the slightest difference. It is the intention and not the word that tells. *Fourth: They distort true values,* **23-24** – (Lk 11:42). The minutiae of the tithe-laws (based on Lev 27:30) on all comestible plants were truly astonishing, Edersheim 2, 412. Even the small seasoning herbs, **mint, dill, cummin,** were not forgotten. The practice is not condemned, nor is it enjoined, despite the misleading Semitic downrightness of the phrase "these things (**justice** etc.) you should have practised without neglecting the

27 may be clean.   Woe to you, scribes and Pharisees, hypocrites! for you are like white-washed tombs, which outwardly appear beautiful, but within they are full of dead
28 men's bones and all uncleanness.   So you also outwardly
appear righteous to men, but within you are full of
29 hypocrisy and iniquity.   Woe to you, scribes and Pharisees, hypocrites! for you build the tombs of the prophets
30 and adorn the monuments of the righteous,   saying, 'If
we had lived in the days of our fathers, we would not have
taken part with them in shedding the blood of the
31 prophets.'   Thus you witness against yourselves, that
you are sons of those who murdered the prophets.   Fill
32 up, then, the measure of your fathers.

Approaching punishment of scribes and Pharisees 23:33-36
33 "You serpents, you brood of vipers, how are you to escape
34 being sentenced to hell?   Therefore I send you prophets
and wise men and scribes, some of whom you will kill
and crucify, and some you will scourge in your synagogues
35 and persecute from town to town,   that upon you may

other (**tithe**)". But it surely should not be found incompatible with the weightier matters of the Law – justice to one's neighbour (cf Deut 10:18), sympathy for him (**mercy**), good faith in dealings with him (**faith**; cf Ps 33 (32):4; Gal 5:22 (23)). **24** – This fantastic situation is illustrated in massive hyperbole. Such conduct is compared to that of one who would carefully filter from his cup a tiny gnat (lest he incur some legal impurity) leaving there a camel. Attention is sometimes called to the play on the Aramaic words (*gml, qlm, qml;* respectively **camel, gnat, filter**) which probably indicates that the saying was proverbial. *Fifth: They are formalists,* **25-26** – (Lk 11:39-41). Meticulous ceremonial care to avoid legal impurity (cf Mk 7:4) was not matched by moral scruples. The surface of the crockery was, no doubt, clean, but it held the product of plunder and the means of intemperance: "*inside they* (the vessels) *are filled from* (*ex*) *robbery and excess*". First things first: see that the inside is morally pure; it will then confer all necessary purity on the surface of the container. *Sixth: They are hypocrites,* **27-28** – (Lk 11:44). The "inside" and "outside" contrast of 25-26 leads on to a formal accusation of hypocrisy. The comparison, deliberately nauseating, is borrowed from the tombs whitened with chalk four weeks before the Passover to warn pilgrims of the danger of contact and legal impurity; cf Num 19:16. The eye sees them gleaming in the sun, but they cover corruption. By the same paradox the Law-abiding Pharisee is full of lawlessness (**iniquity**) cf 1-7, note. *Seventh: They are murderers of God's envoy,* **29-32** – (Lk 11:47-48). As in 23 it is not the act of honouring their great ancestors, 29, that is condemned but present murderous intention which lays bare the hypocrisy of their protestations. They admit, 30, that it was their fathers who murdered the prophets but seek to disclaim responsibility. Nevertheless, they and Jesus know their murderous intent towards him; cf 21:38, 45. The situation of their **fathers** has reappeared and their conduct shows, 31, that they are worthy sons, and that their protest, 30, is empty. Bitterly ironical, Jesus urges them to their deadly work: their fathers have killed the servants, 21:35, 36, it is theirs to complete the work and kill the Son. In these words, recalling those of the Baptist (33; cf 3:7), but unexpected and terrible on the lips of Jesus, the crafty Pharisees are warned of the judgment that condemns to hell.

Approaching punishment of scribes and Pharisees 23:33-36 (Lk 11:49-51)
    Jesus in his turn (lit. "therefore behold I . . .) is sending (cf 10:16) his own **prophets** to declare the divine message, and **wise men** and **scribes** (cf 13:52) to apply it. The old order will repeat itself, and with it the opportunity for sacrilegious murder. **35** – Thus the chosen race will fitly bear the responsibility for all the innocent blood shed **on earth** (or "on the ground"?) in the whole course of sacred history. The names of Abel and Zechariah are chosen, because Abel's murder is the first

come all the righteous blood shed on earth, from the
blood of innocent Abel to the blood of Zechariah the son
of Barachiah, whom you murdered between the sanctuary
36 and the altar.   Truly, I say to you, all this will come upon
this generation."

Jerusalem admonished 23:37-39
37 "O Jerusalem, Jerusalem, killing the prophets and stoning
those who are sent to you! How often would I have
gathered your children together as a hen gathers her brood
38 under her wings, and you would not!   Behold, your house
39 is forsaken and desolate.   For I tell you, you will not see
me again, until you say, 'Blessed is he who comes in the
name of the Lord.' "

mentioned in the Scriptures, Gen 4:8, and that of the priest Zechariah, 2 Chr (Par) 24:20-22, the last in the Hebrew order of books. In each case there is question, as here, of a just reckoning to be made, Gen 4:10f; 2 Chr (Par) 24:22. The reference to Zechariah is certainly to the priest of 2 Chr (Par) 24:20 – "son of Jehoiada" and slain in the temple precincts (cf Lk 11:51) – and not to the prophet, who is called "son of Berechiah" in Zec 1:1. There are some faint indications that the reading **son of Berechiah** in Mt is not original: the phrase is absent altogether from the Sinaitic MS and from four cursives; it becomes "son of Jehoiada" in the "Gospel of the Nazarenes" known to Jerome and thought by him to be the original Matthew. Its absence from the parallel place in Lk suggests to many critics that it may be an ancient and mistaken gloss. This theory is accepted by many exegetes. The question remains unsolved. **36** – For all these crimes the nation will shortly answer. The fall of Jerusalem came forty years later.

Jerusalem admonished 23:37-39 (Lk 13:34-35)

37 – The sorrow underlying the anger of the denunciations rises to the surface. The city of God, 5:35, assassin of his envoys (cf 30, 34; 2 Chr (Par) 24:20f; Jer 26:20ff; 2 (4) Kg 21:16, etc.) and finally rejecting the reconciliation through the Son! By repeated appeal to Jerusalem (unmentioned in the Synoptics but told in Jn) Jesus has used the most anxious care to protect his own. **38** – The city with its temple (**your house**) will be left forsaken as the prophet had threatened, Jer 22:5 – a repetition of the sorrow of the Babylonian exile. **39** – But Jesus does not yet speak openly of material ruin. He speaks rather of the spiritual loss his absence will bring. They have heard his last appeal. His mission to them is over. Yet, it seems, he ends on a note of invitation. If Jerusalem should come to hail him as her king, as many on Sunday had saluted him (cf 21:9, note), she will find him. But not till then. The words are perhaps merely a farewell exhortation though many see in them a promise of the future conversion of Israel to Christ – a conversion which is in fact prophesied by Paul, Rom 11:25.

Introduction to the discourse on the "End" 24:1-3

¹ Jesus left the temple and was going away, when his disciples came to point out to him the buildings of the ² temple. But he answered them, "You see all these, do you not? Truly, I say to you, there will not be left here one stone upon another, that will not be thrown down." ³ As he sat on the Mount of Olives, the disciples came to him privately, saying, "Tell us, when will this be, and what will be the sign of your coming and of the close of the age?"

II

Discourse: The "End" 24:1 – 25:46

Introduction 24:1-3 (Mk 13:1-4; Lk 21:5-7)

1 – Jesus leaves the temple by the eastern gate and, crossing the Kedron, climbs the slope of Olivet. Turning to look backward down upon the temple buildings the disciples, admiring provincials, exclaim at their massive beauty. **2** – Our Lord's reply is disconcerting. This Herodian temple, begun more than forty years before (20/19 B.C.) and not completely finished until thirty years later (64 A.D.) was even now threatened with total ruin – it was burned and overthrown in 70 A.D. **3** – The remark is unexpected and the disciples walk on, perhaps in silence, perhaps in agitated discussion until, reaching the summit, all stop to rest. The four privileged disciples (Mk) put the double question: "When?"; "What warnings?". It is difficult to determine whether these questions refer to one event, the time and herald-signs of the destruction of Jerusalem, or to two, the time of the destruction of Jerusalem and the signs of the end of the world. Luke's words and to a slightly less extent Mk's seem to suggest one; Mt's suggest two. It is usual to reconcile the two forms of the question, Mt as against Mk, Lk, by pointing out that for a Jew the destruction of the temple would spell the end of the world itself. In this hypothesis the disciples thought that the two events were to be simultaneous, and Jesus in his reply treats of them side by side because the first is a figure of the second ("end of a world", "end of the world"); nevertheless, it is claimed, he removes the disciples' chronological confusion. It is said that two separate events are certainly discussed in the discourse because one is described as local, imminent, forseeable through historical happenings, while the other is universal, of unknown date, without warning signs.

Another and important theory has been recently presented, a revival of Augustine's tentative opinion but revised and supported with powerful new arguments. The theory defends the unity of the discourse and holds that *the reference throughout is to the destruction of Jerusalem with its double aspect:* the end of the old order ("times of the Jews") and the opening of the new ("times of the Gentiles"). The hypothesis does not deny the possibility of a further sense (fuller? typical?) in the discourse. Indeed it follows from the nature of the case that the divine judgment which closes the first act of world-history (the Age of Israel) is the destined model or type of the Last Judgment which is to mark the end of the next (the Age of the Gentiles). This fusion of perspective is in the style of the prophets. For them the "Day of Yahweh" (i.e. of Yahweh's judgment) has a shifting perspective, the reason being that this "day" is considered more from the theological, transcendental, plane than

The beginning of sorrows 24:4-14

⁴ And Jesus answered them, "Take heed that no one leads ⁵ you astray. For many will come in my name, saying, ⁶ 'I am the Christ,' and they will lead many astray. And you will hear of wars and rumours of wars; see that you are not alarmed; for this must take place, but the end is ⁷ not yet. For nation will rise against nation, and kingdom against kingdom, and there will be famines and ⁸ earthquakes in various places: all this is but the begin- ⁹ ning of the sufferings.   Then they will deliver you up to tribulation, and put you to death; and you will be hated ¹⁰ by all nations for my name's sake. And then many will fall away, and betray one another, and hate one another. ¹¹ And many false prophets will arise and lead many astray. ¹² And because wickedness is multiplied, most men's love ¹³ will grow cold.   But he who endures to the end will be ¹⁴ saved.   And this gospel of the kingdom will be preached throughout the whole world, as a testimony to all nations; and then the end will come.

from the historical and contingent point of view. But the hypothesis denies that the two themes (end of Jerusalem, end of the world) are *juxta*posed so that one part of the discourse refers to the end of Jerusalem. the other to the end of the world; it does not deny that the themes are *super*imposed. St Paul, therefore, could resume certain phrases of the discourse and refer them to the end of the world. Strictly literal interpretation, the theory claims, is satisfied by the historical reference (destruction of Jerusalem) and, in fact, sometimes demands such a reference (e.g. 24:16-20). **3** – The disciples' question in Mk, Lk is explicitly concerned with the destruction of Jerusalem and Mt's form is capable of the same interpretation. The phrase **your coming** (*parousia*, a term not used in the Gospel except Mt 24) has in the Greek papyri the meaning of a royal visit. Paul certainly uses the word of Christ's final coming at the end of the world (1 Cor 15:23 etc.) but it may be that in this case as in others he has taken over Mt's terminology and adapted it to the final coming. The **close of the age** (a more exact translation than "the consummation of the world") sounds more decisive for the end of the world reference than does the term *parousia*. Nevertheless the word "age" (*aion*) signifies not the physical world or universe, but "era, epoch" of human history. The "era" here might therefore be that of the old dispensation. In 28:20, where the perspective changes, it is the new, messianic era.

The beginning of sorrows 24:4-14 (Mk 13:5-13; Lk 21:8-19)
4-5 – Jesus does not yet reply directly to the disciples' question: he is concerned primarily with spiritual issues and with the conduct of the disciples. He supposes his own death after which many would come usurping the title that belonged to him – as in fact they did, with grievous results for themselves and their followers. For these political pseudo-Messiahs who appeared in considerable numbers before the destruction of Jerusalem cf Jos., *Bellum Judaicum* 2, 13, 4; 6, 5, 4. **6-7** – Still anxious to warn his own rather than to foretell the future, Jesus speaks of the inward peace the disciples must preserve in a troubled world. The prophetic style he uses does not call for minute verification though this is not lacking for the years before 70 A.D. It was a period savage in its wars, ferocious in its very peace (Tacitus, *Hist.* 3, 2, 1) with war's usual concomitants: plagues (Tacitus, *Annales* 16, 13) and famine (Ac 11:28; Jos., *Ant.* 20, 2, 5); even earthquakes (in towns of Asia Minor, 61-2 A.D.; Pompeii in 63 A.D. etc.). All this does not closely concern the apostles, as the Jerusalem catastrophe will; cf 15ff. The "end" of Jerusalem with its final break with the old order is still to come. **8** – These calamities are "the beginnings of *the pangs of childbirth*" (*arché odinon*). The world is in travail for a new age (cf Mic 4:9-10; Rv (Apoc) 12:2) though the pangs have not reached their climax; cf 15, note. The sentence, though ominous, is designed to console the disciples; cf

The great tribulation 24:15-25

15 "So when you see the desolating sacrilege spoken of by
the prophet Daniel, standing in the holy place (let the
16 reader understand), then let those who are in Judea
17 flee to the mountains; let him who is on the housetop
18 not go down to take what is in his house; and let him
19 who is in the field not turn back to take his mantle. And
alas for those who are with child and for those who give
20 suck in those days! Pray that your flight may not be in

Jn 16:20-22. **9** – Pursuing the theme of his disciples' conduct (cf 10:17-23, notes) Jesus fortifies them against the future by showing that their fate is neither outside his knowledge nor divorced from his interest (**for my name's sake**). **10-12** – Under the pressure of persecution many will defect and even hand one another over to the persecutors. In this divided field religious impostors (cf 5) reap a rich harvest. (Such a situation in fact developed some years before the destruction of Jerusalem; Rom 16:17-18; Gal 1:6-9; 2 Cor 11:13 etc.) Faced with this disedifying spectacle the love of God will freeze in the hearts of many. **13** – But he will save his life (cf Lk 21:19) who shows perfect fortitude (translating **to the end,** *eis telos* as "perfectly" as in 2 Cor 1:13 and perhaps Jn 13:1). **14** – But before the **end,** which in view of the following verses, probably now means the end of Jerusalem, the good news of the kingdom must be announced to **the whole world**. This last phrase, suggesting to modern ears the inhabited world as we now know it, is already used, equivalently, in Rom 1:8 "in the whole world", and the **testimony to all nations** finds its echo in Rom 1:5. Paul registers this universal preaching as a *fait accompli* as early as 60 A.D., Col 1:23, ten years before the fall of Jerusalem. The verse does not hint, therefore, that the perspective has passed beyond the fall of Jerusalem. Through all the hostile circumstances described, 5-12, the Gospel will go steadily forward. 14, too, thus holds a note of consolation for the disciples.

The great tribulation 24:15-25 (Mk 13:14-23; Lk 21:20-24)
At last Jesus proceeds to answer the disciples' question, but he is still concerned primarily with practical advice and comfort. **15** – **The prophet Daniel** (Dan 9:27; cf 11:31; 12:11) had spoken of the "devastating hateful thing" which "will be upon the temple" (LXX). The words were verified in 168 B.C. (cf 1 Mac 1:57; 2 Mac 6:1-5) by the conduct of the hellenizing tyrant Antiochus Epiphanes who set up in the temple an idol and altar to Olympian Zeus. Jesus speaks of a repetition of such sacrilege and he invites the reader of Daniel to penetrate the deeper prophetic sense of the allusion. (Possibly it is the evangelist himself who invites to this or to an attentive consideration of our Lord's words.) If Jesus is referring explicitly to the desecration of the temple (**the holy place**), the warning would be recognized by the Christians when, in 68 A.D., the Jewish Zealots tyrannized in the temple which they had turned into a fortress. If he is referring to the desecration of the sacred soil of Palestine, it would be the Roman armies bearing down on Jerusalem in 69 A.D. that would be the signal for flight; cf Lk 21:20. **16** – The Christians are to flee from Judea to the mountains (across Jordan, seemingly). In effect they did leave Jerusalem for Pella before the siege. **17-20** – Haste will be imperative. Should anyone be taking his ease, eastern-fashion, on the flat-roof, let him run down the outer staircase but not go into the house to encumber his flight with

²¹ winter or on a sabbath.   For then there will be great
tribulation, such as has not been from the beginning of
²² the world until now, no, and never will be.   And if
those days had not been shortened, no human being
would be saved; but for the sake of the elect those days
²³ will be shortened.   Then if any one says to you, 'Lo, here
²⁴ is the Christ!' or 'There he is!' do not believe it.   For
false Christs and false prophets will arise and show great
signs and wonders, so as to lead astray, if possible, even
²⁵ the elect.   Lo, I have told you beforehand.

baggage. Should he be at work in the field let him not wait even to pick up his cloak. And alas for those forbidden by necessity or by love to leave their burden behind! The disciples must pray that God's judgment be tempered with mercy. In winter, rushing torrents would stay their flight; sabbath-scruples (cf Ex 16:29), still felt by the Christians in the early days of the Church, would restrict it to less than one useless mile.

Many exegetes see in **21** the beginning of a discourse on the end of the world, 21-32. If this is so, its opening conjunction **For** is a merely formal connective after the manner of apocalypse (cf e.g. Dan 11:45 with Dan 12:1). But it appears preferable to see a close connexion and refer 21 to the destruction of Jerusalem. In support of this reference is the parallel Lk 21:23*b*. The **great tribulation,** it is urged, like the "great distress" of Lk 21:23*b*, may still be the concomitant of the destruction. The extravagance of the terms (not, however, entirely absent from 6-7 which certainly refer to the period before the destruction) is not incompatible with this restricted reference. The prophets present local historical events connected with the fortunes of God's people in grandiose language; cf, e.g. the "apocalypse" of Is 24-27 dealing with the overthrow of the arch-enemy, Assyria. The mere mention of a world-judgment is no proof that the section deals with the end of time. Every intervention of God is a world-judgment. For terms very like those of Mt and referring to the destruction of Jerusalem by Nebuchadnezzar, cf Bar 2:2; cf Is 13:6-10; Jer 4:23-26; 30:7. **22** – This verse may suggest the period immediately preceding the end of the world; the time, with its physical trials and moral seductions, 24, is mercifully to be shortened; otherwise the salvation of the chosen Christian faithful would be threatened. The mention of these **elect** is said to prove that the destruction of Jerusalem is not here referred to since the "elect" can be neither the Jewish factions besieged in Jerusalem nor the Christians, because these last left Jerusalem before the siege, 16, note. Nevertheless the argument is not peremptory: St John Chrysostom, for example, identifies the "elect" with Christians who remained in Jerusalem and explains that it was owing to their presence that God shortened the siege and so preserved a remnant of the Jews. Alternatively it is possible to identify this "remnant" itself with the "elect" of 22 and 24. The "remnant of Israel" is the recurrent theme of the prophets; it indicates the survivors of the particular national calamity the prophet has in mind, some of whom, not all, will prove worthy of God's promise. In this view the calamity is the destruction of Jerusalem and the "elect" are the surviving Jews for whom the offer of the messianic kingdom still lies open. St

The coming of the Son of man 24:26-28

²⁶ "So, if they say to you, 'Lo, he is in the wilderness,' do not go out; if they say, 'Lo, he is in the inner rooms,' do ²⁷ not believe it.   For as the lightning comes from the east and shines as far as the west, so will be the coming of ²⁸ the Son of man.   Wherever the body is, there the eagles will be gathered together.

Paul (Rom 11:7; cf Rom 11:15) names the "remnant" "the elect", but refers the term to those Jews who have already (c. 56 A.D.) embraced Christianity. This is because, in his perspective, the crisis has already occurred – the advent, death, resurrection of the Messiah; this crisis is entirely a spiritual one, and its "survivors", therefore, are necessarily those who have actually entered the messianic kingdom. Our Lord's perspective is different: the crisis is national and yet to come. This difference of perspective means, as in the case of the prophets, that the personnel of the 'remnant' is different also. The prophetic flavour of the passage is perceptible: divine decree has **shortened** (cf Dan 9:24) the time of tribulation (the siege of Jerusalem lasted five months) – otherwise no single inhabitant (lit. "no flesh"; cf Jer 12:12) would have survived. **23-25** – The words are addressed indeed to the apostles but only in so far as these represent the faithful who live to see the end (i.e. of Jerusalem, in our view). The pseudo-liberators, 5, appear again. Their deceits are described in the terms of Deut 13:1 where the false prophet offers (lit. "gives" in Dt and Mt) various portents. The fulfilment of such predictions, however, is to be taken only as a trial of faith permitted by God, Deut 13:2-3. Their purpose will be to win supporters even among the elect. The reappearance of the deliverers in this part of the discourse may seem to argue for a reference to a second epoch – the end of the world. But, on the other hand, it may be that our Lord's intention is simply to indicate that they multiply, as might be expected, as the threat to Jerusalem grows more alarming.

The coming of the Son of man 24:26-28 (Lk 17:23-24, 37)

26 – The impostor must be left severely alone under whatever guise, whether coming like a second Moses from the desert as happened under the procurators Felix, 52-60 A.D., and Florus, 60-62 A.D. (cf Jos, *Bellum Judaicum*, 2, 13, 4; *Ant*. 20, 5, 10) or hidden in the inmost rooms, surrounding his preparations with the mystery sometimes expected of the Messiah. **27** – The **lightning** image suggests a suddenness which might forbid reference to the destruction of Jerusalem which, 15, gives warning of its approach. Yet the argument is not conclusive since the suddenness is not such as to exclude a period of activity for pseudo-Messiahs, 24, and the "lightning" image is used by the prophets, Is 30:27ff; Zec 9:14, of divine judgments in the course, and not at the end, of history. The **coming** (*parousia*, 3, note) of the Son of man is therefore not necessarily a coming for the final and universal judgment; it may be his coming for the judgment on Israel. **28** – A sentence in proverb-form reminiscent of Job 39:30. It possibly means that the final coming of the Son of man will leave none untouched, but similar language is used by the prophets to describe divine judgment on Jerusalem (Jer 7:33f etc.) in which case the **body** is the carcase of destroyed Jerusalem where the birds of prey will have work to do.

The significance of the coming 24:29-31

29 "Immediately after the tribulation of those days the sun
will be darkened, and the moon will not give its light, and
the stars will fall from heaven, and the powers of the
30 heavens will be shaken;   then will appear the sign of the
Son of man in heaven, and then all the tribes of the earth
will mourn, and they will see the Son of man coming on
31 the clouds of heaven with power and great glory;   and
he will send out his angels with a loud trumpet call, and
they will gather his elect from the four winds, from one
end of heaven to the other.

The significance of the coming 24:29-31 (Mk 13:24-27; Lk 21:25-28)
Impressed by the cosmic dimensions of the imagery, most commentators refer 29-31 to the end of the world theme. This seems unnecessary: it is possible to maintain the single reference of the whole discourse and that Jesus still speaks of the fall of Jerusalem or rather of its counterpart which is the establishment of the Messianic kingdom in power. **29** – The consequence of the great disaster is expressed in the prophetic style we have already noted, 21. The serried ranks (perhaps "marshalled hosts" rather than **powers**) of God's heavenly army are in turmoil. As in Is 13:6-10, foretelling the ruin of Babylon, the very heavens are presented as involved in the catastrophe. All agree that these stereotyped terms of prophecy and apocalypse are not to be taken literally, whether the reference be to the end of the world or to the end of Jerusalem. It follows that 29 does not settle the problem. It should be noticed however, that Peter, Ac 2:19f, uses the very similar language of Joel 2:30f, not of the end of the world but of the new era formally and spectacularly inaugurated on Pentecost Day. For Peter, Joel's "great and manifest day of the Lord" has come with the messianic age. It is instructive (cf 31, note) that Joel heralds this "day" with a trumpet, Jl 2:1. **30** – Commonly taken as decisive for the end of the world reference: the Son of man appears as sovereign judge; the sign is of his triumphant and avenging Cross: the lamentation is not of repentance, which would come too late, but of despair. But here again another view is possible: **the coming of the Son of man on the clouds** (cf Dan 7:13) may well refer (as in 26:64; see note) to the glorious establishment of his kingdom on earth. The **mourning** of the tribes may be taken from Zec 12:10-14, where the mourning is not of despair but of repentance for the death of one untimely slain, apparently of David's house. The repentance is followed, Zec 13:1ff, by an era of grace.   These references to Daniel and Zechariah both suggest the messianic era rather than the end of the world (cf the grouping of the same texts in Apoc 1:7, probably in the same sense). The **sign** of the Son of man in heaven is taken to mean the rallying-signal which is the Messiah himself (*semeion* as in Is 11:12). It is a sign perhaps experienced rather then seen; cf 26:64. It is a "heavenly" sign (once asked for and now to be given, cf 12:38ff), like the **coming on the clouds**, because the Son of man's heavenly glory is perceived in the triumphal establishment of his kingdom on earth. The mourning, as in Zec 12:10, is consequent upon the realization of the glory of the Son whose death is thus shown to have been a hideous crime. In this theory, therefore, the sign is Christ the King seen in symbolic vision bearing the marks of his shameful death now as glorious wounds – a vision which forces itself upon the attention of men. **31** – The **gathering of the elect** is variously

The time of the coming 24:32-36

32 "From the fig tree learn its lesson: as soon as its branch becomes tender and puts forth its leaves, you know that 33 summer is near. So also, when you see all these things, 34 you know that he is near, at the very gates. Truly, I say to you, this generation will not pass away till all these 35 things take place. Heaven and earth will pass away, 36 but my words will not pass away. But of that day and hour no one knows, not even the angels of heaven, nor the Son, but the Father only.

interpreted according to the sense given to the word "elect" (22, 24, notes). It is usually understood as the fulfilment of the Christian hope for the end of time, 1 Thess 4:17, 2 Thess 2:1, while the **trumpet,** 1 Thess 4:15f, is to awaken the faithful who are supposed dead, but again another interpretation is possible. This second opinion holds that whereas v. 30 refers to the conversion of the nations ("all tribes of the earth") who perceive that Christ has risen and reigns, v. 31 calls attention to those other members of the messianic kingdom – the "remnant of Israel" (22, note). The "trumpet", it is held, is only the signal that the messianic era has opened; it is the rallying-call for God's people precisely as in Is 27:13. We are reminded that in the Jewish daily prayer (*The Eighteen Benedictions*) the "trumpet" of 31 and the "sign" of 30 are joined in a petition for the coming of the messianic age: "Sound the great *trumpet* for our deliverance and raise a *standard* for the rallying of our exiles!". The "trumpet" in Mt, as so often in St John's Apocalypse, unlike the "last" trumpet of 1 Cor 15:52, announces perhaps the intervention of God in the course of history and not at its end. In this view the symbolical trumpet is to rally Christ's own elect – the remnant of Israel dispersed over the known world.

The Time of the coming 24:32-36 (Mk 13:28-29; Lk 21:29-31)
On the assumption that the preceding verses refer to the end of the world the context of this section causes difficulty, particularly in view of 34. Some suggest that our passage refers back to the destruction of Jerusalem section; others find this procedure arbitrary and, yielding to the force of the context, apply 32-35 to the end of the world (34, note). The view adopted here, which holds for the destruction of Jerusalem theme throughout the discourse, claims to offer the more natural explanation of the text, and also to save the context. **32-33** – Just as the happy season of summer has its herald-signs, Cant 2:12f, so the establishment of the messianic era, counterpart of the destruction of Jerusalem, has its portents, *viz.* **all these things** (*panta tauta*), 33; cf "these things" (*tauta*) in 3. The events of 5-28 will, as they mature, proclaim the imminence of the kingdom whose powerful establishment is described, according to the view we have preferred, in 29-31. **34** – And indeed none of "these things" is far distant. All will take place within the lifetime of many now living (**this generation:** cf 11:16; 12:39; 17:7 etc.). Here, as in 23:36f, Jesus appears to intend a chronological indication; the alternative explanation of "this generation" as "the Jewish race" is much less probable. **35** – That **heaven and earth will pass** may mean that the old order is to give way to a new world (19:28, note) – the messianic era, 29. Possibly, however, 35 which is apparently parenthetical and occurs elsewhere (5:18, note) has no reference to the symbolism of 29 and indicates that our Lord's words (his doctrine in general) are more stable than the physical universe.

Readiness for the coming 24:37-44
[37] "As were the days of Noah, so will be the coming of the
[38] Son of man.   For as in those days before the flood they
were eating and drinking, marrying and giving in
marriage, until the day when Noah entered the ark,
[39] and they did not know until the flood came and swept
them all away, so will be the coming of the Son of man.
[40] Then two men will be in the field; one is taken and one

36 – Not, in our view, a return to or continuation of a conjectured end of the world theme, but a continuation of the destruction of Jerusalem theme. Jesus refuses an exact date, though in 34 he seems to define a date within 30-40 years. From this apparent incompatibility the inference is usually drawn that 34 and 36 refer to two different events, respectively the destruction of Jerusalem and the end of the world. It is admitted however that 36 is unexpected in its present place. For this reason, and for others, it seems necessary to emphasize the indefiniteness of the time-indication in 34 as opposed to the refused precision (**day and hour**) in 36. Thus 34 and 36 may refer to the one event – the establishment of the messianic kingdom, the great "day" of Yahweh according to the prophets. In support of this is the close similarity between 36 and Ac 1:7f where Jesus, asked the time of this establishment, refuses to give it and says only (Ac 1:8; cf Mt 24:14) that the Gospel must first be spread abroad. In either case, the exact day and hour is the Father's secret. No man, no angel, **nor the Son** (this last phrase, certainly authentic in Mk 13:32, is probably authentic in Mt) knows that. The crescendo is instructive, but there remains the dogmatic difficulty of our Lord's proclaiming his ignorance. It should however be remarked in passing that the inclusion of the phrase is a strong witness to the complete honesty of the evangelists. The difficulty (similar to that of 19:17; 20:23) is to some degree solved if we remember that it is the constant practice of the incarnate Son to claim no knowledge beyond that which the Father has instructed him to use. That is true even of the Gospel of John who indubitably teaches the divinity of Christ; cf Jn 7:16; 14:10. On the dogmatic side it may be said that in the incarnate Word were two planes of knowledge – divine and total on one plane, human and limited on the other; direct communication between the two being established only by his supernatural "infused knowledge". This last was infused in proportion to the dignity of the man-God and to the needs of his redemptive work (e.g. knowledge of his own divinity and messianic character; gift of prophecy). It is doubtful if the knowledge of the time of the world's ending or of the *exact* "day and hour" of Jerusalem's destruction was thus needed.

Readiness for the coming 24:37-44 (Lk 17:26-27, 30, 34-35)
37-39 – The exact time of the coming (*parousia*) is uncertain and will be unexpected. This "coming" is to overtake people at their usual occupations, careless of impending disaster. **40-41** – The sudden event will make a sharp distinction between the fate of individuals who up to that moment were in close association. The sense of **taken** and **left** will depend upon the identification of the disaster. For those who accept the end of the world context the terms mean "taken to God", "left unaccepted". In the destruction of Jerusalem hypothesis, "taken" means "swept away by the catastrophe" and "left" means spared (as

⁴¹ is left.   Two women will be grinding at the mill; one
⁴² is taken and one is left.   Watch therefore, for you do not
⁴³ know on what day your Lord is coming.   But know this,
that if the householder had known in what part of the
night the thief was coming, he would have watched and
⁴⁴ would not have let his house be broken into.   Therefore
you also must be ready; for the Son of man is coming at
an hour you do not expect.

Parable of the conscientious steward 24:45-51

⁴⁵ "Who then is the faithful and wise servant, whom his
master has set over his household, to give them their food
⁴⁶ at the proper time?   Blessed is that servant whom his
⁴⁷ master when he comes will find so doing.   Truly, I say
⁴⁸ to you, he will set him over all his possessions.   But if
that wicked servant says to himself, 'My master is de-
⁴⁹ layed,'   and begins to beat his fellow servants, and eats
⁵⁰ and drinks with the drunken,   the master of that servant
will come on a day when he does not expect him and at
⁵¹ an hour he does not know,   and will punish him, and
put him with the hypocrites; there men will weep and
gnash their teeth.

Noah was "left", Gen 7:23) to form part of the chosen "remnant". **42-44** – This comparison, like that of the deluge, 39, presents a man overtaken by disaster. It warns the disciples to *be wakeful (gregoreite)*. Though you do not know the hour (cf 36), proceeds our Lord, this at least you must appreciate: that if a householder knew exactly when the thief would come he would be prepared. The saying is strange because the disciples themselves do not know "the hour", 36. We are evidently to understand the suppressed implication that the house-holder, if forewarned of the event but ignorant of the exact hour, would watch all night. As before, 4ff, Jesus is concerned with the conduct of his disciples. The coming disasters will overwhelm their hope and faith and lead them to rash action (cf 25-26) unless they stand in calm fortitude awaiting the hour of deliverance; cf Lk 21:28.

Parable of the conscientious steward 24:45-51 (Lk 12:41-48)
    The parable as it stands is a warning for those in authority in the Church to be ready for the coming of Christ in final judgment, however delayed this judgment may be. It appears however (and the preceding context as explained above supports this) that the parable as Jesus spoke it was one of crisis: a warning for the authorities in Israel to make their decision now, before the coming of God's judgment on the nation. Reinterpreted in the perspective of the early Church (cf p. 165), the "coming" is now seen as the final coming at the Last Day, and the servants are not now the Jewish but the Christian leaders. The new emphasis falls not on the fate of Israel as a people in world history but on that of the individual Christian leader in the world to come. **45-47** – The parable is a diptych. The first picture presents the faithful superin-tendent of the household; from supervision of the servants he is promoted to superintendence of all his master's affairs; loyal to his earthly responsi-bilities in the kingdom, the Christian leader will be associated in heaven with the glorified Son of man presiding thence over his earthly kingdom; cf 19:28 note. **48-51** – In the companion picture the steward sees in his master's absence an opportunity for oppression and debauch. The "delay" of v. 48 appears to be a suggestion that the Last Day may be a long way off. The **punish him** of v. 51 is difficult (lit. "cut in two"), though the sawing of a slave's body was a punishment not unknown in the Greek and Roman periods; but it may possibly mean "cut him off", i.e. from the association with the reigning Christ in heaven, v. 47. His lot is henceforth with the "hypocrites"; this last term invites us (cf 23:13, 15) to think of the scribes and Pharisees who had cut them-selves off from the kingdom, 23:13; though it is possible that Luke's "the unfaithful" is here a better translation of the ambiguous Aramaic. The **weeping and gnashing of teeth** (cf 8:11-13), not found in Lk, has already been associated with individual reprobation, 22:13, and recurs, significantly, in 25:30.

Parable of the ten virgins 25:1-13

¹ "Then the kingdom of heaven shall be compared to ten
maidens who took their lamps and went to meet the
² bridegroom.   Five of them were foolish, and five were
³ wise.   For when the foolish took their lamps, they took
⁴ no oil with them;   but the wise took flasks of oil with
⁵ their lamps.   As the bridegroom was delayed, they all
⁶ slumbered and slept.   But at midnight there was a
cry, 'Behold, the bridegroom!   Come out to meet him.'
⁷ Then all those maidens rose and trimmed their lamps.
⁸ And the foolish said to the wise, 'Give us some of your
⁹ oil, for our lamps are going out.'   But the wise replied,
'Perhaps there will not be enough for us and for you; go
¹⁰ rather to the dealers and buy for youselves.'   And while
they went to buy, the bridegroom came, and those who
were ready went in with him to the marriage feast; and
¹¹ the door was shut.   Afterward the other maidens came
¹² also, saying, 'Lord, lord, open to us.'   But he replied,
¹³ 'Truly, I say to you, I do not know you.'   Watch therefore, for you know neither the day nor the hour.

Parable of the talents 25:14-30

¹⁴ "For it will be as when a man going on a journey called
¹⁵ his servants and entrusted to them his property;   to one
he gave five talents, to another two, to another one, to
¹⁶ each according to his ability. Then he went away.   He
who had received the five talents went at once and traded

Parable of the ten virgins 25:1-13

There has probably been the same shift of perspective in this parable as in the previous one: the "coming" (not now of the master but of the bridegroom) is a coming in final judgment. **1-4** – The background is that of a marriage but wants detail, and it has elements of improbability – thus probably suggesting allegory. It is not entirely clear that the virgins are bridesmaids, since no mention is made of any bride (the reading "and the bride", v. 1, found in many MSS is probably not original), nor is there any hint that the maidens go to the bride's house first: it is to the groom's they go. The parable is concerned only with the relationship of maidens and groom. The small clay lamps hold little oil. The prudent, foreseeing possible delay (cf the delay of v. 48), carry refuelling vessels also. Such lamps are most unsuitable for the open-air procession. They are introduced into the parable deliberately, possibly because the more practical torch would not bring in the necessary idea of replenishing-vessels, possibly as symbols of vigilance, Lk 12:35. The *bridegroom* (called "Lord" in 11; cf 7:22; 24:50) is Christ himself (cf 9:15; 22:2; Eph 5:25ff; Apoc 19:7-9; 21:2. For rabbinic ideas of the Messiah wedded to his people cf Edersheim 1, 722f). **5-8** – Wearied with waiting, all **grew drowsy** and fell asleep. This detail serves to underline the delay of the groom. It is not reproved: both wise and foolish have allowed themselves to be overtaken by sleep. The guilt does not lie in this but in the carelessness that had made no provision for all eventualities. The wise, though asleep, are prepared. **9** – The rather selfish complacency of the prudent may not be admirable but (as elsewhere; cf Lk 16:8) it is only their one quality (of preparedness) that is set as a model. It emerges that this quality is a personal one and cannot be supplied by others (note the emphatic pronouns of 3, 7, 9: **their lamps, for yourselves**). **10-13** – It is too late now: the groom's arrival (like the master's in 24:50) has caught them unprepared. The wise go in with the groom to the marriage-feast; cf 22:2, note. The door fast-shut, the invocation "Lord", the strange and solemn repudiation by the bridegroom, are all unlifelike and betray the application of the parable. This is explicitly made in 13: prudent provision for the Lord's coming, whenever it be.

Parable of the talents 25:14-30 (cf Lk 19:11-27)

Jesus had said, 24:45, that the true servant must be faithful and prudent. The parable of the virgins illustrates the prudence that makes the Christian live with a view to the coming of the Bridegroom. The parable of the talents, as it now stands, illustrates the faithfulness required of each Christian in the administration of goods committed to him by the master. **14-15** – The "watchfulness" mentioned in 13 is necessary because the situation under discussion is comparable to the one about to be described. In proportion to the financial ability of each of his

¹⁷ with them; and he made five talents more. So also, he
¹⁸ who had the two talents made two talents more. But he
who had received the one talent went and dug in the
¹⁹ ground and hid his master's money. Now after a long
time the master of those servants came and settled accounts
²⁰ with them. And he who had received the five talents
came forward, bringing five talents more, saying, 'Master,
you delivered to me five talents; here I have made five
²¹ talents more.' His master said to him, 'Well done, good
and faithful servant; you have been faithful over a little,
²² I will set you over much; enter into the joy of your
²² master.' And he also who had the two talents came
forward, saying, 'Master, you delivered to me two talents;
²³ here I have made two talents more.' His master said to
him, 'Well done, good and faithful servant; you have
been faithful over a little, I will set you over much; enter
²⁴ into the joy of your master.' He also who had received the
one talent came forward, saying, 'Master, I knew you to
be a hard man, reaping where you did not sow, and
²⁵ gathering where you did not winnow; so I was afraid,
and I went and hid your talent in the ground. Here you
²⁶ have what is yours.' But his master answered him, 'You
wicked and slothful servant! You knew that I reap where
I have not sowed, and gather where I have not winnowed?
²⁷ Then you ought to have invested my money with the
bankers, and at my coming I should have received what
²⁸ was my own with interest. So take the talent from him,
²⁹ and give it to him who has the ten talents. For to every
one who has will more be given, and he will have abundance; but from him who has not, even what he has will
³⁰ be taken away. And cast the worthless servant into the
outer darkness; there men will weep and gnash their teeth.'

servants (with the intention, therefore, of their making profit for him) the master commits to them various sums. A huge sum to the first, a small fortune to the second, a not inconsiderable amount to the third. For the "talent" cf 18:24. **16-17** – The first and the second lose no time (translate: And he went away. 16 Immediately he who . . .) in doubling each his master's money by hard work. Presumably this result was achieved only **after a long time,** 19, when the master returned; cf 25:5; 24:48, note. **18** – The third hid his talent, doubtless in the form of current coins, in a hole in the ground for safety. **19** – The long absence of the master (and cf 24:48; 25:5) throws into relief the sustained diligence of the first and second servants and the persistent laziness of the third. **20-23** – The faithful conduct of some few business-matters (the amounts, though huge, are as nothing to the master and in comparison with the reward) is rewarded by a post of greater importance. The application of the parable shines through the sentence: **Enter into the joy** (i.e. the joyful banquet; cf 25:10, note) **of your master!** The faithful servant shares with Jesus (cf 25:34) the joy of the Father's kingdom and apparently (cf 25:21, 23) is associated with the king's administration of the earthly kingdom so long as it lasts; cf 19:28, note. **24-25** – The lazy servant throws the responsibility upon the master. Experience tells him, he suggests, that the master is a **hard,** exacting man. It seems that he stops short of an accusation of dishonesty. He develops the term "exacting" in two farming-images. They are operations in which the master has had no personal share, from which nevertheless he expects profit. The servant alleges that his timidity proceeded from a knowledge of this. He considers that the return of the talent absolves him from blame. **26-27** – The master immediately unmasks the true motive of the servant's conduct: sloth. Even granted this caricature of himself, he argues, the servant should have had the wit and will if not to trade, as the others would have done, at least to bank the money. On Jewish bankers cf Edersheim 2, 463f. The master would thus have received the **interest. 28-29** – To the first servant, who has shown himself able to bear great responsibility, the master transfers the idle "talent". Yet the servant had already "entered into the joy of his master". One, therefore, again receives the impression (cf 21, 23) that the faithful servant of Christ is awarded a stewardship of a higher order in heaven (cf Lk 16:9-12) and associated more closely than ever with the furthering of the kingdom's interests. In human affairs responsibility is increasingly added to the able and willing. This is true, *mutatis mutandis*, of the kingdom, 29. **30** – The punishment is directly contrasted with the reward. The lazy servant is thrust out from the joy and light of the king's banquet-hall; cf 8:12. The parable primarily teaches that God's gifts, of nature and especially of grace, are held in stewardship and must not be allowed to lie idle. They are to be used to further his kingdom; cf 5:13-16. It emerges, secondarily, that the standard of

The Last Judgment 25:31-46

31 "When the Son of man comes in his glory, and all the angels with him, then he will sit on his glorious throne. 32 Before him will be gathered all the nations, and he will separate them one from another as a shepherd separates 33 the sheep from the goats, and he will place the sheep 34 at his right hand, but the goats at the left. Then the King will say to those at his right hand, 'Come, O blessed of my Father, inherit the kingdom prepared for you from 35 the foundation of the world; for I was hungry and you gave me food, I was thirsty and you gave me drink, I was 36 a stranger and you welcomed me, I was naked and you clothed me, I was sick and you visited me, I was in prison 37 and you came to me.' Then the righteous will answer him, 'Lord, when did we see thee hungry and feed thee, or 38 thirsty and give thee drink? And when did we see thee 39 a stranger and welcome thee, or naked and clothe thee? 39 And when did we see thee sick or in prison and visit 40 thee?' And the King will answer them, 'Truly, I say to you, as you did it to one of the least of these my 41 brethren, you did it to me.' Then he will say to those at his left hand, 'Depart from me, you cursed, into the 42 eternal fire prepared for the devil and his angels; for I was hungry and you gave me no food, I was thirsty and

God's judgment is relative to the opportunities offered: "the greater the gifts the greater the account demanded" (Gregory the Great).

The Last Judgment 25:31-46

The preceding parables have dealt with God's particular assessment of the conduct of individuals – he now passes to a description of the universal and final assize. Between 24:1-44 and 25:31-46 there is this in common, *viz.* that in each case a collective **judgment** closes an era in the history of salvation, and there is a solemn intervention of the Son of Man . . . But the analogy stops there . . . The first tableau, 24:1-44, presents a purely collective judgment, taking place in time, without any reference to sanctions in the eternal world; this is followed by a new stage in the history of man's religious evolution – a new cosmos. The second tableau describes a judgment not only collective but individual also; when it is finished, human history is at an end; man goes to eternal life or to eternal loss. Contemporary Jewish thought, too, appears to distinguish a judgment inaugurating the messianic era ("days of Messiah"; cf 19:28) and another judgment, strictly eschatological, which introduces the eternal world. Even the second of these has, for the rabbis, a tinge of nationalism: Israel would receive preferential treatment from God the Judge. Jesus, speaking here of this second and final judgment, shows no trace of nationalism. The judgment by which the kingdom of the Son is purified before becoming the kingdom of the Father is decided exclusively on religious grounds. **31** – Of this final judgment the Messiah had not been imagined as the independent Judge. Jesus, however, unhesitatingly assumes this office. He goes further (cf 40, 45) and decides the issue on man's attitude to himself. This situation constitutes a declaration of divinity almost as solemn as the one he was to make when he presented himself to the Sanhedrin as Son of God. **32-33** – Man is fitly judged by the Son of man and the judgment is universal. The **sheep,** for their whiteness, mild expression and docility, are a suitable image of the faithful followers of Christ the shepherd, Jn 10:3, 4, 27. They are distinguished from the **goats** (cf Ez 34:17), black, mistrustful of eye and intractable of conduct, aptly chosen as their wicked counterpart. The **right hand** then, as now, was considered as the place of favour. **34** – The **king,** the enthroned Son of man of 31, invites the good to the kingdom of his royal Father. They are blessed of (i.e. "by" or "belonging to"; cf Jn 11:29) that Father who, in his eternal decree had foreknown his own and prepared for their happiness; cf 5:4, note. **35-36** – Why this reward? Because the king himself had been fed by them, harboured, clothed, visited in sickness and in captivity. The Son of man thus identifies himself with the cause of all men whom, as the Servant of God, Is 53, he purchased with his death. **37-40** – Christian disciples at last could not doubt that they had done these things for the love of

⁴³ you gave me no drink, I was a stranger and you did not welcome me, naked and you did not clothe me, sick and ⁴⁴ in prison and you did not visit me.' Then they also will answer, 'Lord, when did we see thee hungry or thirsty or a stranger or naked or sick or in prison, and did not ⁴⁵ minister to thee?' Then he will answer them, 'Truly, I say to you, as you did it not to one of the least of these, ⁴⁶ you did it not to me.' And they will go away into eternal punishment, but the righteous into eternal life."

Preparations for the Passover 26:17-19 (Mk 14:12-16; Lk 22:7-13)

17 – It is the **first day of Unleavened Bread,** normally indicating the period from sunset 14th to sunset 15th Nisan (cf p. 287 note); it appears from Mk 14:12, however, that the lambs, sacrificed in the afternoon of 14th Nisan, had not yet been slain; the expression must therefore be used in the wider sense found once or twice in contemporary Jewish literature. Nevertheless if the hypothesis is adopted (p. 288) that Jesus celebrated his Supper on 13th Nisan, we shall have to go still further and adopt the translation of many early Greek writers; "on the day before" instead of "on the first day", i.e. 13th and not 14th Nisan. **18** – Jesus is outside the city (having spent the night in prayer on Olivet? cf Lk 21:37; Jn 18:2) but it was obligatory to eat the passover lamb in the city itself. The disciples (Peter and John in Lk 22:8) are therefore sent into the town to one whose name the evangelists suppress, perhaps for prudence sake. Mt's account is less circumstantial than Mk (whom Lk follows), but it appears from all three evangelists (**the Teacher says**) that the man was a friend of Jesus and willing to put a private room at his disposal despite the crowded conditions of the town at festal times (about 100,000 pilgrims in a town with a population of about 30,000). The hour of our Lord's destiny has struck (his **time** – as in Jn 7:6-8).

Prophecy of betrayal 26:20-25 (Mk 14:17-21; Lk 22:14, 21-23; Jn 13:21-30)

20 – When the sun had set (cf Ex 12:8), the thirteen *lay* at table. At the great feasts the Jews reclined on mats or mattresses, resting on the left arm, the right being used for eating. If the order was that of the Roman *triclinium*, three sides of the square (or oval) were used by the guests, the fourth being left open for convenience of service. (For positions at table cf Jn 13:23ff). **Judas,** keeping up appearances, was still with the apostles, but in the course of the meal Jesus attempts to touch his conscience. **21-23** – Our Lord's answer to the question of the troubled apostles insists on the intimacy, not the identity, of the traitor. The traitor is at table now; he *has* dipped into the dish of sauce (the *charoseth?* p.289) that passes round the table. **24** – That the Son of man goes freely to his death (cf Jn 8:14, 21f, etc.) is no excuse. **As it is written** must be a reference to Is 53. **25** – Judas probably puts his question in a low voice or possibly in concert with the others, 22. The answer is not a direct affirmative (Aramaic has *hen* for "yes") but it agrees with the statement made and at the same time calls attention to the fact that the first speaker has provoked agreement; it therefore implicitly invites the first speaker to salutary reflection; cf 26:64; 27:11. Judas must have left the table almost immediately – his knowledge of discovery

Last Supper 26:26-29

²⁶ Now as they were eating, Jesus took bread, and blessed, and broke it, and gave it to the disciples and said, "Take, ²⁷ eat; this is my body." And he took a cup, and when he had given thanks he gave it to them, saying, "Drink of ²⁸ it, all of you; for this is my blood of the covenant, which ²⁹ is poured out for many for the forgiveness of sins. I tell you I shall not drink again of this fruit of the vine until that day when I drink it new with you in my Father's kingdom."

would make his position intolerable; it is therefore improbable that he was present for the institution of the holy Eucharist. Lk 22:21 gives the impression that Judas was still at table for the Institution but his phrase is placed before the Institution by Mt 26:23 and Mk 14:18.

Last Supper 26:26-29 (Mk 14:22-25; Lk 22:19-20; 1 Cor 11:23-25)
If this was in fact a Paschal supper, the traditional Jewish elements have gone unemphasized in all the accounts (there is no mention even of the lamb); this, however, is understandable in view of the importance of the institution of the *new* covenant. **26** – It appears that the main meal has begun and therefore, if this is the Passover supper, the second cup drunk but the lamb not yet eaten (p. 289). Jesus **blessed** the bread, i.e. blessed God for giving it (not "blessed" *eulogesas* in Lk 22:19 and 1 Cor 11:24, but "gave thanks" *eucharistesas*, hence "Eucharist"). As he gave it to the disciples he said, **"This is my body"** (Lk adds "which is given for you"; 1 Cor "which is for you") In Aramaic: *den hu bisri:* this it (i.e. is) my body, or simply *den bisri:* this my body ("'is" being understood). The sacrificial character of Christ's gesture is clear from v. 27, and to eat of the sacrifice was, in the O.T., to appropriate its blessings. At the Supper, the disciples are invited to appropriate the blessings of Christ's atoning death. **27** – The taking of the **cup** did not follow immediately: 1 Cor 11:25 (and the longer reading of Lk 22:20) says "after supper". If this was the Paschal supper, the lamb was eaten after the blessing of the bread and before the cup (the third cup, cf p. 289) was taken. This third cup of the Passover was called by the Jews "the cup of blessing" (the term actually used by Paul in 1 Cor 10:16). At the Paschal meal the eating of the lamb was followed by a prayer of thanksgiving said by the paterfamilias: Mt and Mk use the word *eucharistesas* in connection with the cup. **28** – As Jesus handed the cup to the disciples he echoed the words Moses spoke when he ratified the old covenant by sacrifice ("Behold the blood of the covenant" cf Ex 24:4-8). He said *den adam keyami:* this (is) the blood of my covenant, adding "which is **poured out**" (the participle used is present but the context demands "which is about to be poured out", as the corresponding Aramaic permits): the blood still to be shed is liturgically offered now. **for many:** apparently an echo of Is 53:12 where the suffering Servant of God "pours out (LXX: "hands over") his soul to death" and "bears the sins of *many*" (or, as we should say *"the many"*). The reference to Isaiah is confirmed by Lk 22:37. **29** – Lk places this sentence with his thanksgiving over a cup before the thanksgiving over the bread; he goes on to speak (in the longer reading, Lk 22:19b-20, which we accept against RSV) of the Eucharistic cup. Lk seems to be closer to the facts, and his "fruit of the vine" refers to the previous cup (probably the first cup of the Paschal meal, cf p. 289). Mt and Mk, having omitted the first cup are forced to put the "fruit of the vine" saying with the

Prophecy of denial 26:30-35

³⁰ And when they had sung a hymn, they went out to the
³¹ Mount of Olives. Then Jesus said to them, "You will
all fall away because of me this night; for it is written,
'I will strike the shepherd, and the sheep of the flock will
³² be scattered.'   But after I am raised up, I will go before
³³ you to Galilee."   Peter declared to him, "Though they
all fall away because of you, I will never fall away."
³⁴ Jesus said to him, "Truly, I say to you, this very night,
before the cock crows, you will deny me three times."
³⁵ Peter said to him, "Even if I must die with you, I will not
deny you." And so said all the disciples.

Gethsemane 26:36-46

³⁶ Then Jesus went with them to a place called Gethsemane,
and he said to his disciples, "Sit here, while I go yonder

Eucharistic cup to which it did not originally refer. The sentence is at once a promise and a farewell. The "wine" they will share at the messianic "banquet" in heaven ("the kingdom of my Father", cf 13:43; 25:34) will be **new** – a joy of which the fruit of the vine is only a symbol. St Luke, on the other hand, appears to have in mind the "kingdom" on earth, the Christian church, and the Eucharistic banquet which is the "Passover" of the messianic era. These two interpretations are complementary. Like the Passover, the Eucharist is an act of family union – it unites the Christian with Jesus in the act of his redemptive death (1 Cor 10:16), and therefore each with his fellow; one bread, one body. It is therefore a pledge of heaven, of union at the "marriage supper of the Lamb" Rev (Apoc) 19:9. Note: Mt (and Mk) omit the command (Lk 22:19; 1 Cor 11:24f) "Do this in memory of me" probably because their texts record liturgical practice (cf e.g. their close juxtaposition of the two "consecrations"), and liturgy has no need to recite a rubric.

Prophecy of denial 26:30-35 (Mk 14:26-31; Lk 22:39, 31-34; Jn 13:36-38; 16:32)

30 – The Jewish Paschal supper ends with the singing of the "Hallel" ("praise") psalms, (cf p. 289), and, the religious rite over, conversation turns to other topics. At the Last Supper it is Jesus who discourses, Jn 14:1 – 17:24, but the discourse is not reported in the Synoptics. The time is probably nearing midnight, and the little company passes through the town in an easterly direction, crosses the Kedron valley and turns left along the western slope of Olivet. A walk of nearly a mile brings them to Gethsemane. **31** – Either on the way or while still in the supper-room (cf Lk, Jn; Mt's "then" is often merely stylistic and not chronological) the disciples are told of their impending desertion. Jesus quotes Zec 13:7 to illustrate the general principle that the flock owes its strength and unity to the shepherd (especially this flock to this shepherd). The illustration is borrowed from the history of king Zedekiah, a timid "shepherd" who, attacked by the Babylonians, abandoned the capital and its inhabitants to their fate, 2 (4) Kg 25:4. **32-35** – In the general consternation the Resurrection prophecy again goes unheeded as also, it would appear, 28:10, the Galilean assignation. Peter's indignation outdoes his respect and draws upon him a detailed prophecy of his own moral fall. The cock crow in Mt is probably the second – the dawn-crow at about 3-4 a.m. Mk mentions two 14:30; the author has heard a cock crow in Jerusalem in April at 2 a.m. Between vv. 35 and 36 there is a pregnant silence. Our Lord leaves the event to make reply, 26:56.

Gethsemane 26:36-46 (Mk 14:32-42; Lk 22:40-46; Jn 18:1)

36-38 – They come to a plot of land (*chorion*) at the foot of the western slope of Olivet, facing the temple; a garden, Jn 18:1, called "the oil-press", *gath shemani(n)*, doubtless because of some rustic installation

³⁷ and pray." And taking with him Peter and the two sons
³⁸ of Zebedee, he began to be sorrowful and troubled. Then
he said to them, "My soul is very sorrowful, even to death;
³⁹ remain here, and watch with me." And going a little
farther he fell on his face and prayed, "My Father, if it
be possible, let this cup pass from me; nevertheless, not as
⁴⁰ I will, but as thou wilt." And he came to the disciples
and found them sleeping; and he said to Peter, "So,
⁴¹ could you not watch with me one hour? Watch and
pray that you may not enter into temptation; the spirit
⁴² indeed is willing, but the flesh is weak." . Again, for the
second time, he went away and prayed, "My Father, if
⁴³ this cannot pass unless I drink it, thy will be done." And
again he came and found them sleeping, for their eyes were
⁴⁴ heavy. So, leaving them again, he went away and prayed
⁴⁵ for the third time, saying the same words. Then he came
to the disciples and said to them, "Are you still sleeping
and taking your rest? Behold, the hour is at hand, and
the Son of man is betrayed into the hand of sinners. Rise,
⁴⁶ let us be going; see, my betrayer is at hand."

Arrest 26:47-56
⁴⁷ While he was still speaking, Judas came, one of the twelve,
and with him a great crowd with swords and clubs, from
⁴⁸ the chief priests and the elders of the people. Now the
betrayer had given them a sign, saying, "The one I shall
⁴⁹ kiss is the man; seize him." And he came up to Jesus at
once and said, "Hail, Master!" And he kissed him.
⁵⁰ Jesus said to him, "Friend, why are you here?" Then they
came up and laid hands on Jesus and seized him. And
⁵¹ behold, one of those who were with Jesus stretched out
his hand and drew his sword, and struck the slave of the
⁵² high priest, and cut off his ear. Then Jesus said to him,
"Put your sword back into its place; for all who take the
⁵³ sword will perish by the sword. Do you think that I

among the olive-trees. Eight of the apostles remain near the gate but Peter, James and John, witnesses of Jesus' glory (17:1-2; cf 2 Pet 1:17-18) are invited to see him in his suffering. The prospect of his passion brings *distress* and *dismay* and mortal sadness. He asks his friends to remain wakeful (**watch**) with him. **39-44** – In an attitude of complete prostration but with his human will deliberately turned to the Father he asks that the cup of sorrow (cf 20:22) may pass him by if this may be done without upsetting the divine redemptive plan. There are two wills in Christ: the divine will and the human will. We may distinguish a double act in the human will: the act of the will which may be called "instinctive" (*voluntas ut natura*) and the deliberate, considered act (*voluntas ut ratio*). Our Lord's instinctive will, true to its nature, shrank from suffering and death considered in themselves; his deliberate will embraced them for the sake of what they were to bring: the redemption of man in the way God willed it. With the restlessness of sorrow he seeks the solace of his disciples, but he asks them to pray not for him but for themselves, that they may not be faced with the crisis, the trial (*peirasmos* cf Rev (Apoc) 3:10) of strength with Satan which Jesus himself has undertaken. In his second prayer Jesus uses the words he taught his disciples to say, 6:10.

Arrest 26:47-56 (Mk 14:43-52; Lk 22:47-53; Jn 18:2-12)
47-49 – Judas was familiar with this garden and with our Lord's habits, Jn 18:2. He knew, too, that Jesus would not have gone to Bethany because Paschal night was to be spent in Jerusalem or the immediate neighbourhood, including the western slope of Olivet. He now leads what is (to judge by their impromptu weapons) a casual gang hired for the purpose, but there is evidently an escort of Roman soldiery, Jn 18:3. For a disciple to embrace his master would not be unusual. **50** – The clipped, and therefore obscure Greek phrase (lit. "for what you are come") is interpreted here as a question but is perhaps better translated as an exclamation: either "(A kiss), friend, for such a purpose!" (cf Lk 22:48), or "Do what you have come to do!" **51-54** – Peter's half-parried blow at Malchus, Jn 18:10, is rebuked by Jesus. Firstly, it is useless – violence must always take the consequence of violence and, in this case, the power is apparently on the wrong side. Secondly, it is unnecessary and undesired – the Son does not choose to exercise his power: twelve times six thousand armed angels, not eleven impotent apostles, waited his word. But how, were he to give that word, would this conform with the prophecies (e.g. Is 53) of a meekly suffering Messiah? **55-56** – Jesus objects to the absurd drama of his arrest and to the show of violence. It implies that he is a dangerous bandit. Yet it must have been clear from his general habit of public teaching ("daily" in the temple; cf especially Jn 7:14; 8:2, 20, 59; 10:23) that he was no secret conspirator and that he could have been

cannot appeal to my Father, and he will at once send me
54 more than twelve legions of angels? But how then
should the scriptures be fulfilled, that it must be so?"
55 At that hour Jesus said to the crowds, "Have you come
out as against a robber, with swords and clubs to capture
me? Day after day I sat in the temple teaching, and you
56 did not seize me. But all this has taken place, that the
scriptures of the prophets might be fulfilled." Then all the
disciples forsook him and fled.

Before the Sanhedrin 26:57-68

57 Then those who had seized Jesus led him to Caiaphas the
high priest, where the scribes and the elders had gathered.
58 But Peter followed him at a distance, as far as the courtyard of the high priest, and going inside he sat with the
59 guards to see the end. Now the chief priest and the
whole council sought false testimony against Jesus that
60 they might put him to death, but they found none,
though many false witnesses came forward. At last two
61 came forward   and said, "This fellow said, 'I am able
to destroy the temple of God, and to build it in three
62 days.' "   And the high priest stood up and said, "Have
you no answer to make? What is it that these men testify
63 against you?"   But Jesus was silent. And the high priest
said to him, "I adjure you by the living God, tell us if you
64 are the Christ, the Son of God."   Jesus said to him, "You
have said so. But I tell you, hereafter you will see the Son
of man seated at the right hand of Power, and coming
65 on the clouds of heaven."   Then the high priest tore his
robes, and said, "He has uttered blasphemy. Why do we
still need witnesses? You have now heard his blasphemy.
66 What is your judgment?" They answered, "He deserves
67 death."   Then they spat in his face, and struck him; and
68 some slapped him,   saying, "Prophesy to us, you Christ!
Who is it that struck you?"

seized at any time. He thus lays bare the leaders' fear of overt unpopular action, 26:5. v. 56 is perhaps more probably Mt's own observation (in Mt – not Mk – Jesus has already said this, v. 54): the whole incident is a prelude to the fulfilment of prophecy. Mt does not think it necessary, however, to point out that the flight of the apostles verifies Christ's recent forecast, 31.

Before the Sanhedrin 26:57-68 (Mk 14:53-65; Lk 22:54, 66-71; Jn 18:24, 15-16)

57 – The prisoner is taken back along the Kedron to the Gate of the Fountain at the S.E. angle of the city walls and so up the graded road into the city. But not (it seems from Lk and Jn) taken immediately before the Sanhedrin; there was a preliminary, nocturnal interview with Annas according to Jn 18:13, 19, 24. The official, decisive trial before the Sanhedrin must have taken place in the morning: a night trial would have been illegal. Mt and Mk do indeed refer to a second trial in the morning (Mt 27:1; Mk 15:1) but they have transferred its interrogation to what was in fact a nocturnal interview with Annas. **58** – Peter has followed at a safe distance; having reached the *palace* (rather than "courtyard") he ventures inside, Mk 14:54, to await the upshot (**end**). **59-62** – All three classes of the council are represented (chief priests, elders, scribes; cf 57).) This council (or "Sanhedrin" – the Greek *sunedrion* in Aramaic form) totalling 71 members was the supreme judiciary body of the Jewish nation and met under the presidency of the reigning high-priest. For capital trials a quorum of 23 sufficed; it is not, therefore, necessary to understand **whole council** strictly. The object of the meeting is to formulate a capital charge to present to the procurator, who alone had power to order execution of sentence; cf Jn 18:31. For appearance sake the formalities had to be observed (Num 35:30 etc.) and eventually the necessary two witnesses are found though even these are not in complete agreement, Mk 14:59. They pervert what Jesus had said, slightly in words, profoundly in sense; cf 2:19. The high-priest is not satisfied; he seeks a capital charge and hopes to condemn Jesus out of his own mouth. **63** – Ignoring the trumped-up charge of the witnesses, Jesus will not refuse an answer to an independent and formal demand from the highest authority (**by the living,** and therefore avenging **God**). The rabbis never give the title "Son of God" to the Messiah and the Jewish writings about Christ's time are shy of it. The titles "Son of God", "Christ", are therefore probably not equivalent for Caiaphas. But the term "Son of God" had been used of Jesus in his own circle, Mt 16:16; Jn 11:27, and the fact was known outside that circle, 27:39-40. It is probable that Caiaphas, aware of all this, adds the title to the term **Christ** and so feels his way to a charge of blasphemy, a capital crime, Deut 13:2-6. **64** – Mt's **You have said so** (lit. "It is you who have said it") is equivalent to Mk's "I am" with a faintly ironical touch as if Caiaphas

Peter's denials 26:69-75

⁶⁹ Now Peter was sitting outside in the courtyard. And a maid came up to him, and said, "You also were with ⁷⁰ Jesus the Galilean." But he denied it before them all, ⁷¹ saying, "I do not know what you mean." And when he went out to the porch, another maid saw him, and she said to the bystanders, "This man was with Jesus of ⁷² Nazareth." And again he denied it with an oath, "I do ⁷³ not know the man." After a little while the bystanders came up and said to Peter, "Certainly you are also one ⁷⁴ of them, for your accent betrays you." Then he began to invoke a curse on himself and to swear, "I do not know ⁷⁵ the man." And immediately the cock crowed. And Peter remembered the saying of Jesus, "Before the cock crows, you will deny me three times." And he went out and wept bitterly.

by using the terms already assumed their truth. Taking this fictional assent as starting-point Jesus proceeds to build on it. *"Moreover"*, he says solemnly, *"from now onwards* (cf 23:39) you will be witnesses of" the situation described by Daniel. **See,** in regard to apocalyptic vision is not so much physical vision as intellectual appreciation. The sentence is better punctuated: "You will see 'the Son of man' " (cf Dan 7:13) "seated at the right hand of the power" (i.e. of the Almighty; cf Ps 110 (109):1 and "coming on the clouds of heaven" (Dan 7:13). This punctuation by indicating a mere juxtaposition of tableaux removes the confusion of imagery. In effect, the "sitting at the right hand" and the "coming on the clouds" indicate the same thing. The twin-thrones for God and the Messiah suggested by the psalm (and cf Dan 7:9) indicate a participation in the divine administration of the world. The same idea is found in the Daniel text where one "like a son of man" "comes" (i.e. to the Ancient of Days for investiture, not to the earth for Judgment) riding on the clouds to receive his kingdom. In Daniel there is no suggestion of a "coming" in a distant perspective of "Last Judgment": it is a question of the new messianic era. Jesus, too, speaks of the new era which begins now on earth; its glory is paradoxically inaugurated by the whole process of the Passion indeed; cf Jn 12:31-33. **65-66** – The second of Caiaphas's two questions (Christ? Son of God?) may have been asked after the reply of 64 as in Lk 22:66, 70. In any case, it is clear that the high-priest takes our Lord's transcendental messianism for capital blasphemy. Jesus, therefore, is not claiming a mild, political messianity, though Caiaphas will find the "Messiah" admission useful before the pagan tribunal. He tears his garments, from the neck downwards for a palm's length, in the ritual manner prescribed for the hearing of blasphemous speech. For the religious court the case is clear, Lev 24:16; it remains to secure sentence from the procurator, 27:1. **67-68** – Mt leaves us to understand that Jesus was blindfolded; cf Mk 14:65; Lk 22:64. Those who strike him (not necessarily the Sanhedrists, even in Mt) defy him to use his prophetic or clairvoyant gifts; cf Ac 23:2 for similar action of another high-priest.

Peter's denials 26:69-75 (Mk. 14:66-72; Lk 22:56-62; Jn 18:17, 25-27)
69-70 – Peter is in the open-air courtyard round which the palace was built. Meanwhile, Jesus is on trial in an upstairs room, Mk 14:66, of the building itself. In the light of the fire, Lk 22:56, Peter is recognized by a maid; his public denial is not less real for being indirect. **71-72** – He moves from the light towards the gate, and another maid (the portress?) challenges him. The denial is formal this time. **73-75** – Then ("about an hour later"; Lk 22:59) Peter is once more at bay among many accusers. His Galilean dialect (confusion of the gutturals, difficulty with the vowels: a, i, o) proclaim him a northerner. The third denial is emphasized by oath and straightway signalized by the crowing of

Jesus taken to Pilate 27:1-2

¹ When morning came, all the chief priests and the elders
of the people took counsel against Jesus to put him to
² death; and they bound him and led him away and
delivered him to Pilate the governor.

Death of Judas 27:3-10

³ When Judas, his betrayer, saw that he was condemned,
he repented and brought back the thirty pieces of silver to
⁴ the chief priests and the elders, saying, "I have sinned
in betraying innocent blood." They said, "What is that
⁵ to us? See to it yourself."   And throwing down the pieces
of silver in the temple, he departed; and he went and

the cock for the second time; cf Mk 14:68-72. It is a bitter reminder of our Lord's words, 26:34.

Note: The evangelists do not, as a rule, purpose to give the exact words of speeches – of accusations and denials in this case – nor the exact order of events. From 26:34 we should expect three denials, but the combined Gospel accounts may seem to suggest more by naming five different accusers at least. If we seek, perhaps unnecessarily, a harmonization, the solution probably lies in assigning the multiplicity of accusers to three groups only, thus:

First Denial: in the courtyard (Mt, Mk, Lk) by the fire (Mk, Lk). Accused by a maid (Mt, Mk, Lk), the portress (Jn). The cock crows for the first time (Mk). *Second Denial:* in the forecourt (Mk) near the door (Mt) a little later (Lk). Accused by the same maid (Mk "*the* maid") whose accusation is supported by others (Jn) including another maid (Mt), a man (Lk). *Third Denial:* apparently by the fire again, a little later (Mt, Mk) including another man (Lk) and a relation of Malchus (Jn). The cock crows for the second time (Mk) immediately (Mt, Mk, Lk, Jn).

Jesus taken to Pilate 27:1-2 (Mk 15:1; Lk 22:66; 23:1)

The second meeting of the Jewish council was at dawn, Lk 22:66; it was evidently short because it was still early morning when Jesus reached Pilate's residence, Jn 18:28. The meeting was held probably in the Sanhedrin's assembly-hall (the *gazith*), on the southern side of the "court of the Israelites". Its purpose was to pass sentence of formal condemnation and to formulate a charge which would impress the governor. They decided upon a political one (27:11; cf Lk 23:2). In the Roman province of Judea only the procurator (Pontius Pilatus, 26-36 A.D.) could order execution of the death-sentence. Normally resident at Caesarea Palestinae, the procurator established his military headquarters ("praetorium") in Jerusalem for the dangerous periods of the great feasts, probably in the palace of Herod on the N.W. height of the city, though possibly in the Antonia, the fortress abutting on the N.W. corner of the temple enclosure.

Death of Judas 27:3-10 (cf Ac 1:18-20)

The whole incident, presented by Mt (only) parenthetically, serves to underline the Sanhedrin's contempt for justice and the hypocrisy of its members. **3-5** – Mt's "then" (here translated **when**) as so often, is vague – the time may be after the condemnation by Pilate. Possibly Judas had thought that the evidence would prove insufficient for condemnation or possibly his crime came home to him only when he saw its fruit and handled the bribe. Filled with remorse (not true "repentance" because empty of hope) he sought to dissociate himself from the affair by proclaiming his master's innocence. The unscrupulous cynicism of the judges showed the attempt hopeless and drove him to a desperate decision. The money, now worse than useless, he flung down in the

⁶ hanged himself. But the chief priests, taking the pieces of silver, said, "It is not lawful to put them into the ⁷ treasury, since they are blood money." So they took counsel, and bought with them the potter's field, to bury ⁸ strangers in. Therefore that field has been called the ⁹ Field of Blood to this day. Then was fulfilled what had been spoken by the prophet Jeremiah, saying, "And they took the thirty pieces of silver, the price of him on whom ¹⁰ a price had been set by some of the sons of Israel, and they gave them for the potter's field, as the Lord directed me."

Jesus before Pilate 27:11-26
¹¹ Now Jesus stood before the governor; and the governor asked him, "Are you the King of the Jews?" Jesus said to ¹² him, "You have said so." But when he was accused by

temple (*naos*, a word which, to judge from its use in Jn 2:20, may include the temple buildings such as the *gazith*). The place of his suicide is unknown. **6-8** – The Law, Deut 23:18, forbade the price of chastity to be put to sacred use; the Sanhedrists now extend the principle to blood-money – it must not be put into the temple-treasury. With it they buy "Pottersfield" (hitherto a well-known name, evidently, and doubtless so called because it contained potter's clay); thenceforth it was called in Aramaic *haqel dema*, "field of blood", because bought with blood-money, but cf Ac 1:18f. This cemetery for strangers (probably Jews who died on pilgrimage in Jerusalem – pagans were the Romans' affair) lay on the southern slope of the Hinnom valley. **9-10** – Mt, as usual, hastens to associate the O.T. with the event; cf Zec 11:12-13; Jer 18:2-4; 19:1-2; 32:7-9. The prophet Zechariah, a true shepherd of Israel, is assessed by the false shepherds, the political authorities, at the mean price of thirty pieces: it is an insult to God whom Zechariah represents. "Throw it to the potter! (i.e. to the cheap shop) a fine price at which to be assessed by them!". The words are God's. The striking similarity of situation and the concurrence of the "thirty pieces" with "the potter" call Mt's attention to a text which he freely adapts, apparently from the Hebrew text, changing "And I" (Zechariah himself) to **And they** (the priests) and adding **as the Lord directed me** in compensation for his own change of pronoun. In the experience of the sixth century prophet, rejected representative of God, Mt sees a prophetic rehearsal of the present situation. *The attribution of the text to Jeremiah*, strongly supported by the MSS is strange. It is possible however, that the text is a fusion of Zec and Jer. Jer ch. 32 recounts the purchase of a field, symbolic of confidence in Judah's rehabilitation; Jer 19:11 has a curious *rapprochement* of the potter's vessel and Hinnom; Jer 18 tells of a visit to a potter of which the text in Zec is possibly an "adaptation". In this case, Mt assigns the text to Jer (as Mk 1:2-3 assigns a composite Isaiah-Malachi text to Isaiah only) as being the more "important" prophet or as heading the fifteen prophets in the Jewish canon of the time. It may, however, be preferable to read "by the prophet" only, omitting "Jeremiah" (with the *Bellum Judaicum*). And indeed it is psychologically improbable that the evangelist, who appears to have adjusted a Hebrew text which he had in front of him, could have made such a mistake. The omission of Jeremiah is also supported by the Syriac versions and some MSS. The name may have been inserted by an early copyist, misled by the faint echoes of Jer.

Jesus before Pilate 27:11-26 (Mk 15:2-15; Lk 23:2-5, 18-25; Jn 18:28-40; 19:4-16)

11 – The scene is Pilate's praetorium, 27:2. The interview would take place indoors where the accusers could not be present: the pollution

¹³ the chief priests and elders, he made no answer. Then
Pilate said to him, "Do you not hear how many things
¹⁴ they testify against you?" But he gave him no answer,
not even to a single charge; so that the governor wondered
¹⁵ greatly. Now at the feast the governor was accustomed
to release for the crowd any one prisoner whom they
¹⁶ wanted. And they had then a notorious prisoner, called
¹⁷ Barabbas. So when they had gathered, Pilate said to
them, "Whom do you want me to release for you, Barabbas
¹⁸ or Jesus who is called Christ?" For he knew that it was
¹⁹ out of envy that they had delivered him up. Besides,
while he was sitting on the judgment seat, his wife sent
word to him, "Have nothing to do with that righteous
man, for I have suffered much over him today in a dream."
²⁰ Now the chief priests and the elders persuaded the people
²¹ to ask for Barabbas and destroy Jesus. The governor
again said to them, "Which of the two do you want me to
release for you?" And they said, "Barabbas". Pilate said
²² to them, "Then what shall I do with Jesus who is
called Christ?" They all said, "Let him be crucified."
²³ And he said, "Why, what evil has he done?" But they
²⁴ shouted all the more, "Let him be crucified". So when
Pilate saw that he was gaining nothing, but rather that a
riot was beginning, he took water and washed his hands
before the crowd, saying, "I am innocent of this man's
²⁵ blood; see to it yourselves." And all the people answered,
²⁶ "His blood be on us and on our children!" Then he
released for them Barabbas, and having scourged Jesus,
delivered him to be crucified.

of pagan ground would have prevented them from eating the Passover (Jn 18:28). But they are active outside on the *Lithostroton* (Jn 19:13) or paved square in front of the palace, and Pilate communicates with them freely (Jn 18:28, 29, 33, 38; 19:4f, 9, 13). It seems that he used the balcony on the façade of the palace and on the same floor as the *secretarium* where the interview took place with Jesus. The balcony would be used as the tribunal, the curule chair in the middle, room for secretaries on either side. Here sentence would be publicly pronounced, and from here could be watched the public scourging (the usual preliminary to crucifixion) in the square. The charge is political (not as in 26:65) and drawn from the "tribute" incident (22:15-22) according to Lk 23:2. Jesus answers "It is you (emphatic) who say it" (cf 26:64): the title is not refused but the acquiescence is reserved. John's fuller account (18:33-38) explains how Pilate, despite the claim to kingship, remains unconvinced of Jesus' guilt – a kingdom of "truth" (whatever that may be) is not a political entity within Pilate's competence. **12-18** – Impressed by the dignified silence of Jesus, Pilate seeks to apply the Roman *abolitio* (suspension of criminal proceedings) in his favour. Such a concession was made on certain festal occasions in the provinces (cf the papyrus of 85 A.D. for a similar occurrence in Egypt). Pilate offers the one alternative (there were others possible, cf Mk 15:7) of the murderer Barabbas ("Jesus Barabbas" is a probable reading). The contrast, he thinks, will decide the case in favour of Jesus Christ. He appeals to the people because he has been informed, reliably enough, that the cause of our Lord's arrest was precisely the leaders' envy of his popularity with them. **19** – (Mt only). For the evangelist the incident of Pilate's wife (Claudia Procula by name according to the apocryphal Gospels) underlines the malice of Israel – a pagan woman pleads the cause of Jesus against his own people. For Pilate it confirms his own uneasy wonder by thickening the atmosphere of mystery. For the Jewish leaders it provides an opportunity of organizing their supporters. **20-23** – The modern technique of mob-management shows how a multitude, even well-disposed, can yield to a vociferous and violent minority – moreover, Barabbas was suffering for a nationalist cause, Mk 15:7, and would have noisy supporters among the crowd. **24-25** – (Mt only). By an action familiar to Jews, Deut 21:6, and Gentiles, Pilate disclaims responsibility. It is an act rather of private superstition than of public administration. This latter Pilate is as impotent to decline as the Jews are powerless to assume. It is before God and not before Tiberius that the Jews take responsibility upon themselves and their descendants. **26** – Mt omits Pilate's further attempt to release Jesus after the scourging, Jn 19:4-15. The scourge was normally the prelude of the cross. Its leather thongs usually carried pieces of bone and metal. The naked victim's hands were tied to a low column. In Roman practice the number of blows was limited only by the endurance or taste of the executioner.

Crowning with thorns 27:27-31

²⁷ Then the soldiers of the governor took Jesus into the praetorium, and they gathered the whole battalion before ²⁸ him. And they stripped him and put a scarlet robe ²⁹ upon him, and plaiting a crown of thorns they put it on his head, and put a reed in his right hand. And kneeling before him they mocked him, saying, "Hail, King of the ³⁰ Jews!" And they spat upon him, and took the reed and ³¹ struck him on the head. And when they had mocked him, they stripped him of the robe, and put his own clothes on him, and led him away to crucify him.

Crucifixion 27:32-38

³² As they were marching out, they came upon a man of Cyrene, Simon by name; this man they compelled to ³³ carry his cross. And when they came to a place called ³⁴ Golgotha (which means the place of a skull), they offered him wine to drink, mingled with gall; but when he tasted ³⁵ it, he would not drink it. And when they had crucified him, they divided his garments among them by casting ³⁶ lots; then they sat down and kept watch over him there. ³⁷ And over his head they put the charge against him, which read, "This is Jesus the King of the Jews." Then two ³⁸ robbers were crucified with him, one on the right and one on the left.

It was not uncommon for victims to die under the lash.

Crowning with thorns 27:27-31 (Mk 15:16-20; cf Jn 19:2-3)
27-28 – Jesus is led back presumably from the balcony into the praetorium itself where Pilate's personal (cf 27:27) *cohors praetoria* would be lodged – the permanent troops having their barracks in the Antonia, the fortress looking down on the temple area from its N.W. corner. The *speira* (here **battalion**) is not necessarily a cohort of 500 men; the term is used of smaller units. The **scarlet robe** is probably some soldier's military cloak: it is evidently meant as an ironical symbol of the imperial purple. **29-30** – The emphasis is on the ridicule, rather than on the pain of the crowning. The **thorn** is, with some probability, the *poterium spinosum* which abounds about Jerusalem and was used then, as now, for firewood; its spikes are slender. The form of the **crown** may have been that of a head-dress, as in the 2nd cent. representation in the Catacomb of Praetextatus, though the phrase **plaiting a crown** suggests a fillet. The earliest (5th cent.) representations of the Crucified show him without the crown; it was perhaps laid aside with the **reed** (his "sceptre"). **31** – Jesus carried his own cross, Jn 19:17, from the praetorium until the procession left the town, 32.

Crucifixion 27:32-38 (Mk 15:21-27; Lk 23:26-34; Jn 19:17-24)
The shape of the cross is not certainly known. The X, Y and T forms were in use, but in our Lord's case the T-shape with upward prolongation of the vertical (*crux immissa*) is witnessed by the best authority (Irenaeus) and leaves room for an inscription "over his head", 37. The transverse beam was called the *patibulum* and, in Rome at least, it was customary for the criminal to carry only this beam. This may be true of our Lord; the *stauros* of Jn 19:17 may mean *patibulum* only. In the middle of the upright was usually a small block to serve as a seat and so take some weight from the hands which were sometimes bound to the *patibulum*, but usually nailed, as in our Lord's case; cf Jn 20:25, 27; Lk 24:39. In Christian art the seat has become a foot-support, doubtless for aesthetic reasons. There is no reason to think that our Lord's feet were nailed together: all representations of the Crucified up to the 12th cent. show them nailed separately. (But cf Barnes, *The Holy Shroud of Turin*, London 1934.) **32** – Simon, born in Cyrene (N. Africa; a town with a large Jewish colony) is conscripted (the Gk verb means to press into governmental service) into carrying the cross in place of Jesus (cf Lk 23:26) who seems to have collapsed. **33** – Golgotha (simplified form of Aramaic *gulgoltha* "skull"; Latin *calvaria*) was the name for the mound, rising about 15 ft. from the surrounding soil, just outside the city-walls less than half a mile from the palace of Herod. **34** – It was the custom for pious women to administer narcotics to condemned criminals. The **gall** (cf Ps 69 (68): 22) of Mt is used, as in LXX, in a general sense:

Mockery 27:39-44

39 And those who passed by derided him, wagging their
40 heads and saying, "You who would destroy the temple
and build it in three days, save yourself! If you are the
41 Son of God, come down from the cross." So also the
chief priests, with the scribes and elders, mocked him,
42 saying, "He saved others; he cannot save himself. He is
the King of Israel; let him come down now from the cross,
43 and we will believe in him. He trusts in God; let God
deliver him now, if he desires him; for he said, 'I am the
44 Son of God.' " And the robbers who were crucified with
him also reviled him in the same way.

Death 27:45-56

45 Now from the sixth hour there was darkness over all the
46 land until the ninth hour. And about the ninth hour
Jesus cried with a loud voice, "Eli, Eli, lama sabachthani?"
that is, "My God, my God, why hast thou forsaken me?"
47 And some of the bystanders hearing it said, "This man is
48 calling Elijah." And one of them at once ran and took
a sponge, filled it with vinegar, and put it on a reed, and
49 gave it to him to drink. But the others said, "Wait, let
50 us see whether Elijah will come to save him." And Jesus
cried again with a loud voice and yielded up his spirit.
51 And behold, the curtain of the temple was torn in two,
from top to bottom; and the earth shook, and the rocks
52 were split; the tombs also were opened, and many bodies
53 of the saints who had fallen asleep were raised, and
coming out of the tombs after his resurrection they went
54 into the holy city and appeared to many. When the
centurion and those who were with him, keeping watch
over Jesus, saw the earthquake and what took place, they

bitter drug (more precisely "myrrh", cf Mk 15:23). Jesus refuses the alleviation. **35** – The soldiers take their customary perquisite of the criminal's possessions, but Mt does not need to call attention to this fulfilment of Ps 22 (21):19, since his account is here permeated with O.T. reminiscences which are sufficiently perceptible. **37** – The exact form of the inscription is not known (four different forms are found in the four Gospels) but would certainly include the name of the crucified and the charge: Jesus, the "king of the Jews"; this proves too laconic for the chief priests' liking. **38** – The episode of the robbers (bandits), like the gesture and words of the passers-by and the mockery of the priests, are all verbally reminiscent of O.T. passages (Is 53:12, cf Lk 22:37; Ps 22 (21): 8; Wis 2:13, 18; Ps 22 (21):9).

Mockery 27:39-44 (Mk 15:29-32; Lk 23:35-37)
39 – Criminals were usually crucified by the roadside as a warning. Again the wording of the verse is reminiscent of O.T. (Ps 22 (21):8 and Lam 2:15). **40** – They (or rather Mt interpreting their thoughts) use the words by which the sufferer is mocked in Ps 21 (22):9 and cf Wis 2:18-20.

Death 27:45-56 (Mk 15:33-41; Lk 23:44-49)
45 – From noon until three in the afternoon darkness covers Jerusalem and its horizon. The great day of God's decisive intervention in the affairs of men (the "Day of Jahweh") is marked, in the conventional imagery of the prophets, by eclipse and earthquake (Am 8:8f, cf Ac 2:19f; Is 13:10; Jer 15:9). It is possible that Mt here and in vv. 51-54 is doing the same, though the precision in v. 45 (from the sixth to the ninth hour) does not suggest this. **46** – The words of Jesus are in Aramaic (*sebaqtani*, not – as in Hebr. – *azabtani*). They are the opening words of Ps 22 (21) which is not a cry of despair but a hymn of supreme confidence in God despite profound suffering. As in Christ's case the divine "forsaking" in the psalm is no more than a poetical expression of acute physical and mental pain to which God has "abandoned" the psalmist without, however, having "turned his face away", Ps 22 (21): 2, 25. In Christ's mouth, indeed, the words are not even a complaint because his intention is simply to show that the fruitful martyrdom of the innocent psalmist was a shadow of his own. It is worth noting, however, that the mental shock that the words, coming from the God-man, must produce, powerfully argues the fidelity of the evangelists who ran this risk in the interest of honest report. It will be observed that in our explanation of this quotation on our Lord's lips the question does not formally arise of his enjoyment of the beatific vision even during the passion (the common opinion of theologians). That the uninterrupted beatific vision in the highest faculty of the soul is compatible with bodily, mental and even spiritual suffering becomes clear to our

were filled with awe, and said, "Truly this was the Son
55 of God!"   There were also many women there, looking
on from afar, who had followed Jesus from Galilee,
56 ministering to him;   among whom were Mary Magdalene, and Mary the mother of James and Joseph, and the
mother of the sons of Zebedee.

Burial 27:57-61

57 When it was evening, there came a rich man from
Arimathea, named Joseph, who also was a disciple of
58 Jesus.   He went to Pilate and asked for the body of Jesus.
59 Then Pilate ordered it to be given to him.   And Joseph
took the body, and wrapped it in a clean linen shroud,
60 and laid it in his own new tomb, which he had hewn in
the rock; and he rolled a great stone to the door of the
61 tomb, and departed.   Mary Magdalene and the other
Mary were there, sitting opposite the sepulchre.

intellect, not to our imagination, if we remember that the formal object
of the vision and the formal object of the suffering are different. **47-49** –
Misunderstanding (deliberately?) the **Eli** articulated with the difficulty of a dying man, the Jews, 47, 49, think or affect to think that this
"Messiah" may have his precursor, Elijah, at hand; 17:10ff, notes.
A soldier, moistening a sponge with the sour wine (*posca*) of his flask,
places the sponge on the end of a long reed (or javelin? cf Jn 19:29,
note). He was moistening our Lord's lips with it; others, apparently Jews,
adopting the Elijah-jest, bid him to desist – not wishing to spoil the
atmosphere of empty expectation. In Mk 15:36 the soldier, too, weakly
makes his compassionate action part of the joke. **50** – At about three
in the afternoon when, a few hundred yards away, the paschal lambs
of the old rite were being slain in the temple, the Lamb of God died;
cf 1 Cor 5:7. Mt's phrase (Mk: "breathed his last") is close to Jn 19:30;
in Lk it becomes a saying of Jesus. **51** – **The curtain of the temple** may
be the curtain of the inmost sanctuary, the Holy of Holies, of the appearance of which nothing certain is known; or possibly the enormous and
elaborate curtain to the outer sanctuary, the Holy Place. If the first, the
priests, many of whom were converted, Ac 6:7, could verify and report
the prodigy. The symbolism seems to favour this inner veil, Heb 10:20f;
9:7, 25. **52-53** – The earth, too, was torn (Mt, alone, mentions the
earthquake) and opened some of the rock-tombs: vertical earthquake-
fissures are still to be seen in the rock of Calvary. It seems probable
that the bodily resurrection and apparition of many dead just ones did
not occur until after Christ's Resurrection (cf 1 Cor 15:20-23) and that it
is mentioned here because the earthquake prepared their exit from the
tombs. **54** – The manner of our Lord's death, the darkness, the earthquake, all impress the pagan guards. They confess the justice of the title
Son of God with which they had heard Christ's foes ironically taunt
him, 20:40, 43, however little they may realize all this title holds.
55-56 – The Galilean women stood watching from some distance: Mary
of Magdala (el-Mejdel on the lakeside c 3 m. N. of Tiberias); Mary,
mother of James (the "Less") and of Joseph, 13:53-54, note; the
mother of the sons of Zebedee (20:20, note) probably the "Salome" of
Mk 15:40.

Burial 27:57-61 (Mk 15:42-47; Lk 23:50-55; Jn 19:38-42)
57-58 – The body had to be removed and buried before the first stars
announced the beginning of the Sabbath, Jn 19:31. It would be about
four o'clock in the afternoon when Joseph, sympathetic throughout to
Jesus, Lk 23:51, approached Pilate to whom, as an influential member
of the Sanhedrin, Mk 15:43, he would have access. He was of Arimathea
(Ramathaim; cf 1 Kg 1:1, 19 etc.) c 12 m. N. of Lydda. **59-61** – He
had purchased a worthy linen shroud, Mk 15:46, and Nicodemus,

The guard at the tomb 27:62-66

⁶² Next day, that is, after the day of Preparation, the chief
⁶³ priests and the Pharisees gathered before Pilate and
said, "Sir, we remember how that impostor said, while
he was still alive, 'After three days I will rise again.'
⁶⁴ Therefore order the sepulchre to be made secure until
the third day, lest his disciples go and steal him away,
and tell the people, 'He has risen from the dead,' and the
⁶⁵ last fraud will be worse than the first." Pilate said to
them, "You have a guard of soldiers; go, make it as
⁶⁶ secure as you can." So they went and made the sepulchre
secure by sealing the stone and setting a guard.

The empty tomb 28:1-8

¹ Now after the sabbath, toward the dawn of the first day
of the week, Mary Magdalene and the other Mary went
² to see the sepulchre. And behold, there was a great earthquake; for an angel of the Lord descended from heaven
and came and rolled back the stone, and sat upon it.
³ His appearance was like lightning, and his raiment white
⁴ as snow. And for fear of him the guards trembled and
⁵ became like dead men. But the angel said to the women,
"Do not be afraid; for I know that you seek Jesus who was
⁶ crucified. He is not here; for he has risen, as he said.
⁷ Come, see the place where he lay. Then go quickly and
tell his disciples that he has risen from the dead, and

Jn 3:1-15, had bought a quantity of spices, Jn 19:39, to place on the shroud and round the body. In the presence of the women, and doubtless with their help, they laid Jesus in Joseph's own unused tomb about fifty yards from the cross. The more well-to-do Jews cut the family tomb in the rock, usually on the side of a slope; a low entrance closed by a thick disc of stone led to the vestibule which in turn led to the tomb proper by a small communicating cavity. Joseph's tomb had one shelf on the right of the entrance, Mk 16:5, for the reception of the body. The two Marys (56, cf Mk 15:47) remained. Others of the holy women prepared spices for a further and less hurried anointing, Lk 24:1.

The guard at the tomb 27:62-66

The night of Friday (**Preparation**, i.e. for the sabbath) passes. On the Saturday there is no formal meeting of the Sanhedrin (Mt does not mention "ancients") but it occurs to a few of the priests and Pharisees that the dead "impostor" promised his Resurrection after three days; cf 12:40. The disciples must be prevented from removing the body during these crucial three days. The first "imposture" – our Lord's claim to Messiahship and more – had been effectively answered by crucifixion; the second (Resurrection, possibly to be alleged by the disciples) would be more difficult to counter should the body be stolen. Pilate, who sounds tired of the whole affair, allows the Jews to use their supporting posse of Roman troops (cf Jn 18:12) for the guardianship of the tomb. The stone is then joined to the surrounding rock, presumably by means of a tape and the official seal.

The empty tomb 28:1-8 (Mk 16:1-8; Lk 24:1-12; cf Jn 20:1-10)

1 – The sabbath-rest was observed, Lk 23:56. When the sabbath was over, as the sky was lightening towards sunrise on **the first day of the week** ("the Lord's – Resurrection – Day", as the Christians came to call it, Ac 20:7) the women (Mk 16:1; Lk 24:10), including Mary Magdalene and Mary the mother of James, 27:56, came to watch at the tomb (Mt) with a view, no doubt, to completing the hasty anointing of Friday, Mk 16:1, Lk 24:1. 2-4 – Before their arrival as it seems (2-4 are probably parenthetical) a considerable earth-tremor declared the advent of the angel in human form. His purpose was to declare the physical Resurrection of Christ and to confirm his message by the spectacle of the empty tomb. He therefore rolled away the stone not to enable the already risen Christ to emerge (cf Jn 20:19, 26) but to allow the women to enter. Mt gives the impression that the angel was still seated on the stone when they arrived but that he preceded them into the tomb. Terror made the guards powerless to interfere; it is probable that they made off citywards before the coming of the women since the angel and the women ignore them completely and there is no trace of their presence in Mk 16:1-8 or Lk 24:1-8; and see on Mt 28:11.

behold, he is going before you to Galilee; there you will see
⁸ him. Lo, I have told you." So they departed quickly
from the tomb with fear and great joy, and ran to tell his
disciples.

Apparition to the holy women 28:9-10
⁹ And behold, Jesus met them and said, "Hail!" And they
came up and took hold of his feet and worshipped him.
¹⁰ Then Jesus said to them, "Do not be afraid; go and tell
my brethren to go to Galilee, and there they will see me."

Precautions taken by the Jewish leaders 28:11-15
¹¹ While they were going, behold, some of the guards went
into the city and told the chief priests all that had taken
¹² place.   And when they had assembled with the elders and
taken counsel, they gave a sum of money to the soldiers
¹³ and said, "Tell people, 'His disciples came by night and
¹⁴ stole him away while we were asleep.' And if this
comes to the governor's ears, we will satisfy him and keep
¹⁵ you out of trouble." So they took the money and did
as they were directed; and this story has been spread
among the Jews to this day.

5-8 – But for the women (true seekers of the Crucified) there was no cause for such terror ("No need for you" emphatic "to be afraid!"). The Lord's promise was fulfilled; cf 16:21; 17:22; 20:19. Escorted by the angel they saw the empty tomb for themselves. The physical body had risen. Now they were to tell the disciples that the risen Christ would be found in Galilee. It is possible that the verb "go before" is to be translated "lead, conduct", in which case Mt clearly supposes that Jesus appeared to the disciples in Judea. But in any case it is Mt's plan to describe only the Galilean episode. By a kind of factual "inclusion", having presented Galilee as the starting-place, 4:12-16, of the first restricted preaching of the kingdom, he now presents it as the starting-place of the universal mission. Hence he is careful, unlike Lk and Jn, to report the angel's message concerning the Galilean rendezvous and to reinforce it, 10, with Christ's instruction to the same effect.

Apparition to the holy women 28:9-10 (cf Jn 20:14f)

Some authors identify this apparition, the first mentioned by Mt, with the apparition to Magdalene alone, Jn 20:11-18. In this hypothesis Mt attributes to the women-group (as opposed to the "brethren" in 10; i.e. the disciples; cf 12:49) what happened to their single representative. Such a "plural of category" is perhaps not unfamiliar to Mt; cf 2:20; 24:8; 27:44. The identification would also explain Lk 24:22-24 where it seems that the women had reported no more than the angel and the empty tomb. Others oppose the identification and explain that 9 refers to a second visit of the women (without Magdalene). Whatever the solution, it must take account of the extreme telescoping of Mt's last chapter.

Precautions taken by the Jewish leaders 28:11-15

As the women were still on their way, certain of the guard were in touch with the priests. It is probable that the guard had already left for the city before the women arrived at the tomb; 28:2-4, note. The Gk tenses used do not contradict this suggestion ("whilst they [the women] were on their way [from the tomb] the guards *having reached* the city told . . . "). The situation of the guards is awkward: the true, supernatural, explanation of their discomfiture would be laughed at in a court-martial. The priests, therefore, have no difficulty in bribing them to suppress an explanation that would have been useless in any case. The main point of the priests' instruction was the alleged theft by the disciples. This the soldiers agreed to and this story became the current explanation in Jewish circles; cf 15 and Justin, *Contra Tryphonem*, 108. The "sleep" excuse is thrown out carelessly as a suggestion. It could be used only before the general public; clearly if it came to an official inquiry (14) sleeping on duty would be no adequate excuse. The priests undertake, in this case, to *bribe* in high places (for the Gk verb – here translated "satisfy" – cf 2 Mac 4:45; 10:20).

Apparition in Galilee. Mission to the world 28:16-20

16 Now the eleven disciples went to Galilee, to the mountain
17 to which Jesus had directed them.   And when they saw
18 him they worshipped him; but some doubted.   And Jesus
came and said to them, "All authority in heaven and on
19 earth has been given to me.   Go therefore and make
disciples of all nations, baptizing them in the name of the
20 Father and of the Son and of the Holy Spirit,   teaching
them to observe all that I have commanded you; and lo,
I am with you always, to the close of the age."

Apparition in Galilee. Mission to the world 28:16-20

The Eleven remained in Jerusalem until the end of paschal week, Jn 20:26, then, naturally, they went back to their homes with the assurance, 7, 16, that they were not leaving the risen Christ in Jerusalem. Mt is aware of the fact (though, like the other evangelists, he does not report Christ's own words) that Jesus had indicated a particular "mountain" in Galilee. The "mountain" is doubtless the high ground above the lake (as in 5:1; 14:23; 15:29) – perhaps, fittingly, the hill of the discourse which inaugurated the kingdom, 5:1. **Some doubted,** says Mt. It is probable that he is simply recording a fact (mentioned by the other evangelists, Mk 16:11, 13, 14; Lk 24:11, 21ff; Jn 20:25) without reference to this particular occasion. The reason may lie in the summary nature of Mt's final chapter or possibly the phrase is to be translated: "they, *the very ones who had doubted,* adored".

18 – The obedience unto death of the man-Christ has resulted in the Resurrection which constitutes his formal investiture as king of the kingdom of heaven and earth, cf Phil 2:8f. Sovereign powers were his before (11:27; cf Jn 3:35), a necessary consequence of the Incarnation, but now the Son of man has formally taken possession of his throne, Dan 7:14. The Resurrection inaugurates the new and worldwide epoch of the kingdom. The kingdom has come "in power". **19** – Consequently the old restriction of apostolic preaching, 10:5f, is abrogated. Enrolment of disciples, baptism, religious and moral instruction are for Gentiles also. The exact conditions of Gentile-reception will cause difficulty later (cf Ac 15) but the principle is already clear. The rite of enrolment is baptism according to Mt (all MSS and versions) and Mk 16:16, and indeed the rigorous and universal practice of the early Church is explainable only by the historical fact of Christ's command. **In the name of** is not "on the authority of" (*en to onomati;* cf Ac 2:38; 10:48) but "by way of consecration to" (*eis to onoma*). By baptism the neophyte becomes the property, and therefore the *protégé*, of the person named. In the case of the "baptism of John" in the Gospels, there would be no need to name a person: since John himself administered the rite, it would be evident that the recipient accepted John's message. In the case of Christian baptism, not administered by Jesus himself (Jn 4:2), the baptizing disciple would presumably have to mention the name of Jesus, since it was into the company of Jesus that the baptized was to be admitted. This mention of the name is supported, if not proved, by Ac 2:38; 8:16; 10:48, and cf Jas 2:7. The Trinitarian formula of Matthew (the reading is textually certain) is attested also for the early second century. It may be his own expansion of the simple formula "in the name of Jesus", since to be affiliated to Christ is to be consecrated to the Father who sent him and to receive the Spirit bestowed by Christ.

Further Reading

M.-J. Lagrange, O. P., *The Gospel of Jesus Christ*, Burns Oates.

J. C. Fenton, *The Gospel of Saint Matthew*, Pelican Gospel Commentaries, 1963.

A. W. Argyle, *The Gospel according to Matthew*, Cambridge University Press, 1963.

J. Jeremias, *The Parables of Jesus*, S.C.M., 1949.

Gospel Parallels, Nelson, 1949. The Revised Standard Version of the first three Gospels in parallel. The use of such a *Synopsis* in the study of any one of the Synoptic Gospels cannot be too highly recommended.

A. Edersheim, *The Life and Times of Jesus the Messiah*, New York. Of great use for Jewish background.

Index